BRITISH LOCOMOTIVE PRACTICE & PERFORMANCE

Patrick Stephens Limited, part of Thorsons, a division of the Collins Publishing Group, has published authoritative, quality books for enthusiasts for more than 20 years. During that time the company has established a reputation as one of the world's leading publishers of books on aviation, maritime, military, model-making, motor cycling, motoring, motor racing, railway and railway modelling subjects. Readers or authors with suggestions for books they would like to see published are invited to write to: The Editorial Director, Patrick Stephens Limited, Thorsons Publishing Group, Wellingborough, Northamptonshire NN8 2RQ.

BRITISH LOCOMOTIVE PRACTICE & PERFORMANCE

Extracts from the pioneering
Railway Magazine articles of
1902-1908
by Charles Rous-Marten

Compiled and edited by
Charles Fryer

Foreword by O.S. Nock

Patrick Stephens Limited

Front endpaper *GWR 4-6-0 'Star' No 4039* Queen Matilda *on an up express between Reading and London. The restored 'chocolate and cream' coach livery shows that the picture was taken after 1922. The 'top-feed' pipes encircling the boiler were fitted to the whole class after 1911, when they were also given superheaters.* (NRM)

Rear endpaper *GWR No 3440* City of Truro, *built in 1903, as restored and preserved, at the head of a train of modern stock. Timed by Rous-Marten, this was the first steam locomotive to reach 100 mph, hauling an Ocean Mails Special of five vans from Plymouth to Bristol on 9 May 1904. The maximum was reached near Wellington when descending from Whiteball summit (see pages 12 and 56).* (NRM, T.J. Edgington Collection)

To Jonathan

This selection first published in 1990

This selection and new material © Charles Fryer, 1990

These articles first appeared between April 1902 and March 1908 in *The Railway Magazine*, whose co-operation in the preparation of this edition is gratefully acknowledged.

British Library Cataloguing in Publication Data
Rous-Marten, Charles
    British locomotive practice and performance: extracts
    from the pioneering ''Railway magazine'' articles of
    1902–1908.
    1. Great Britain, Locomotives
    I. Title II. Fryer, Charles III. Railway magazine
    625.2'6'0941

ISBN 1–85260–222–8

Patrick Stephens Limited is part of the Thorsons Publishing Group, Wellingborough, Northamptonshire NN8 2RQ, England.

Typeset by Burns & Smith Ltd, Derby
Printed by Bath Press, Bath, Avon

10 9 8 7 6 5 4 3 2 1

All photographs credited to 'NRM' are by courtesy of the National Railway Museum, York.

Contents

ACKNOWLEDGEMENTS

I am grateful to the Editor of *The Railway Magazine* for permission to reprint the extracts from Charles Rous-Marten's articles in that Magazine which appear in the following pages.

I am also greatly obliged to the National Library of New Zealand for information about Rous-Marten's earlier career, and to the railway writer John Wrottesley for other helpful information; also to the staff of the Mitchell Library, Glasgow, who provided photocopying facilities without which the preparation of this book could not have been done in the comfortable surroundings of my own home.

FOREWORD

by O.S. Nock BSc DIC CEng FCGI FICE FIMechE

The writing of the serial article 'Locomotive Practice and Performance' in *The Railway Magazine* each month for a period of twenty years was a pleasurable task, and when my kind publishers intimated that they would like to see the individual articles covering some of the most significant topics republished in book form I was naturally gratified. Arrangements for republication were quickly and cordially arranged, and editorial work was well advanced when I was delighted to learn that after a suggestion by an author resident in Scotland my publishers were going to reprint extracts from the pioneer serial of these articles written by Charles Rous-Marten, written between 1902 and 1908. Even at that relatively early date, compilation of train running logs was already a practiced art with a few locomotive enthusiasts, such as the Rev W. J. Scott, Norman D. MacDonald, R. E. Charlewood and R. Collier, he who afterwards inherited a peerage and became Lord Monkswell. But as Charles Fryer explains in the succinct biographical reference in the introduction to his own book, Rous-Marten, as an experienced practical journalist, was the 'arch-priest' of them all. The remarkable thing was that none of them, not even Cecil J. Allen who carried on the authorship of 'British Locomotive Practice and Performance', for so many years subsequently, was a professionally trained mechanical engineer!

In selecting the extracts for re-publication, Mr Fryer has been careful to segregate those dealing with 'Practice' and 'Performance', and subconsciously, perhaps, has produced a period piece of locomotive-enthusiast thought at the turn of the century, and just after. For although Rous-Marten and his friends were 'persona grata' with most of the principal locomotive engineers of that period, they did not converse upon the more intimate details of locomotive design, with the consequence that most of Rous-Marten's dissertations on practice now appear to us as slightly naive as well as being a little verbose. It is a matter of history that the wheels of 'British Locomotive Practice and Performance' rolled on in *The Railway Magazine* in much the same way for 20-odd years under Rous-Marten's eventual successor, Cecil J. Allen.

Then, in 1926, one of his regular correspondents, E. L. Diamond, one of the most erudite of the pupils of Sir Henry Fowler on the Midland Railway at Derby, presented a remarkable paper to the Graduates Section of the Institution of Mechanical Engineers, and then indeed the eyes of the railway literary world were opened to the outstanding merit of the development of valve gears that had taken place on the Great Western Railway more than 20 years earlier. I found it strange that my old teacher at Imperial College, Professor W. E. Dalby, in writing his mighty 760-page tome

Steam Power in 1951, in which 60 pages were devoted to valves and valve gears, should have made no mention of the Great Western Railway development under Churchward.

Valve gears apart, however, thanks to Mr Fryer one can relax in the company of one of the most talkative of railway writers and read once more of the days when the great McIntosh 4-6-0s of the Caledonian were bringing the 'Corridor' up Clydesdale, when the 'Scarborough Flyer' ran from Leeds non-stop to that seaside town and was hauled by a NER 4-2-2 single, and when the first Midland compounds were attaining speeds of more than 90 mph on the Settle and Carlisle line.

INTRODUCTION

Charles Rous-Marten[1] was born in London in 1841. His father, William Marten, was a member of a long-established Sussex family whom business had drawn to the capital, where he became a merchant, and it was there that the young Charles grew up and received his education. As a boy he had many interests and hobbies, one being the contemporary railway scene. From quite an early age he travelled on passenger trains and made copious notes on the performances of their locomotives. Probably he was the first person ever to do this.

When he was 15, calamity struck the Marten family when the bank in which his father's assets were invested failed. The decision was taken to emigrate to New Zealand, where colonization by white settlers had already begun and where land allotments were being sold to suitable persons by a Government ready to advance money on loan to enable them to be purchased. The allotment which the Martens took was in the southern part of the South Island. Marten Senior now began a new life as a farmer and stockbreeder, and rose in the esteem of the local community so that eventually he was made a magistrate. He seems to have lived a placid and uneventful life, eventually slipping out of ex-istence quite undramatically, his death certificate simply stating that he died from 'decay of vital energy'. This was in 1892, his wife having pre-deceased him by four years. He had three sons and three daughters, Charles being the eldest.

The latter turned towards engineering as a study and, eventually, journalism as a profession, and his boyhood interest in the mid-nineteenth century British railway scene transferred itself to the system which was then beginning to develop in New Zealand and which eventually extended itself to the vicinity of his parents' home in Invercargill. He had never had any formal instruction in engineering principles, but he was fortunate enough to become acquainted with William Conyers, manager of the Southland Provincial Council's railway system, who first offered him employment on the railway and then promoted him to be a stationmaster. Deciding to fly higher, Rous-Marten tried to enter politics as a member of the New Zealand Parliament, but his nomination was bungled and he failed to get elected. In 1877 he became a journalist, rose to become one of the editorial staff of the *Wellington Evening Post*, and was eventually appointed Chief Editor.

As to his personal life, records are scanty. In January 1876 he married Emily Jane Hickson, daughter of a prominent Wellington citizen. They had no children. She presumably went

[1] He was given two forenames at birth, as plain C. R. Marten, and collected the hyphen at some point during his adult career.

with him to England when he settled in London in 1893, and she outlived him for some years. It seems strange that the obituaries that appeared in the journals to which he had contributed lack the usual condolences extended to a widow. He certainly formed many firm friendships with like-minded people, and had many personal interests which he actively pursued. One obituary notice refers to him as 'a cultured musician and able musical critic', and notes that he had amassed the largest musical library in the Southern Hemisphere. It was not his practice to do things by halves! He took a keen interest in astronomy, and for ten years supervised the southernmost meteorological observatory in the world, near Foveaux Strait, which divides the South Island of New Zealand from Stewart Island. Here, in 1885, he observed a total eclipse of the sun and wrote a description of it. The *Railway Magazine* obituarist also describes him as a 'theologian', but this probably means no more than that he was a practising Anglican churchgoer. While he lived in Wellington he functioned as a church organist and sang tenor parts in oratorios.[2]

New Zealand was then a relatively sparsely populated country, and Rous-Marten soon became well-known to all the locomotive engineers of its railway systems. The enthusiasm he had early shown in observing and timing trains in the land of his birth soon found expression in his adopted country. In 1892 he created something of a stir by announcing that he had travelled behind a Baldwin-built 2–6–2 locomotive which had covered 15 miles in 15 minutes and reached a maximum speed of 64 miles an hour. In Great Britain this would have been nothing remarkable, but on the New Zealand gauge of 3 feet 6 inches it seemed so unlikely that many questioned, to quote one critic, whether he had not been 'carried away in

his enthusiasm as an amateur railway engineer of a pronounced type with a weakness for high speed'. Critical scrutiny of his records in regard to this particular claim, however, appears to have confirmed its plausibility.[3] At any rate, the engine in question has been preserved in New Zealand. A photograph shows it to be a rather ungainly machine, small-wheeled with two massive domes, a huge headlamp in front of the chimney and a cowcatcher fixed to the buffer beam—certainly no sprinter to look at.

Rous-Marten's name became enough of a household word in New Zealand railway circles to bring him to the notice of the country's government, and in 1884 the latter commissioned him to make a study of the United Kingdom's railway system for the guidance and benefit of New Zealand railway companies. He threw himself into this enterprise with zest, and at the end of three years produced a Report which he despatched to the New Zealand Minister for Public Works. Duly published, it became something of a standard work of reference. To compile it he travelled over almost every main line in Great Britain, covering some 40,000 miles in all, and also paid close attention to the workings of rail traffic at the larger terminal stations and junctions. He visited the Locomotive and Carriage works of the various companies, and made the acquaintance of many locomotive superintendents, who rewarded his enthusiasm with invitations to be present at tests, experiments and trial runs. By the time his

---

[2] It is interesting to notice how a propensity for religious observance and organ-playing can co-exist with an interest in railways. One of his successors, who continued his series of articles in *The Railway Magazine*, Cecil J. Allen, was also a church organist and had strong religious affiliations. One thinks, too, of the late Bishop Eric Treacy.

[3] Twelve years later his personal history repeated itself with a vengeance, when, travelling in a van on an Ocean Mail Special between Plymouth and London, he believed himself to have clocked a maximum of 102.3 miles an hour descending towards Taunton from Whiteball summit. He did not reveal this openly at the time, though he gave a number of broad hints. Later, after the Great Western Railway had acknowledged that their 4–4–0, *City of Truro*, was the locomotive in question, Cecil J. Allen and others examined the records carefully and came to the conclusion that, whatever the maximum speed might really have been, the figure of 8.8 seconds for a single quarter-mile was suspect, as not being borne out by the figures for the previous quarter-miles. However, it does seem probable that the 'hundred' was attained, and *City of Truro* has been preserved in York Railway Museum as a record-breaker.

Report was completed he probably knew more about railways in all their aspects than any other person in Great Britain.

Between 1887 and 1893 he visited other countries, Australia in particular, to study their railway systems, and then returned to the land of his birth, to remain there for the rest of his life as the London representative of the chief New Zealand newspapers. Railways continued to be his chief interest, not only in Great Britain but also in France, where he studied the practice of compounding in steam locomotives and was very impresssed by what it could achieve. The French government of the day felt so much obliged to him for his sympathetic interest that they offered him a decoration, which he declined to accept in case it might appear that his advocacy of the French compound locomotive had been for personal reasons and not as the consequence of impartial observation.

It was now that he began to contribute articles to railway and engineering journals, especially the newly-established *Railway Magazine* under G. A. Sekon's editorship. An article by him appeared in its first issue, and others followed in later issues; in September 1901 he commenced the regular sequence on *British Locomotive Practice and Performance*, extracts from which make up the bulk of this book. They became the *pièce de résistance* in the fare offered by the new magazine, and, with a slight alteration in the title, have continued to the present day.

In his own time, Rous-Marten became a legendary figure. Cecil J. Allen referred to him as 'the high priest of the craft of train timing'. The phrase is apt. Like other distinguished ecclesiastics he had his own special liturgical garb by which he could be recognized from afar, his frock-coat and tall hat. He also had his professional gadgetry, though it was the stop-watch, not the censer, which he wielded.[4] Anecdotes gathered around him. The best-known is probably the one about his performances during the 1895 Railway Race to Aberdeen, when he was one of a team observing the running of the East Coast Route's record-breaker. He not only remained awake during the whole of one of the fastest of these night runs (though a sleeping berth was available had he wished to use it) but when the express was drawing into Aberdeen station he realized that he would just be able to catch the early morning service back to King's Cross if he made a quick rush across the station platform. So he gathered his paraphernalia together, leapt from the carriage door while the train was still in motion, legged it across the intervening space, coat-tails flying, and clambered into the south-bound train which had already begun to move out, with some assistance from the guard, who drily remarked that he wasn't staying long in Aberdeen that morning.

He died at the age of 67 after contracting influenza, making a partial recovery and then having a relapse. The last article which he wrote for *The Railway Magazine* was produced while he was recuperating in the supposedly mild climate of Bournemouth, though that particular winter it turned out to be unwontedly chilly. During his convalescence he imprudently took time off to attend a conference in Liverpool. Over-exertion brought on a return of 'flu and he suffered a heart attack; he lingered for a fortnight and passed away on the afternoon of Easter Monday, 1908. A funeral service was held for him at St Paul's Church, Clapham, where he had worshipped on Sundays when travelling did not take him elsewhere, and his friend, the Reverend W. J. Scott, delivered the encomium. His remains were later cremated at Golders Green. One hopes that they were conveyed there by train.

* * *

If every railway journalist, like every dog, has his day, then Rous-Marten's day, the years during which he wrote for *The Railway Magazine*, was an interesting one in the story of British railways. It was at once a decade of climax and of transition. From being an ungainly object surrounded by rods and brackets and barnacled with excrescences, the British express passenger

---

[4] He had four stop-watches when he went into action, one in each hand and one in each trouser pocket.

locomotive had attained a kind of maturity and perfection during the final few years of the nineteenth century, and had become a handsome machine which could haul loads of up to 200 tons at an average speed between stops of from 50 to 55 miles an hour. The 4–4–0 wheel arrangement had now become general with new designs, though on some lines the 4–2–2 single-wheeler had been given a fresh lease of life since the introduction of steam-sanding had improved wheel grip at starting, and improved steel rails now allowed loads of up to 10 tons to be placed on each driving wheel, thus increasing adhesion. The general positioning of cylinders within frames, and the tidying up of external features had produced on nearly all new locomotives a sleekness of line and contour which made them good to look at. Some subtle influence, too, caused locomotive superintendents and their chief draughtsmen, men who had never darkened the doors of any Art College, and who would have pooh-poohed the notion that they were aesthetes, to build engines whose proportions harmonized with the canons of artistic good taste and which, seen sideways on, caused the eye to appreciate them as it would pictures painted in accordance with the principle of the Golden Sec-

tion. External liveries, which shed staffs were expected to keep bright and clean, enhanced the effect of line and shape. By the turn of the century, all passenger locomotives, even the 'blackberry black' ones of the London and North Western Railway, were good to look at, and some were utterly splendid. Was it, one wonders, the springtime glory of South Eastern and Chatham engines, with their Brunswick green boilers, cabs and tenders, polished brass domes and splasher edges, red frames and copper-capped chimneys, which caused Rous-Marten to travel so frequently behind them, on a line not famed for high speed? Cabs adequate for the protection of drivers and firemen from wind and weather were now invariably provided, and on some lines, such as the Great Eastern and North

GER 4–4–0 No 1900 Claud Hamilton, *designed by J. Holden and built in 1900, the prototype for 120 others. Many, like the one illustrated, were adapted to burn oil. In their royal blue livery, lined out in red and yellow, with brass splasher beadings and red coupling rods, these engines presented a magnificent spectacle, and their haulage capacity was also remarkable, though Great Eastern schedules were admittedly easy compared with those on many other lines.* (NRM)

Eastern, they were really commodious. Boiler pressures had generally risen to 160–180 lbs per square inch. On almost any main line the best engines could have coped successfully with the best trains on almost any other.

As for the trains themselves, the provision of comfort and convenience was now seeping down the social scale. All expresses now conveyed third class passengers; on the Midland, indeed, second class had been abolished and the third class brought up to its standard. Four-wheeled coaches had now disappeared from long-distance services, and eight-wheeled bogie coaches were replacing six-wheelers. Lines whose trains ran for any considerable distances had now introduced corridor coaches with toilet compartments. Restaurant cars had begun to appear, so that the former lengthy refreshment stops like those at York and Preston were no longer necessary. On some night trains, first class sleeping carriages were being introduced, so that one could doze away the miles. Automatic brakes, working by vacuum or compressed air, were now the rule on all passenger trains. The permanent way had been much improved by the replacement of short iron rails by longer steel ones, though the later refinement of welding their ends together, so that rail-knock was eliminated for long stretches, had not yet been found feasible.[5] Average speeds were increasing. The express passenger train in Great Britain (and, one should add, also in France and some parts of the United States) had now become the fastest thing on earth, and was to remain so for some years yet. It was also available at a penny a mile, or even less when special excursion facilities were available.

If railways seemed to have reached a high point in regard to social utility, however, that did not mean that locomotive engineers were sitting back complacently and just turning out

more of the same when new engines were required. Shareholders wanted the largest possible return on their invested capital, so boards of directors were always pressing for economies in operation. Locomotive superintendents were accordingly continually asking themselves whether they might be able to reduce operating costs through changes in design. Could double-heading be eliminated by making locomotives more powerful? Did coupling driving wheels together really improve haulage ability without sacrificing speed, or was it true, as Patrick Stirling of the Great Northern Railway had once said, that an express engine with coupled wheels was 'like a laddie running wi' his breeks doun'? How high might boiler pressure be safely raised? If axle loads were increased to obtain better adhesion, how many bridges would need to be strengthened, and would the cost be prohibitive? For a locomotive to run freely at speed, did driving wheels need to be very large? Could one increase the heating surface inside a boiler without greatly enlarging it externally? Was a wide grate more conducive to steam-raising than a narrow one? Was the interior of a steam dome the best place from which to supply steam to the cylinders without priming occurring? Or was a perforated pipe running the length of the boiler just beneath its highest point equally efficient? Or was there some better method still? Could the water from the tender tank, injected into the boiler to replace what was evaporating away, be heated up first, using heat that would otherwise be wasted? What was the best internal profile for a locomotive's chimney, so that the exhaust blast would produce the greatest sucking effect through the fire-tubes? Was a square-topped firebox better than a round-topped one? Did compounding really save coal in the long run, and was it worth experimenting to find out?

These and similar questions occupied the minds of locomotive superintendents and their assistants, and were extensively dwelt upon in Rous-Marten's articles. There were of course many developments that came after his time—the practice of super-heating steam, for example, and the replacement of the slide valve

---

[5] I recall that during my schooldays in the 'twenties we were told in science classes of the dreadful buckling that would occur in hot weather, with consequent disastrous accidents, if no gaps were left between the butt-ends of the rails so that they could expand.

by the piston valve to enable finer adjustments of cut-off and easier flows of steam into and out of cylinders.

Other changes which were to alter the railway's image were also still in the future when Rous-Marten passed from the scene. The provision of special luxury trains on ultra-fast schedules, which he recommended, had not yet begun, expect that the London, Brighton and South Coast line had introduced its 'Brighton Sunday Pullman', forerunner of the later daily 'Southern Belle'. Electric traction was beginning to come in on short selected portions of line, but no one as yet envisaged its use on long-distance trains. The first diesel locomotive had yet to appear. Steam railcars had begun their short vogue on some branch lines. As yet there was no competition from road vehicles, and here and there new lines were still being constructed.

When the twentieth century opened, the cult of speed had not really begun, though the Railway Races to Edinburgh and Aberdeen in 1888 and 1895 had aroused some enthusiasm; crowds were prepared to turn out during the small hours at places like Newcastle and Carlisle to see the rivals arrive and depart. The old Queen, who had always insisted that no train should exceed 40 miles per hour when she was in it, would certainly have disapproved of ultra-rapid transport on railways. It was a token of things to come when her coffin was hurried from Portsmouth (she had died in the Isle of Wight) to London in record time, reaching a speed of 80 miles an hour at one point, twice what she would have sanctioned if she had still been alive, so that Victoria station could be reached on time after a delayed start. During the earlier part of the new reign the first stirrings of the streamline age began to be felt. In 1904 a contraption of wood, wire and fabric carrying two men actually *flew* across a beach in America. In 1906 the Navy built its first full-sized battleship capable of 20 knots. Transatlantic liners began to compete for the Blue Riband. Edward VII, who had liked living a fast life in the days when he was still Prince of Wales, approved of his trains running fast also, and arranged for his son and daughter-in-law to carry out a Royal Tour of the West Country by travelling down to Plymouth in a train that set out to reach that place in record time, and succeeded.[6] It was left to Rous-Marten, however, to time the first train to reach 100 miles an hour.[7]

However, the new enthusiasm for speed on the railway took a bad knock when a number of serious accidents, each with many fatalities, occurred within months of each other, because of derailments on sharp curves. A period of caution followed when on some lines drivers were officially discouraged from much exceeding the mile-a-minute rate. Rous-Marten felt the caution was overdone; not speed itself, but speed in the wrong place, was to be deprecated.

At the time of Rous-Marten's death, the British locomotive scene was beginning to change. Single-wheelers disappeared from main-line expresses, except as pilots, and were relegated to branch lines; by 1920 they were almost all gone. Webb's famous compounds had all been either scrapped or radically rebuilt. The 4-4-0 no longer reigned supreme in express passenger work, though its day was by no means over. Six lines had begun to build 4-4-2s as their principal express type. The Great Western also tried this wheel arrangement, but later reconstructed their 'Atlantics' as 4-6-0s. On a number of lines the latter type was beginning to be built for the heaviest work. Compounding, after trials on a number of lines, persisted only on the Midland. The Brighton line began to build express tank engines. Most portentous of all developments was Churchward's huge 'Pacific', *The Great Bear*, completed at Swindon in 1908. It was something of an experiment, and Churchward himself was not over-enthusiastic about it; it proved too large for all the Great Western routes except the main line from Paddington to Bristol. Swindon eventually rejected its monstrous offspring, rebuilding it as a 'Castle' 4-6-0 after its boiler had worn out.

---

[6] See page 83.
[7] See note 3, page 12.

In regard to coaching stock during the Edwardian period, variety increased. The clerestory roof enjoyed a brief vogue. Six-wheel bogies were fitted to many dining and sleeping cars to give a smoother ride. Electric lighting powered from dynamos driven from the coach wheels took the place of gas lamps fuelled from cylinders slung under the frames. Carriages with separate compartments were still the rule, unless one were wealthy enough to hire a family saloon to be attached to the train of one's choice, but on nearly all lines the dangers of isolation were mitigated on long non-stop runs by the provision of side-corridors and end-vestibules allowing access to toilets and refreshment cars. The 'Southern Belle' began to run daily between London and Brighton, foreshadowing many future 'Belles' on other lines; for a while to travel by Pullman was the acme of luxury. On the Lancashire and Yorkshire 'Club Car' trains appeared, to convey business men from Southport and Blackpool to Manchester and back, but the idea did not spread widely; what Manchester thought today, London in this case did *not* think tomorrow. In 1908 the London and South Western introduced four first class sleeping cars for use on night services between London and Plymouth; they came just too late for Rous-Marten to use, but he would have loved their removable iron bedsteads complete with brass knobs. They did not long outlast him, since they did not attract enough custom; in 1911 they were sold to the Great Western Railway.

The Edwardian age was the high noon of rail travel. Lines penetrated everywhere. There were companies innumerable, both large and small. Between any two places there were alternative routes. You could travel from Liverpool Street to York, from King's Cross to Cromer, from Edinburgh to Kirkcudbright, in through carriages. You could book from St Pancras to Stratford-on-Avon (though you would have to change *en route* if you wanted to go that way). Railways now long closed and overgrown with vegetation or obliterated by motorways then carried passengers and paid their ways. It was an expansive, optimistic age, cheerful and inclined to be bumptious. Progress was inevitable. Britannia ruled the waves and exported her products, including locomotives, to all parts of the globe. We had actually made friends with the French at last. As for the Kaiser, a few more Dreadnoughts would keep him in his place. It could not last, but while it did it was bliss to be alive—if you had an income to match your extravagances. Of this period's railway travelling Rous-Marten was the great scribe.

* * *

The first thing that strikes one when one reads his articles is Rous-Marten's enthusiasm for his subject, which comes bubbling out like champagne from a shaken bottle. The obvious delight he takes in writing about the objects of his affection is infectious. His encyclopaedic knowlege of everthing to do with railways is very evident. It was said of him that if he were put down beside the track on any main line route in Great Britain he would infallibly know where he was to within a quarter of a mile. His comments are usually pleasant, his criticism never carping or sour. The only persons about whom he allowed himself to be scornful were those who passed derogatory remarks about railway shortcomings out of the depths of their ignorance, or who invented impossible feats of locomotive performances for publication in the popular press; on such he poured out the vials of his wrath. In general it is praise that he dispenses, and one is carried along on the crest of a wave. Things are excellent, or capital, or first-rate, or remarkable. Performances are creditable, or smart, or, at worst, respectable.

He certainly succeeded in his aim of making his articles informative and readable. The steam locomotive is easier to understand, as regards its mode of working, than electronic devices of the present day, but it is not simply a machine for boiling water in order to turn wheels. It has its complications. In design, one desideratum has to be balanced against another. The controls inside its cab are more numerous than those that a car driver has to operate. Fuel varies in quality and needs to be placed skilfully on the fire. Steam has to be delivered to the cylinders dry, not mixed with droplets of water. Bearings run hot unless properly oiled. Rous-Marten was good at explaining the complications in simple language which a railway enthusiast who knew little about mechanics could follow; he did not pile on engineering jargon.

However, he had his faults, some of which seem more serious to us than they did to his first readers, and one was what seems in our more laconic age an undue verbosity. He was an adept at using two or three words where one would do. Like the character in W. S. Gilbert's verses, 'he argued high, he argued low, he also argued round about him'. He could go on repeating himself over and over again. One is sometimes tempted to wonder uncharitably whether this had anything to do with being paid by the length of his articles. Adjectives sprinkled in profusion, phrases saying the same thing twice in a different way, anecdotes not always relevant to the occasion, quotations from poets, novelists and Shakespeare, Latin tags—they all mount up. However, all these were no doubt to the taste of the Edwardian reader who, after a busy day clerking in an office, and after a good meal, put on his carpet slippers, relaxed in an easy chair before a cheerful coal fire, and proceeded to savour the orotundities of his favourite magazine. We like our literary fare with less gravy on it, but Rous-Marten wrote for his own time, not for ours.

He also goes in for frequent literary interpolations, acceptable to our great-grandfathers, no doubt, but we tend to find them somewhat tiresome and overdone and I have not gone out of my way to include them in the extracts which follow. Latin quotations, in particular, were more in vogue in the days when that language figured more largely in the education of gentlemen, and Members of Parliament threw them at each other across the floor of the House. No doubt *The Railway Magazine* reader who had only been to a Board School was suitably impressed; they sounded sonorous, and what exactly they signified didn't really matter. *O tem-*

pora, O mores: *O si sic omnes*: *Tempora mutantur et nos mutamur in illi*: out they came at the slightest provocation. The habit died hard; Cecil J. Allen, of blessed memory, was addicted to it; after his time the practice faded away. We do not now wallow in the classics like our ancestors. I fancy, too, that in these box-watching days we read the classics of our own language less. I confess to never having come across Silas Wegg, whom Rous-Marten trots out more than once. No doubt the loss is mine.

I personally also find his frequent use of inverted commas, which appear like froth on the beer of his eloquence, rather tiresome. There is no article of his in which at least a dozen pairs fail to appear. A journalist has to live, and they certainly help towards the profitable filling-up of space. Inspection shows that other contemporary *Railway Magazine* contributors also made copious use of them. This, too, is now an almost extinct habit. It is some 50 years now since *The Times* stopped referring to a record as a 'record'.

Another feature which slightly raises the eyebrows, now that we have passed out of the age of mensurating in rods, poles and perches, is Rous-Marten's use of *chains* as sub-divisions of the mile. In the present decimal age it is perhaps as well to mention that a chain was 22 yards, the length of a surveyor's chain-measure (and also the length of a cricket pitch) and that there were 80 in every mile. The Rous-Marten addict should have his pocket calculator with him all the time; he has then only to divide the figure given him by 80 to get the fraction of a mile as a decimal. For such a person, Rous-Marten, like Karl Marx's workers, has nothing to lose but his chains. Another habit which I personally find rather irritating is his frequent use of the abbreviation 'viz'. This, too, is never met with now. However, these are small matters.

Am I doing the great man an injustice, in finding a certain flavour of adulation in his articles when he is referring to the great men of the railway world, while they are still in office and in a position to refuse him a footplate pass if they dislike anything he has written? They are always referred to in an excessively complimentary manner; they are the able Mr This or the excellent Mr That, to whom he pays tribute or takes off his hat. If one of them seems to have done something questionable, punches are at once pulled, and it is suggested that there must be a good reason for what is being done. One may instance here his attitude to F. W. Webb, Locomotive Superintendent of the London and North Western Railway for so long. A little while before he began his Practice and Performance articles, Rous-Marten wrote two long pieces in praise of Webb's compounds, saying how generally satisfactory he had always found them when he sampled their performance. Webb was then still enthroned at Crewe. Just how satisfactory or otherwise they really were was shown in the rapidity with which they disappeared, or were radically modified, once George Whale had succeeded Francis Webb, and by the long subsequent hostility displayed against the very idea of compounding by London and North Western drivers. Locomotives were required which were simple, sturdy and reliable, and Whale built his new 4-4-0 non-compound 'Precursor' 4-4-0s as fast as he could, and despatched to the scrap heap engines which in Mr Webb's eye had been the last word in locomotive design in their time. Locomotives were needed which were reliable, whose driving wheels kept in phase with one another and did not start to spin round in opposite directions when they felt like it. Rous-Marten certainly knew of the compounds' failings, as later articles, written after Webb had retired, show. By now Whale was the one issuing footplate passes. So, like the Vicar of Bray, Rous-Marten began to disown what he had once been concerned to defend. But perhaps I am just being cynical.

One very definite criticism one *must* make is of his manner of presenting locomotive performance. Almost never does he give a sufficiency of detail; all too often it is vagueness helped out by verbiage. As an example one may take the case of a journey described in his August 1904 article, made on the South Eastern and Chatham line between Cannon Street and Folkestone. He omits to give the number of the 'D' Class 4-4-0 which hauled the train, or the latter's tare weight in tons; he gets a fact wrong, quoting a speed at the top of a 1 in 100 incline, when there is no such incline on the line; he says nothing at all about the journey after the descent from Sevenoaks tunnel; he gives no passing times anywhere. Instead we get compliments for the railway's new General Manager, Mr Vincent Hill, 'not only on this excellent and very comfortable train, but also on the admirable punctuality usually maintained by the suburban business trains to Victoria and Ludgate Hill since his accession to the chief command'. It looks suspiciously like a case of 'You scratch my back and I'll scratch yours'. If only he could have foreborne to flatter the great Mr Hill and used the space taken up by including a log of the journey and some speeds at critical places. On the relatively few occasions when he *does* provide a log, he never includes speeds, and he gives it exactly as he took it, in the form of watch-readings in hours, minutes and seconds. His successors adopted the much more helpful practice of showing a run as beginning with '00.00', so that one can see at a glance how long it took from start to pass, and of giving speeds at the logged points of the journey. It never occurred to Rous-Marten to do this. In transcribing such of his logs as I have included, I have taken the liberty of altering them to conform with later practice.

More than once in his sequence of articles Rous-Marten insists on his concern to be accurate. Alas, he was frequently the opposite. When he mentions a gradient or a distance he is often in error. For someone with such an immense knowledge of the routes over which he travelled this seems very surprising . In regard to gradients, one supposes he had access to official documents. His friend the Rev W. J. Scott certainly must have had, for he published a series of articles entitled *Gradients of our Chief Railways*, between 1902 and 1904, in which all the main line routes are dealt with and diagrams given. Unfortunately they are not always accurate. Some of Rous-Marten's mistakes may have arisen from using them, but certainly not all did.

GWR 4–6–2 No 111 The Great Bear *as built in 1907 — the first 'Pacific' to be constructed in Britain. Why Churchward built it is something of a mystery since in his time the 'Stars' were adequate for the heaviest trains, and the engine's dimensions limited its operation to the main line between London and Bristol. It was too big for its routes. Rous-Marten's reaction was that it left him 'gasping with sheer amazement'. It was eventually dismantled in 1924, parts of its motion being incorporated in a new 'Castle' 4–6–0.* (NRM)

Perhaps he relied on his memory, which sometimes let him down. Perhaps, writing his articles in longhand, in a hurry to get them in on time, he sometimes wrote illegibly and the compositor mistook one figure for another. But he really ought to have been more careful. It will be noticed, in the 'Performance' section, that the mistakes sometimes came thick and fast. I have corrected all serious errors with appropriate footnotes, basing my judgements on a recent issue of *British Main Line Gradient Profiles*, which in turn are based on earlier profiles published in *The Railway Magazine* during the 'thirties. Gradients may have *slightly* changed in the 30 years which followed Rous-Marten's death, but not all that much.

Having said all these things in criticism, I still avow that his articles make enjoyable reading. They were not written for the assiduous researcher, out to debunk in order to get a doctorate, but for the railway enthusiast. They were intended to carry the reader along and convey a shared pleasure and excitement. This they do, and that is the justification for re-printing some of them. Like the plays of Shakespeare they are 'God's plenty'. He brings before our eyes a pageant of the great engines of bygone days, the 'Spinners' and 'Highflyers', the 'Cities' and 'Greyhounds', the 'D' Class dandies of the South Eastern and Chatham and the 'Dunalastairs', the 'Precursors' and the 'Jersey Lilies', all (in Wordsworth's phrase) 'characters in the Great Apocalypse'. We share his enthusiasm, and wonder what he might have made of a Gresley or Bulleid 'Pacific', or a 'Britannia'. Fate allowed him just one glimpse into what was for him 'Tomorrow's World'. Churchward's 'Pacific', *The Great Bear*, emerged from Swindon in February 1908, and in his article two months later he tells us that it left him 'gasping with sheer amazement'. But he was never able to sample its performance, for he died in that same month.

PART 1
Practice

APRIL   1902

On the introduction of the 4–6–0 type for express passenger work on the Great Western Railway

The event of the past month in respect of British locomotive practice is Mr W. Dean's[1] enlistment of the Great Western Railway in the small and select corps of British railways that use six-coupled express engines. The latest locomotive designed by him and turned out early in March from the Swindon works[2] forms the third British instance of this arrangement being adopted for express service . . .

The new Great Western engine is intended, I understand, for use on the steep grades of Devon and Cornwall, which are as steep as 1 in 55 to 1 in 60 for many miles together both ways, whilst at some points on the Dartmoor, Rattery and Hemerdon banks they even rise at 1 in 43, 1 in 41 and 1 in 40. I am not aware that express trains having an inclusive speed of over 40 miles an hour are run anywhere in the world over gradients so severe as these. Yet the Great Western Railway accomplishes the feat, and does it in good style, too, with the 5 ft 8 in four-coupled bogie engines of the domeless 'Camel' or 'Avalon' type, which have cylinders 18 in by 26 in, as it did with their similarly dimensioned but smaller-boilered predecessors, *Duke of Cornwall*, *Pendennis Castle*, and the rest of the class. Only with loads of 200 tons and upward, which are of daily occurrence during the summer months, recourse was compulsorily had to pilot assistance.

Herein was found the usual experience as to the 'double-heading' practice. The train engine could often have kept time with the load had one coach been taken off. The extra coach was the 'last straw which broke the camel's back'—I do not refer to the powerful locomotive so-named—on such grades as 1 in 40. Thus the second engine was often run for the sake of that single coach. When such loads as 12 or 13 of the large corridor clerestoried bogie coaches had to be hauled the recourse to piloting seemed more justifiable, but, even so, a full load for *two* locomotives never could be provided, because such a train would have extended beyond the station accommodation available, and would in other respects, too, have been an unwieldy, if not unmanageable length on such a road. Consequently, at the best, two engines only took the load for one and a half—regarding the train engine as entitled to be credited with its own load and allotting the odd half to the pilot.

Even the main line of the Great Western from Paddington to Newton Abbot, although it has

---

[1] References to Mr Dean in this extract should really be understood as applying to his assistant, G. J. Churchward, who later succeeded him as Locomotive Superintendent on the GWR. At the time when the article was printed, Dean was suffering from progressive mental deterioration, and it was Churchward who was actually, and tactfully, doing his work for him.

[2] No 100 *William Dean*.

GWR 4-6-0 'Saint' No 98, as yet un-named; unlike the first of its class, No 100, it was built with a coned boiler. Its exterior appearance and that of its sister-engines was later modified by curving the running-boards downwards at either end and substituting a more conventional two-step approach to the foot-plate for the original ladder-like contraption. (NRM)

the reputation of being, and indeed is, one of the easiest roads in the kingdom over the greater portion of those 214 miles, has a few stiff little bits scattered about, On the down journey it has no adverse gradient of any consequence until the Wellington bank is reached, 169 miles from London, but then several miles of steep grades have to be breasted until the Whiteball summit is attained, near the west end of the tunnel, and much of the rise is at 1 in 89.[3] This, however, could be conveniently tackled with heavy trains by the aid of a bank engine after the plan adopted by the Caledonian Railway at Beattock. But in the opposite direction there are three fairly stiff ascents rather widely separated, but none exceeding two miles in length, viz, that near

Burlescombe at 1 in 115, in Box tunnel at 1 in 100, and near Wootton Bassett, also at 1 in 100. It would be manifestly awkward and extravagant to rely on bank engines regularly for those three climbs. Each would involve a special stop; and so, when the standard express engines have loads with which they are unable to keep time up those banks unassisted, a pilot is taken from Exeter all the way to Bristol, or from Bristol to Swindon, a special stop being made at the latter place to let it come off. I have noted this on various occasions with the 7 ft 8 in single-wheelers, but it is far less common with the new coupled 'Atbara' and 'Badminton' classes, which appear to be able to grapple with all ordinary train loads, and to be overtaxed only by the extra-heavy expresses of the holiday season. But it is obvious that still more powerful locomotives might be advantageous, even on this easier length of 214 miles, both to save the

[3] Not quite accurate, though not seriously misleading. The last 3 miles before the summit are at 1 in 90 (1 m), 1 in 86 ($\frac{3}{4}$ m), 1 in 80 ($\frac{3}{4}$ m) and 1 in 127 ($\frac{5}{8}$ m).

GWR 4-4-0 No 3340 Marazion, *built in 1900 and still in its original condition with parallel boiler and curved running-plate, heading a Paddington-Plymouth train, re-srarting from Brent, South Devon. This was one of the smaller 5 ft 8 in four-coupled engines intended for haulage over the severe gradients between Newton Abbot and Penzance.* (Ken Nunn Collection, Locomotive Club of Great Britain)

expense of a second engine and to avert the need of an extra stop to pick up or drop the pilot.

It is the special difficulty of the Great Western Railway that its worst banks do not lie within compact limits, like that of the London and North Western Railway at Shap, or those of the Caledonian at Beattock and Dunblane, which can be conveniently worked with the aid of a bank engine stationed at the foot. From Newton Abbot to Penzance, a distance of 112½ miles[4], there is hardly a single level stretch of any material length. Putting aside the relatively easy bit across the table-land extending between the Rattery and Hemerdon summits, about 12 miles, the road is a series of perpetually-recurrent steep-sided gables, far severer than the

Shap, Beattock, Dunblane, Falahill, Whitrope or Barrhead inclines, or than the grades by which the London and South Western crosses Dartmoor; worse, even, on the average, than those of the Aviemore-Culloden out on the Highland line. Such conditions manifestly demanded 'heroic' treatment. Obviously this is how Mr Dean has viewed the case, for he has produced a novel type of locomotive that ought exactly to fulfil the requirements indicated. With a vast boiler 5 ft in diameter and a huge Belpaire firebox more than 9 ft in length, 2,400 sq ft of heating surface, cylinders 18 in by 30 in, six-coupled 6 ft 8 in wheels, some 50 tons of adhesion weight, and a steam pressure of 200 lbs per square inch, the new locomotive necessarily possesses immense nominal strength, which she should be able to develop fully in actual practice. Thus the newest Great Western engine must be

[4] Not accurate: the distance is 111¼ miles.

classed as one of the most powerful ever yet placed on British metals for passenger express duty, weighing as it does no less than 69 tons without the tender.

It may be observed that in this newest locomotive Mr Dean has departed strikingly (1) from the special traditions of his railway in one important respect, viz, in using outside instead of inside cylinders; (2) from British traditions generally in employing so great a length of piston stroke as 30 inches.

The former plan is, of course, no novelty outside the Great Western, even for six-coupled engines, there being many old locomotives of this type on the Caledonian line, built for mineral traffic, while the newer six-coupled express engines of the North Eastern and Highland lines both have outside cylinders. But their employment on the Great Western under the present conditions is quite a fresh departure. It affords another illustration of a fact to which I have more than once called attention—that whenever a particular method appears on the eve of becoming utterly extinct in British locomotive practice, something invariably occurs which gives it a new lease of life.

Time after time outside cylinders have seemed to be on the extreme verge of extinction on British railways, and then something has always happened to save them. The cases of the London and South Western with its four-cylinder non-compound, of the Great Northern with its '990' class, of the London and North Western with its compounds, of the Midland and North Eastern with their newest compounds, and of the North Eastern and Highland with their six-coupled express type, will at once suggest themselves. And now the Great Western affords a fresh instance. Mr Dean no doubt would as usual have placed his cylinders inside the frames could he have found room for them. But this is not easy with six-coupled wheels of large diameter, while with a piston stroke so long as 30 in, owing to the length of the crank-throw, it would probably be quite impracticable.

Although the point does not necessarily arise in the present connection, it may be worth while to observe that those people who regard the old broad gauge as a mistake, a mere fad of an ambitious engineer, and who declare our standard 4 ft 8½ in gauge equal to all requirements, must begin to realise the serious restrictions which the narrower width and the lowness of our load-gauge vertical limit impose in respect of increased power. If you desire a fairly large driving wheel, you must curtail your length of stroke, else you will raise your boiler so high that the chimney will be knocked down by the first bridge or tunnel. If you desire big cylinders you cannot conveniently or satisfactorily get them inside the frames owing to the narrowness of the available space. If you therefore compulsorily place them outside, then you must 'mind your eye' and not make them too large, or they will strip off the edge of the first station platform you come to, or cut a groove in the side of the next tunnel. These would be awkward incidents, and are wisely avoided by our locomotive designers. But the necessity of avoidance imposes much otherwise unnecessary planning and scheming.

Now, Mr Dean in his new engine has adhered to the cylinder diameter which has given him such excellent results in the 'Atbaras', 'Badmintons', 'Cornwalls', and 'Camels', viz, 18 in. Manifestly he finds that the boiler pressure of 180 lbs to 200 lbs of steam with the relative pressure on the piston area which an 18 in diameter yields, viz, about 255 square inches, provides an initial motive force ample for his requirements. And so, instead of employing cylinders 20 in in diameter, as he did originally in the 7 ft 8 in singles and in the 7 ft coupled 'Armstrongs', with a 24 in piston stroke in the former case and a 26 in stroke in the latter, he has determined to obtain enhanced effective power by multiplying that initial force through the aid of leverage. This was the principle upon which the late Mr Patrick Stirling proceeded when he designed his celebrated 8 ft single-wheelers. He gave them a stroke of no less than 28 in in order to secure augmented haulage power, while the large wheel diameter allowed a slower movement of the reciprocating and revolving parts at a given speed.

But Mr Dean has 'gone one better' than this. By adopting a stroke of no less than 30 in in length he has taken a virtually new departure in British locomotive practice. So far as I am aware this extraordinary length of stroke has only once before been tried in Great Britain, for express work at any rate. That was in the case of a batch of 7 ft coupled express engines designed by Mr W. Bouch, which came into the hands of the North Eastern Railway on the absorption of one of the numerous smaller lines which are now incorporated in its vast system. These engines, which were numbered 1268, 1269, 1270, etc, had leading bogies and 17 in outside cylinders, with 30 in piston stroke. They were built many years ago, and were reported to have done good work, but soon after they came into the possession of the North Eastern Railway Mr Fletcher, who was Locomotive Superintendent at the time, rebuilt them as inside-cylinder, non-bogie engines, with a reduced piston stroke, 24 in, I believe, closely resembling his own well-known and very efficient standard type which so long did all the best express duty on the North Eastern, and did it remarkably well too . . . Those were the only British express engines that I know of which ever had a 30 in stroke, and, as it will be noticed, the peculiarity was not perpetuated, nor has it been revived in this country—although the case is otherwise in America—until this new departure on the part of Mr Dean on the Great Western Railway.

As to the advantages and disadvantages of a long piston-stroke, I have had something to say in earlier articles of this series. The question is one upon which the highest authorities differ *toto coelo*. Mr Dean himself long maintained a maximum limit of 24 in for all his passenger engines excepting the few employed on the South Devon and Cornwall lines. To them he gave 26 in, as he did also to the four 7 ft coupled of the 'Armstrong' Class, and subsequently to his 'Cornwalls', 'Camels', 'Badmintons' and 'Atbaras'. Messrs D. and P. Drummond, Billinton, Kirtley, J. Stirling, Wainwright, Johnson, W. Worsdell, Robinson, Aspinall, Holmes, Manson and M'Intosh, all hold by a 26 in stroke. So

does Mr Ivatt in his numerous '400' and '1321' classes, his twelve single-wheelers and his goods engines, but he prefers 24 in in his '990' or Atlantic type. Mr Holden long kept to a 24 in stroke, but latterly has substituted 26 in, and has also lengthened the stroke of some of the 24 in engines to 25 in. Mr Webb has always consistently and persistently adhered to 24 in. Both the 8 ft single-wheelers and the large mineral traffic engines built by the late Mr Patrick Stirling for the Great Northern had 28 in stroke. The French express engines on M de Glehn's four-cylinder compound principle, which are now the standard type on all the main lines in France, have uniformly a $25\frac{1}{4}$ in piston stroke. Some American engines have 28 in, 30 in and even 32 in stroke.

Thus, 'doctors differ' so widely that it would be presumptuous for an outside engineer to 'lay down the law' on such a point. It will be manifest to everybody possessing even the most rudimentary acquaintance with mechanical engineering that a long stroke has the advantage of increasing by leverage the practical efficiency of the motive force supplied by the steam pressure on the pistons, and that it has the disadvantage—if that be really a disadvantage, which is much disputed, of proportionately accelerating the piston speed, because the piston has so much longer distance to travel in the given time of each stroke. Every locomotive engineer has to weigh the one thing against the other, and then to judge which, in his particular circumstances, must be allowed to send down the scale. Probably in most instances where the highest speeds have to be run on a road of moderate difficulty the shorter stroke of 24 in to 26 in will be preferred as affording a lower piston speed. But when very heavy loads have to be hauled over severe gradients, especially when the descents are too steep or curved to warrant extreme downhill velocities, then the extra long stroke, such as 28 in or 30 in, can undoubtedly be employed with great advantage on the score of increment of power thus often obviating the use of a pilot engine. Mr Dean's experiment will be watched with deep interest by all locomotive engineers.

OCTOBER 1902

On Mr S. W. Johnson's new three-cylinder compounds on the Midland Railway

Last month I illustrated the new compound engine which has been designed by Mr S. W. Johnson and built at the Derby works for the heavy express work of the Midland Railway. Two of these engines have been constructed, differing from one another only in the fact that one has plain 1¾ in copper tubes giving 1,448 square feet of tube-heating surface, while the other has steel Serve tubes, 2¾ in in external diameter, and ribbed internally, thus presenting a heating surface of 1,570 square feet, according to the formula by which the surface of Serve tubes is computed.

In planning this new type of locomotive, which has many features of entire novelty, Mr Johnson has preferred to follow the later North

MR No 2632, one of Johnson's first pair of 4–4–0 three-cylinder compounds, with one inside high-pressure and two outside low-pressure cylinders and 7 ft coupled driving wheels. Introduced in 1902, they were tested out on the Settle-Carlisle line and proved very successful, climbing the gradients well and reaching speeds of 90 mph and upwards on the descents. See pages 102–104 for descriptions by Rous-Marten of runs behind these two compounds between Carlisle and Leeds. (NRM)

Eastern rather than the earlier North Western ideas. That is to say, he follows the general plan of the North Eastern railway locomotive No 1619 as rebuilt, and not that of the North Western 'Experiment', 'Dreadnought', 'Teutonic', 'Greater Britain' or 'John Hick'. His system is common to both of these in the respect that he uses three cylinders, and not either two as the North Eastern did originally, or four as Mr Worsdell has done latterly. It is a little curious to note how in each of those cases the development has been in the direction of adding an extra cylinder. But Mr Johnson not only adopts the North Eastern number of cylinders; he also chooses the North Eastern relative position in preference to that on the North Western engines. That is to say, he has one high-pressure cylinder 19 in in diameter like the North Eastern, instead of two 15 inch like the latest North Western three-cylinder engines. And he places the one high-pressure cylinder inside, and the two low-pressure cylinders outside the frames, as the North Eastern does, instead of putting the two high-pressure cylinders outside and the one low-pressure cylinder inside as North Western does. It may be added that Mr Johnson's compound has various dimensional points in common with Mr Worsdell's; eg each has 7 ft coupled driving wheels and high pressure cylinders 19 in by 26 in. But differences soon begin to appear. Mr Johnson gives both his inside and his outside cylinders his usual length of piston stroke, viz, 26 in. Mr Worsdell shortens the stroke of his outside cylinders by 2 in, giving them only 24 in as against 26 in in the inside cylinder. This is a detail of practice as to which diversity of opinion may exist—indeed, evidently does exist. For whereas Mr D. Drummond in his four-cylinder non-compound engines, class 720, adopts the same length of piston stroke, viz, 26 in, for all four cylinders, Mr J. Manson in *his* four-cylinder compound locomotive on the Glasgow and South Western Railway employs a 26 in stroke for his inside cylinders and one of 24 in for his outside pair, just as Mr Worsdell in No 1619. 'Doctors differ' once more. I shall not attempt to decide as to the

relative merits of their respective methods.

Each of the new Midland compounds has 150 square feet of heating surface in its firebox. Thus, adding this to the tube surface, it will be seen that the two engines possess a total heating surface of 1,598 square feet in the one case and 1,720 square feet in the other. This should be ample for supplying 'live' steam to one cylinder 19 in by 26 in. But a plan of auxiliary working has also to be provided for. I may as well give the official description of the method, which is as follows: 'The middle cylinder takes steam directly from the boiler at 195 lbs pressure per square inch, and this steam is exhausted, without the intervention of any pipe, directly into the steam chest common to the two outside cylinders. Simultaneously with the admission of steam to the high-pressure steam chest, steam, at a predetermined pressure, is automatically admitted to the low-pressure steam chest by a specially-constructed regulating valve placed on the side of the smokebox. The regulating valve is so arranged that when the maximum pressure allowed for in the low-pressure chests is attained, further supply of steam directly from the boiler is automatically cut off; thus excessive strains are avoided on the moving parts, and although the boiler pressure is 195 lbs per square inch, none of the pistons are ever subjected to a pressure equal to that of the pistons in a simple engine working with a boiler pressure of 170 lbs. When working compound, the pressure in the low-pressure chests, according to the position of the reversing gear, varies from 40 lbs to 60 lbs; but for starting and working a heavy train up a steep incline, increased power can be obtained by admitting steam from the boiler through the regulating valve to the low-pressure chests for as long a time as necessary. The amount of steam that can be passed by the regulating valve between the minimum and maximum limits is governed by a controlling valve placed in the cab. By manipulating this valve the driver can vary the low-pressure steam-chest pressure to suit the work in hand . . . A gauge is provided in the cab which shows the driver the amount of pressure that the engine is working with in the low-pressure steam chests. This ought to prove a valuable auxiliary when steep banks have to be encountered like those approaching Blea Moor, Ais Gill or Peak Forest.

The boilers of Nos 2631 and 2632 are 11 ft 7 in in length and 4 ft 8 in in diameter. The fireboxes are very large, exceeding even those of Mr Johnson's penultimate class, as they are no less than 8 ft 6 in long. This, I should say, would take a great deal of stoking, but the advantages as to steam generation are unquestionable. The boiler-axis stands 8 ft 6 in above the rail level.

In respect of steam pressure, Mr Johnson has adopted a rather novel and peculiar figure. Usually, if the steam pressure be not 160 lbs, 170 lbs, 175 lbs, or 180 lbs, it is 200. True, the Glasgow and South Western Railway uses the curious pressure of 165 lbs, but generally round numbers are chosen excepting in the case of 175, which has a special relation to the even 100 or 200. But Mr Johnson, although he employs a higher pressure than 180 lbs, does not quite go up to 200. He has adopted 195. But it appears from the passage in the official description which I quoted just now that through the relief afforded by a special device the pistons will not be subject to a pressure larger than the equivalent of 170 lbs in a non-compound engine. Mr Johnson's new locomotive weighs $59\frac{1}{2}$ tons in working order, and its double-bogie tender weighs $52\frac{1}{2}$ tons; thus the total weight of the motive machinery of the train hauled by this engine is 112 tons.

As No 2631 and 2632 are still in their experimental stage it would be premature to say anything about their performances. No 2631 has been employed for some time stationed at Leeds and has worked the express which starts from Leeds daily at 10.6 am for Carlisle, leaving Carlisle on its return journey on the 3.55 Glasgow diner which is booked to do the $112\frac{35}{4}$ miles to Leeds, without stop, in 2 hours 20 minutes, or at an average speed of 48.3 miles an hour over a road with long banks at 1 in 100. I have seen it once or twice at Carlisle taking out the latter train. It was stationed at Carlisle for a short time at the beginning of last month, but I believe it subsequently went back to Leeds as its regular home. The new compounds are very fine-looking engines, extremely massive in aspect, and I have no doubt they will give a good account of themselves in regular practice.[6]

---

[5] Not quite accurate; the distance is 113 miles, so the train's average speed is fractionally greater than the figure Rous-Marten gives.

[6] See the extract on page 102 which gives a startling account of the locomotive's capabilities.

On the extent to which locomotive power depends upon boiler size and heating surface

It is much to be wished that some consensus of opinion could be arrived at among British locomotive engineers upon the question of locomotive boiler power. Hitherto we seem to have proceeded by a method which savours largely of the empirical. Needing enhanced power, we have increased the length or diameter of our boilers—or both—have enlarged our fireboxes, have augmented our steam pressure by so many pounds to the square inch, and so on. But it is difficult to detect any trace of a definite or uniform system in our manner of advance. We do not seem nearer than ever to the establishment of a formulated principle as to the proper proportions that should exist between boiler and firebox dimensions on the one hand, and cylinder capacity—either absolute or in relation to driving wheel diameter—on the other. Yet it is clearly most desirable that if possible we should know authoritatively whether there can in reality be said to be any such principle, and if so what it is.

It will of course be suggested that one 'principle' has been kept steadily in view during the past few years. That is to say, that the heating surface, alike of the boiler and of the firebox, and also the pressure of steam, have been persistently augmented. But this bears too close an analogy to the popular sentiment so often expressed as regards some political matter in need of reform—'Something must be done' . . . All

these ideas are quite right in themselves; the defect is that they lack precision of detail. It may be asked: What amount of heating surface should a modern express engine have in order to be able to perform satisfactorily the most arduous modern express work? Now if we take this as a starting point and begin to enquire into the view of the leading engineers on the subject we shall find a most curious and inexplicable discrepancy. It is a favourite fashion of the twentieth century to say confidently, 'Oh, a modern express engine ought certainly to have at least 2,000 square feet of heating surface'. Very good; that might do as a standard, only the unfortunate thing is that if we adopt that tentatively we are immediately brought face to face with two reasonable criticisms. First, a heating surface of 2,000 square feet or upward is no modern method at all, for engines built more than fifty years ago had as much as that. Sir Daniel Gooch's 8 ft single-wheelers, on the Great Western Railway, the first of which came out in 1847, had an amount of heating surface which ranged in different engines from 1,952 to 2,080 square feet. Also the London and North Western Railway's 8 ft single-wheeler, designed by Mr T. R. Crampton, and shown in the Great Exhibition of 1851, had as much as 2,290 square feet, which is not exceeded at the present day by a dozen English engines. Thus, in the London Exhibition of 1851, we had at any rate these two engines, each possessing 2,000 square feet of heating surface or more, whereas in the Glasgow Exhibition of 1901, fifty years later and less than three years ago, not one engine was there shown which even approached that amount of heating surface. It is true that on this later occasion there were regrettably few locomotive exhibits, but those that were present showed the most up-to-date British practice. For instance, the London and South Western engine, No 773, built by Messrs Dübs and Co, was one of Mr Drummond's 'last words' up to that date, yet its total heating surface, including that given by the firebox water-tubes, did not exceed 1,500 square feet for cylinders 18½ in by 26 in, while the Midland engine, No 2591, constructed by Messrs Neilson, Reid and Co, which was of Mr S. W. Johnson's latest design, actually had only 1,193 square feet, to fill cylinders 19 in by 26 in. Even the four fine express engines shown by British railways at the Paris Exhibition in the previous year, 1900, all fell far short of the amount of heating surface which is now so freely advocated as a minimum standard.

There is this much that is specially noteworthy as regards the Midland engine, namely that one of that batch of ten built by Messrs Neilson, Reid and Co, and represented at the Glasgow Exhibition by No 2591, notwithstanding her strangely small amount of heating surface, actually gave me the finest run I ever had on the Midland Railway, taking the load and road and speed all into account, up to a few weeks ago, when it was surpassed by one of Mr Johnson's new compounds. It may perhaps be remembered that No 2596, driven by Turner—now, alas, no more—took the 9.30 am fast Scotch express, weighting 300 tons, from St. Pancras to Leicester in a few seconds over 111 minutes, this gaining nearly two minutes on the fast booked time; and, I may add, the run could have been made in 2 or 3 minutes less but for the fact that the tender, being one of the older six-wheel kind, could not carry enough water to provide for 99 miles of such exceptionally hard work. This made it incumbent on Turner to economise the water, and consequently steam,

during the latter part of the journey. Still, the fact remains that that run of roughly 99 miles in 111 minutes, with 300 tons behind the tender, over a road which simply swarms with troublesome banks, was accomplished by an engine possessing only 1,193 square feet of heating surface. With other Midland engines of the same class . . . I have also recorded some excellent work, although never quite equal to that by No 2596 just mentioned. Yet it would seem somewhat rash to conclude that less than 1,200 square feet of heating surface could be taken as sufficient for such work. But, then, where are we to find a standard? In this particular instance . . . 1,193 square feet of heating surface provided steam enough for cylinders 19 in by 26 in to accomplish that remarkable performance. But, on the other hand, I have never obtained anything like approximate results with the very similar '60' class, which differ from the '2591' class mainly in having cylinders ½ in more in diameter, and it is another striking illustration of the singular diversity of practice that prevails, to find Mr Churchward supplying over 1,800 square feet of heating surface for cylinders only 18 in in diameter, whereas Mr Johnson provided less than 1,200 square feet for cylinders 19 to 19½ ins, the piston stroke in both cases being the same.

But perhaps the strangest instance of what appears at first sight topsy-turvydom in this respect was furnished by the late Mr Patrick Stirling. Now I have never met any engineer, at home or abroad, who did not take off his hat most cordially to Mr Stirling's great capacity as a locomotive engineer. His special strength consisted in the marvellous exactness with which he designed his engines for the specific work they were required to do. Whatever was the work that had to be done, his engines, while that work remainded proportionate to their powers, always—bar accident—did it efficiently. It may no doubt be said that Mr Stirling in his later years to some extent lacked foresight and did not realise in its fullness the great advance that was now occurring in the demands made upon locomotive power. I am of course basing my

GNR 4-2-2 No 1007, one of Patrick Stirling's last six 8-footers to be built at Doncaster, which came out in the year of his death, 1895. In these he slightly increased the cylinder diameters to provide extra power, and put a little more weight on the driving wheels. (NRM)

remarks purely on the steps he took to supply the demand that arose, namely in the last class of 8 ft single wheelers which he designed and built, Nos 1003–1008, which came out in 1895, which, while splendid engines, capable of work much beyond any *a priori* estimate of single-wheeler capacity, nevertheless fell far short of modern requirements. But it is also noteworthy that Mr Stirling continued to build his original type of 8 ft single, first designed in 1869, up to so recent a date as the year 1893–4, when he brought out Nos 1001 and 1002, the latest specimens of the earlier type. It is true that in the year 1885, fifteen years after the earliest 8 ft single had been designed, Mr Stirling, when starting to build a fresh batch of the type, did make some minor alterations. He gave the 1884 batch, ten in number, which came out at intervals during the subsequent ten years, an additional 1½ in in boiler diameter. When the first eight of that class had been built No 771 to 778, it appeared as if their author, having now produced forty-five of that type, had determined to build no more, but to continue instead constructing the new six-

wheel 7 ft 6 in single-wheelers, with inside cylinders, which he had started to turn out in 1885, but which were practically mere enlargements of his earlier express type, Nos 4, 6, etc, introduced by him shortly after his accession in 1866. He decided, however, to complete the batch of ten, and accordingly the last two made their appearence in 1893–4. As is generally known, they were originally numbered 264 and 265, taking the place of two older engines which had been converted by him from 7 ft coupled to 7 ft single, which were to go into the duplicate list. I had an interesting run on the footplate of No 264, subsequently No 1001, shortly after she came out, and later with her sister engine, No 265, which had then become No 2002. She took a creditable part in the famous Race to Aberdeen of 1895, running on several occasions between Grantham and York. I have subsequently had many fine runs with both Nos 1001 and 1002, which always excited my interest as being the last of the famous race that had first begun work in 1870.

But the particular phase of interest which attaches in the present connection to that batch of ten is this: The standard heating surface of the previous thirty-seven 8 ft single-wheelers was 1,165 square feet; that was always regarded as quite absurdly small when cylinders 18 in by 28 in had to be filled. It might naturally have been expected that when in 1884 Mr Stirling started his last batch of the first design and gave them boilers 4 ft in diameter, instead of 3 ft 10½ in as in the previous engines, the boiler length in both cases being 11 ft 5 in, he would certainly have secured a material increment of heating surface. But not at all. Nos 771, etc, built in 1884, actually had 110 square feet *less* of heating surface than had No 1, designed in 1869. It is true that some part of the larger surface was due to the employment of a water midfeather in the firebox, which was subsequently abandoned, but even so there was a substantial difference in favour of the earlier set. It may be added that the steam pressure was simultaneously increased from 140 to 160 lbs, but this is not germane to the point at present under consideration.

In the year 1894, in the course of a conversation with Mr Stirling, he remarked to me that he was greatly annoyed at the necessity being forced upon him of using pilots on the heaviest and fastest trains, a proceeding which it had always been his rule to discountenance—indeed, wherever possible, absolutely to forbid. He admitted, however, that the weight of the fastest trains had become much greater than that with which his original type of 8 ft single-wheeler was designed to cope, and he had come to the conclusion that it would be advisable to give the next batch of engines that he should build considerably enhanced strength. He added that his next engines would have greater boiler power and far larger cylinders, the latter of the colossal dimensions of 19½ in by 28 in, and he expressed his conviction that these would be found capable of dealing with modern express duty. I remember asking him whether he did not contemplate multiplying and enlarging his 7 ft 6 in type. He replied in the negative. 'Of course,' he said, 'those are fully more powerful than the

eight-footers, they are cheaper to build, and they do their work very well, but I prefer the 8 ft type, and I believe them to be more suitable for being given increased power. At any rate I am going to try it.'

Accordingly Nos 1003–1007 came out with the colossal 19½ in by 28 in cylinders, and also No 1008, which was indentical with the other five save in having cylinders ½ in smaller. But now came the peculiar feature of the whole affair. The 'more powerful boilers' which the new engines were to have turned out to be the same diameter as the previous ones, but *4 in shorter*, while instead of having increased heating surface they actually had 14 square feet less; that is to say, No 1003, being of the latest class, had only 1,031 square feet of heating surface, whereas No 1002, which belonged to the older class, had 1,045 square feet. So here again was a paradox. Apparently the enhanced steaming capacity was to be found in a slight enlargement of the firebox, which in No 1002 was 6 ft 2 in in length, and contributed 109 square feet of heating surface, whereas in No 1003 the firebox was 6 ft 8 in long and contributed 122 square feet. But here again arose the peculiarity that in the earliest of all 8 ft singles the firebox, while only 6 ft 2 in in length, gave the same heating surface, 122 square feet, as did the latest of the type. What also no doubt made for improved steaming power was the enlargement of the firegrate area from 17¾ square feet in No 1002 to 20 square feet in No 1003, while the steam pressure was also increased from 160 to 170 lbs. Still, the heating surface problem remains, and this becomes still more striking when it is remembered that in Mr Sturrock's first eight-wheeled engine, the celebrated No 215, which was built in 1853 and had 17 in by 24 in cylinders, with 7 ft 6 in driving wheels, the heating surface was no less than 1,719 square feet, of which the firebox yielded as much as 155 square feet, the steam pressure, even in those far-off days, being 150 lbs to the square inch. It is, to say the least, a curious and interesting fact that, whereas the 'crack' express engines designed or built for the London and North Western,

Great Western and Great Northern Railways respectively in the years 1847–1853 should have 2,290, 2,080 and 1,719 square feet of heating surface respectively, the 'crack' new expresss engines designed for the Great Northern forty-two to forty-six years later should be given only 1,031 square feet. Moreover, in the case of his 6 ft 6 in coupled mixed traffic engines, which often took their turn on express duty, Mr Stirling contented himself with considerably less than 1,000 square feet of heating surface.

But, on the other hand, whereas his single-wheelers performed work which has always been admittedly excellent and even astonishing, his coupled engines were unmistakably failures when employed on heavy fast expresses, although they did well enough on light expresses, heavy stopping trains or express goods. I have made many scores of express trips with them, and without exception found their work unsatisfactory, owing to shortness of steam whenever they were required to pull more than a relatively light load or to exceed a moderately high speed. It will be remembered also that the numerous 7 ft coupled engines, designed and constructed by Mr Stirling's brother for the South Eastern Railway, also were provided with a strangely small heating surface—less than 1,000 square feet—to supply cylinders 19 in by 26 in. But on the other hand it must be borne in mind that the duty imposed on these engines was by no means arduous, partly owing to the lowness of the booked speeds, and partly because the loads with which they were required to deal were not so heavy as they appeared from the mode of computation employed. One has read authentic records of their making fair time with loads of 23 coaches, but then that only meant in reality 230 tons behind the tender, the reckoning being at the rate of 10 tons per coach, whereas a 23-coach train nowadays would weigh fully 400 tons on the lines running north and west from London. Thus Mr James Stirling, like his brother of the Great Northern Railway, had designed his engines expressly for the particular duty they would be called upon to perform, and they appear to have done it well enough.

But in view of the achievements of the other classes of engines named it becomes exceedingly difficult to lay down any hard and fast rule as to what ought to be the minimum of heating surface in provision for given work. Experience has abundantly proved that in some cases one engine having only 1,000 to 1,200 square feet of heating surface may be more efficient and prove more powerful than another whose surface is 50 per cent larger. I am of course referring to work performed under approximately identical conditions, and in closely similar circumstances. The puzzle is to explain why the same factors appear so often to yield discrepant results. It is here that we realise the great want to which I referred at the outset, the need of some authoritative statement of principles. I am not unaware that an occasional furtive attempt has been made to indicate roughly how much heating surface ought to be provided for cylinders of a given diameter. But even if one could accept that dictum as final, one is instantly faced by the difficulty that, judging from their practice, every other leading engineer in the kingdom holds a different view on this head. It is quite certain that Mr Sturrock, Mr P. Stirling, Mr James Stirling and Mr S. W. Johnson *did*, and Mr Churchward, Mr D. Drummond, Mr Ivatt, Mr Worsdell, Mr Aspinall and Mr M'Intosh *do* consider that the proportions they have adopted are the best, else why should they choose them? Yet the confusing side of the case is that no two of these very eminent gentlemen agree one with the other. Here some partial explanation will no doubt be offered in the second criticism which I mentioned above, namely that the value of heating surface does not depend wholly on its quantity, but quite as much or more on its nature and disposal. One engineer holds that a comparatively small tube area will suffice provided the firebox dimensions are generous, and lays it down as an absolute law that tube surface is of but little value beyond a very few feet from the firebox. Other engineers declare that they obtain appreciable value throughout the whole length of tubes 14 or 15 ft long. That Mr D. Drummond does obtain, with his water-tubes passing through the firebox, a large excess of steam-generating value over a like area at the smokebox end of his boiler tubes appears to be indisputable; but he further claims that with his water-tube boiler, in which a huge flue some $2\frac{1}{2}$ feet in diameter passes along the whole central length of the boiler barrel, and is crossed by intermediate water-tubes, he can obtain as much steam generation as with double the heating surface in a boiler of the ordinary type.

It is clear, then, that in considering the question of boiler power one has to recognise the fact that the amount of heating surface is only one of several factors that materially count. That is, I admit, a truism. It may justly be retorted that nobody questions this; but what I maintain is that, while it may be tacitly or even verbally admitted in theory, it is not yet recognised in all its fullness as a point of locomotive practice. Perhaps that may seem a little obscure. What I mean is that although undoubtedly many engineers of the present day are acting upon that perception in locomotive building, their action is of such a curiously various kind, the method of one differing so widely from that of another, that undeniably no one general principle has as yet been arrived at. And it does seem extremely desirable that this state of things should not continue. It is admitted that a given nominal quantity, which we may call a, of heating surface in one place or disposed in one way, is worth x or y, as compared with what it would be worth if it were otherwise placed or differently disposed. But what we never seem to arrive at is the precise practical value of a or x or y, else we should not see such an amazing variety of methods and proportions employed as is the case. It may be, of course—I am not prepared to deny it—that all of these multifarious differing methods are equally good one as another.

APRIL 1904

On cylinder dimensions and whether a diameter greater than 18 inches was really necessary for efficient working

Last month I ventured to suggest the desirableness of some definite principle being agreed upon as regards the best proportions between boiler power and cylinder capacity—the former being considered with reference to its efficiency as a steam generator and the latter in relation to the demands made upon it in respect of tractive force—determined by the diameter of the driving wheels and by the nature of the duty to be performed. And I drew attention to the very wide differences of opinion which still exist in this connection among our most eminent locomotive engineers, no two of whom agree even approximately on this point.

I now come to two other details of locomotive practice on which the views of British locomotive engineers are almost equally diverse, viz, cylinder dimensions and driving-wheel diameter. It will be at once recognized that these three points, boiler capacity, cylinder capacity and driving wheel diameter are essentially and inextricably correlated. I desire to avoid confusion by setting aside for the present the sub-details of the steam-generative apparatus and the question of adhesion weight, dealing simply with the actual and relative dimensions of cylinders and driving wheels.

Now, taking first the matter of cylinder diameter, I may offer *in limine* the very audacious and almost profane remark that it has not yet been proved to my own conviction that

for any work so far required on British railways any larger cylinder diameter than 18 in is in reality needed . . . I do not assert that no greater diameter than 18 in *is* needed; I merely say that I am so far without proof that a larger diameter is necessary or advisable. It may be, but hitherto this remains unproved. Let us consider first the case of express engines. For some years even after railway traffic had grown to a substantial magnitude, our engines found 15 in cylinders ample for their purpose. Much excellent work was done by the Gooch engines on the London and South Western, by the 'Jenny Linds' and 'Little Sharps' on the London Brighton and South Coast, by the Cramptons on the South Eastern, by several classes on the Great Eastern (then Eastern Counties), Great Northern and London and North Western, the cylinders of all the locomotives mentioned being only 15 in in diameter. I myself have seen South Eastern Cramptons, unpiloted, gain time with loads respectively of 21 and 24 four-wheeled coaches, and have noted the same thing on other lines. Of course a four-wheeler of those days was comparatively a very small thing, but 20 to 24 even of those small things made an appreciable load. Then in the late fifties and early sixties came the 16 in cylinders of the South Eastern 6 ft Cudworths, both single and coupled; the Great Eastern Sinclair 7 ft singles; the Great Northern Hawthorns and converted Cramptons; the London and North Western 'Bloomers'; the Midland Kirtley singles, etc. But even in the forties 18 in cylinders had been introduced on the Great Western and London and North Western—on the former as a standard size but on the latter only as an experiment, not permanently or generally. It was not until the late seventies that the 18 in cylinder came into widespread use. Just as Sir Daniel Gooch had in 1846 taken the bold step of adopting so large a size on the Great Western for his 8 ft single-wheelers, so did Mr Patrick Stirling pursue a like course on the Great Northern with *his* 8 ft single-wheelers, originally designed in 1869, twenty-three years later. But it was only in these express engines that Mr Stirling used so large a cylinder. In his far more numerous four-coupled type he employed from first to last, for nearly thirty years, cylinders only $17\frac{1}{2}$ in in diameter. And it is noteworthy that in by far the most numerous class of passenger locomotives so far designed by his successor, Mr H. A. Ivatt, the $17\frac{1}{2}$ in cylinders have been continued. I refer of course to the '400' type and its variant as to boiler power, the '1321' class. Of these Mr Ivatt has built no fewer than 116, viz, Nos 400, 1061–1080, 1301–1320 and 1341–1360, with the smaller boilers, and Nos 1321–1340 and 1361–1395, with the larger boilers, all having cylinders $17\frac{1}{2}$ in by 26 in and 6 ft 6 in coupled wheels. As against these he has turned out only twelve single-wheelers and twenty-one Atlantics which have somewhat larger cylinders. Obviously, then, a good deal can still be done with even $17\frac{1}{2}$ in cylinders. Indeed, I have known Mr Ivatt's '1321' class keep time unassisted over and over again with Scotch expresses of 320 to 340 tons weight behind the tender.

At the same time, on the Great Western, Mr W. Dean, after trying 19 in cylinders and even 20 in cylinders, reverted to the 18 in of his famous predecessor, Sir D. Gooch, and Mr Dean's successor, Mr G. J. Churchward, follows his example even with his newest and largest locomotives, alike for the fastest passenger service and for the heaviest goods traffic. Thus Mr Churchward's now famous

'Cities', his huge 'Consolidation' goods type, his newest monster tanks and his ten-wheeled six-coupled express class all have 18 in cylinders, and without making any 'odorous' comparisons I do venture to assert that no *better* work, relatively at any rate, is being done in England than by these 18 in cylindered locomotives.

The position taken up by Mr Churchward and Mr Ivatt is that the diameter of the cylinders is of wholly minor importance as compared with the amount of force that is transmitted *through* the cylinders *to* the wheels *from* the boiler. So both of these distinguished engineers provide in the first instances powerful boilers. I do not mean powerful merely in the sense of extensive heating surface, for Mr Ivatt gives his '1321' class only 1,250 square feet, but rather in the sense of proved efficiency, by reason of the disposition of the heating surface and by the provision of such a firebox as will ensure swift and thorough combustion of fuel. Mr Churchward, in his standard 'City' class, supplies 1,818 square feet of heating surface and a very efficient firebox; the cylinders too are half an inch larger than those of Mr Ivatt's engines, and the driving wheels are 2 in larger, the piston stroke being in both cases 26 in. But when he has to deal with a type of engine whose principal duty is to *pull hard*, alike in weight-hauling and in hill-climbing, then he seeks the extra force by calling in the aid of leverage, and with that object adds no less than 4 in to the length of his piston-stroke, giving it the exceptional length of 30 in. The ten-wheeled, six-coupled expresses, tanks and the Consolidation goods all have 30 in stroke. But my present point is that providing bigger boilers so as to be able to send more steam through the cylinders Mr Churchward and Mr Ivatt have obtained highly satisfactory and even remarkable practical results without using a larger diameter than 18 in.

Turning to other British railways, we find a noteworthy difference of practice. Mr D. Drummond on the London and South Western, Mr R. J. Billinton on the London Brighton and South Coast, Mr H. S. Wainwright on the South Eastern and Chatham, Mr J. Holden on the Great Eastern, Mr S. W. Johnson on the Midland, Mr W. Worsdell on the North Eastern, Mr J. G. Robinson on the Great Central, Mr J. A. F. Aspinall on the Lancashire and Yorkshire, Mr M. Holmes on the North British, Mr J. Manson on the Glasgow and South Western, Mr J. F. M'Intosh on the Caledonian and Mr P. Drummond on the Highland, all have resorted to larger cylinder diameters for their standard express engines, mostly 19 to $19\frac{1}{2}$ in. Mr Ivatt himself has used 19 in and $18\frac{3}{4}$ in cylinders in his single-wheel and 'Atlantic' classes, Mr Worsdell has even gone up to 20 in in his newest engines, and Mr M'Intosh has adopted the diameter, wholly unprecedented in British practice, of 21 in for his latest express and goods engines. Here is surely an amazing discrepancy of method. Yet I say frankly that I have obtained good work from *all* those widely-divergent cylinder sizes. But the fact remains that I have recorded equally good work with cylinders of 18 in and $17\frac{1}{2}$ in diameter, allowing due weight to the circumstances and conditions of the duty required. The explanation is not that the cylinders differ in size according to the boilers which supply them and the work they have to do. This, self-evidently, is not the case, as will at once be perceived by adopting the simple process of collating the dimensions on the one hand and the prescribed duty on the other. No, we can only accept the plain fact that here again, as in regard to heating surface, 'doctors differ'.

It is unnecessary to demonstrate that if the smaller-diametered cylinders can do all that is needed they are preferable. That is obvious. The question is: Why should the larger ones have come into such very general use? There are two main theoretical reasons. One is that steam can be used more expansively and therefore, as a rule, more economically. The other is that in any case of emergency a greater power can be temporarily exercised by the larger cylinders. But these theoretical advantages are not always realised in actual practice. Drivers cannot always be got to use their steam expansively enough, and so they sometimes run their large-cylindered engines 'out of breath', ie short of steam. No doubt if one could rely upon every driver being an ideal engineer this difficulty might be minimised. But the disturbing element of 'personal equation' *will* intrude, and then we find large-cylindered engines behaving unsatisfactorily.

Whether the expedient of a longer piston-stroke will, in addition to giving enhanced tractive force through leverage, also prove advantageous through allowing extended expansion in the cylinders still remains to be proved, but the experiment of a 30 in stroke as against the usual 26 in is well worthy of trial. Mr Worsdell in his latest locomotives—the large 'Atlantics'—has adopted, as did Mr P. Stirling in his 8 ft singles, a 28 in piston stroke. That also is experimental and may prove beneficial. Whether his 20 in cylinders will also yield the full benefit that would be proportional to their vast size is another point that still has to be definitely proved.

Hitherto 20 in cylinders have never been conclusively shown to be satisfactory as compared with cylinders of a smaller diameter. If my memory serves me aright, they were first used in the case of the 7 ft 8 in convertible single-wheelers originally built for the broad—or 7 ft—gauge, and subsequently converted for use on the narrow—or 4 ft $8\frac{1}{2}$ in—gauge, viz, Nos 3001–3030, the 'Amazon' class. But they did not prove satisfactory, and were all lined up to 19 in, while the second batch of 30 engines, virtually of the same type, although differentiated as the 'Achilles' class, Nos 3031–3080, were given 19 in by 24 in cylinders from the first. Next, 20 in cylinders were employed in the four 7 ft coupled 'Armstrong' class engines on the Great Western, Nos 7, 8, 14 and 16, which for some reason proved relative failures and have been rebuilt. Thirdly, 20 in cylinders came out in Mr Worsdell's two North Eastern engines, Nos 1869 and 1870, which were built in 1896, with coupled wheels of the unprecedented diameter of 7 ft $7\frac{1}{4}$ in, but which never seem to have achieved unqualified success. Mr Worsdell's fifteen six-coupled bogie express engines complete the list of the non-compound locomotives which in this country have been given 20 in cylinders. They have always done well in my personal experience, extending over a large number of journeys, but I am very far from being convinced that with only 1,769 square feet of heating surface and with 200 lbs steam pressure they would not have done just as well, if not better, had their cylinders been 18 in in diameter. The new North Eastern Atlantics also have 20 in cylinders. When Mr Aspinall brought out his earliest express engines on the Lancashire and Yorkshire with 7 ft 3 in coupled drivers he adopted 19 in in view of the large size of his wheels. Then he tried one with 18 in cylinders and another with 17½ in, each being in all other respects absolutely identical with the rest. The result, as stated to me by himself, was that the 18 in cylinders gave better results than the 19 in, and the 17½ in even slightly better still. When he reverted to 19 in with his large ten-wheeled 'Atlantic' or '1400' class it was in order to obtain a higher tractive force without reducing the diameter of his 7 ft 3 in wheels, and he further provided a boiler with no less than 2,052 square feet of heating surface. I believe that Mr James Stirling was the first to introduce 19 in cylinders in ordinary practice. He did so in the case of his South Eastern express type, which came out early in 1884, Nos 116, 183 and 198. But Nos 205, 212, 214, etc, which came out in the same year, were identical, save in having 18 in cylinders, and the drivers then declared to me emphatically their preference for the latter. Seeing that they had less than 1,000 square feet of heating surface this is not surprising. In the same year Mr S. W. Johnson built for the Midland ten express engines, Nos 1667–1676, which, with 7 ft coupled wheels, had cylinders 19 in by 26 in, and only 1,120 square feet of heating surface, whereas their predecessors, Nos 1327–1346, with 18 in cylinders, had 1,313 square feet. Although Nos 1667, 1668 and 1675 of that class, when tried by me in the years 1884–1885, when they were brand new, always performed creditably, it is undeniable that the class had a bad name from the first, and was soon rebuilt with more powerful boilers and higher steam pressure. It was not for more than a decade afterward that Mr Johnson again tried 19 in cylinders. Early in the nineties he advanced from 18 in to 18½ in, as in Nos 2183–2202, 7 ft coupled, and Nos 2203–2217, with 6 ft 6 in wheels. More recently he adopted 19½ in cylinders, as in his '60' class which, although they have given me a few good performances, have never as a class done so well as the other Midland engines when I have been with them. In the Belpaire class Mr Johnson retained the 19½ in cylinders, giving them, however, vastly larger boilers, but in the latest engines of his standard type, eg Nos 805–809, 2591–2600 and 2636–2640, he reverted to 19 in cylinders, with 1,193 square feet of heating surface, a combination which, as I mentioned last month, has given me some paradoxically excellent work. Yet here again I am by no means certain that they would not have been quite as efficient and economical had they 18 in cylinders . . . although I do not pretend to assert dogmatically that they would. I merely hint that such is my impression, based upon experience which I could quote if necessary.

On the most suitable diameter for driving wheels in a steam locomotive

Coming now to the third point of locomotive practice upon which it seems to me that the establishment of some definite rule or principle is desirable, I may observe that the diversity of opinion among British locomotive engineers as to the most useful diameter of driving wheels has long been almost as marked as in the case of boiler capacity and cylinder dimensions. At the present moment, however, it exhibits a greater tendency toward conformity than at any previous period of railway history.

This is due, no doubt, in a large measure to the virtual elimination of the single-wheeler from the list of engine types recently built, or now in course of construction, or in contemplation. This may not seem at first sight to be a necessary association of effect with cause. The question is often asked by persons who are not professional engineers, but who are interested in railway engineering: Why should the driving wheels of a locomotive be larger, if single, than when coupled to another pair, or to other pairs of wheels? It might be thought that the advantage of enhanced tractive force, which is obtained with a smaller wheel, could be utilised equally well in either case. But herein enters the condition to which I have previously drawn attention—that of the 'weight available for adhesion', which is not by any means the same thing as the actual weight on the driving wheels. The weight available for adhesion, as it is technically term-ed, or the 'adhesive weight available for the purpose of traction', as it is also and perhaps more accurately expressed, is only so much of the total weight on the axle that can be made to 'bite' the rail; that is, to 'hold on to it' sufficiently to afford a 'grip'.

Now I explained in a previous article that the proportion of weight which can be thus utilised is *never* more than one-third, seldom more than one-fourth, usually only one-fifth and often—as in drizzly or snowy or frosty weather, when the rails are slippery—as little as one-sixth or even less. Well, I believe I made that clear on the former occasion, but from letters I have received from readers it appears that 'some doubted'. I cannot help that. The plain hard fact remains that even if you put 18 tons on the axle of a single-wheeler you cannot possibly ever make more than 6 tons of it *pull*, or usually more than 3 or 4 tons. All the power you set to turn the wheel that is more than equivalent to that adhesion weight simply makes the wheel revolve without 'biting' and so is sheer waste of steam. But, it may be asked, how does this affect the question of the driving wheel diameter? Would not that adhesion weight be just as effective with a 6 ft wheel as with an 8 ft one? I daresay that does puzzle many people. I know that plenty of readers have wondered what the late Mr Patrick Stirling meant when he said that in designing his new single-driver express engines he determined to have a large wheel because *the larger the wheel, the better the adhesion*. It has been put to me: Is not the contact between the wheel tyre and the rail merely that of a *point*? And if so must it not be the same whether the wheel be large or small? Theoretically, no doubt, if you assume the wheel periphery to be a perfect circle, and the rail to be absolutely a right line, then the case must be so. But neither assumption would be correct. That point of the wheel's convexity which rests on the rail is necessarily flattened, in however small degree, by the weight superposed, while wherever it rests upon the rail it depresses the latter to a small extent. Thus the convex surface rests not upon an absolute dead level but in a slight concavity. Consequently it will easily be realised that the larger the circumference of the wheel, the flatter will be the curve of contact, and hence the larger the area of actual adhesion which, although it may be but momentary, is an essential and vital factor in the operation of traction. So when you have to get all your traction out of the adhesion which can be brought to bear by a single pair of wheels, the more you can extend that area of actual adhesion the better, especially as simultaneously you reduce the relative pressure upon any precise point of the rail-length.

It may reasonably be rejoined that what I have said at other times about the loss of relative tractive force due to increased driving-wheel diameter must surely come in here, and that in this way the gain in adhesion would be counteracted by such loss. That is quite true, but the remedy is obvious. Mr Stirling used an 8 ft wheel, yet he got considerable more tractive force than he had obtained from his engines with 7 ft or 6 ft 6 in wheels. How? By increasing the size of his cylinders. His early 6 ft 6 in engines had cylinders 17 in by 24 in; his 7 ft had cylinders $17\frac{1}{2}$ in by 24 in. But his 8 ft engines had cylinders 18 in by 28 in. Thus whereas the 7 ft and 6 ft 6 in wheeled engines had 88 lbs and 87.5 lbs of tractive force for every lb of effective pressure in the cylinders, the 8 ft engines had 94.5 lbs. Hence it follows that a single-driver engine must have a large wheel so as to get better

proportionate adhesion with a limited axle-weight, and that the loss of tractive force, through increased wheel diameter, must be made up by enlarged cylinder power. It will of course be borne in mind also that a large wheel makes fewer revolutions in a given distance than does a smaller wheel, and consequently 'sweeps out' the cylinder proportionately more seldom. All these matters manifestly have to be taken into account in decoding upon the dimensions and proportions of a locomotive.

But there are other considerations, and one of these is the tendency to what is called 'imperceptible slipping'; that is to say, the tendency of the driving wheels to make more revolutions than are needed to cover a given distance. This tendency is inherent in all locomotives, and must be so when a smooth wheel periphery rests upon a smooth rail. But it is seriously larger when the wheel is a 'free' or 'single' one, not coupled to another pair. That might be conjectured *a priori*, but it has been abundantly proved in actual practice. A 7 ft wheel ought in theory to cover a mile in 240 revolutions. But it doesn't. No, it always makes more revolutions than that—often many more, because to some extent there is always more or less of imperceptible slip. I have made various experiments on this head, and at times have found a 7 ft wheel take 65–70 revolutions instead of 60 to cover a quarter of a mile. This sort of slip is quite separate from that violent *perceptible* slip one so often sees, which is characterised by a furious outburst of puffs from the chimney, and a quite gratuitous display of fireworks from the driving wheels as the result of the extreme friction on the rail. The sand-blast has unquestionably been of great service in minimising both classes of slip, and indeed has prolonged for a generation the life of the single-wheeler type, but it has apparently reached its limit of efficiency, and now enhanced adhesion must be secured through coupling two or more pairs of wheels. Various ingenious plans have been suggested from time to time for enhancing the adhesion by means of electro-magnetism applied to the wheels, but so far none of these schemes has come into practical use. Coupling is a far simpler and more direct method, beside giving vastly greater adhesion than ever could be got with a single driving wheel, unless excessive weight were superposed. For if you have two pairs of coupled wheels you may have 36 tons of weight upon the four wheels, and if three, then 54 tons on the six, as Mr J. F. M'Intosh has in the case of his two celebrated Caledonian ten-wheelers, Nos 49 and 50. When you can get such a weight as this for the purpose of traction you are virtually independent of wheel diameter as regards the question of the adhesive superiority of larger wheels, although of course this always remains in greater or less degree a factor in the problem of effective power. But with so large a weight available wheel diameter may be practically ignored in that adhesive connection.

Eliminating, then, that phase of the question—what should be the driving wheel diameter—we come to the real heart of the problem. The force given *out* by—or rather *through*—the cylinders proportionately to the steam admitted is roughly computed by squaring the diameter of each cylinder, and multiplying the result by the length of the piston stroke, both in inches. The amount of that force which is *actually applied* to the driving wheels is computed by dividing the final product by the diameter of the wheel, also in inches. The force *nominally exerted* on the rails is computed by multiplying *that* result by the effective steam pressure in lbs. And the *actual force exerted* on the train is computed by associating that last result with the adhesion weight available for traction, this being reckoned in the manner already explained. Manifestly, then, the tractive force exercisable by a cylinder of given dimensions varies as the diameter of the wheel which takes it up, and consequently the larger the wheel the smaller will be the dividend representing tractive force. This is, I need hardly say, quite a rudimentary application of mechanical principles—a pure matter of leverage.

It might appear on that basis as if the wheel could not be too small, because the smaller the wheel in proportion to the cylinder, the greater the tractive force theoretically educed. Up to a

certain point this is no doubt true. So far as simple brute force goes, it is the case. But once again it has to be remembered that it is not the mere abstract theoretical power that has to be considered for purposes of practical utility, but the extent to which that power can be actually and profitably utilised. Thus, with cylinders of the very common size of 18 in by 26 in, the following respective amounts of tractive force in lbs for every lb of effective pressure on the pistons, will be exercised by wheels of the different diameters specified:

8 ft 0 in	87.7
7 ft 6 in	93.6
7 ft 0 in	100.2
6 ft 9 in	104.0
6 ft 8 in	105.3
6 ft 6 in	108.0
6 ft 0 in	117.0
5 ft 6 in	127.6
5 ft 0 in	140.4
4 ft 6 in	155.9
4 ft 0 in	175.5
3 ft 6 in	200.6
3 ft 0 in	234.0

It may seem absurd to think of 3 ft wheels in connection with express work, but on the narrowest gauges, such as the 3 ft 6 in, or the metre gauge, such an association is by no means unknown. In New Zealand, for instance, where I made a number of experiments some years ago, some fairly fast running has been done with a 3 ft wheel. In one case a distance of 20 miles was run in 32 minutes from start to stop, averaging 37.5 miles an hour, in spite of a bad slack for relaying and several for curves of 7 chains radius. The absolute maximum rate was 53 miles an hour. That was with 3 ft wheels, six coupled, and cylinders 12 in by 16 in. On another occasion with 3 ft wheels, four coupled, and cylinders 10½ in by 18 in, I did three successive stages of 9, 7 and 5 miles in 14, 12 and 8 minutes respectively, from start to stop, in each case making a like maximum speed. But of course no one would advocate the use of so small a wheel for fast running even on the 3 ft 6 in

Caledonian Railway 4-6-0 No 58, built with 5 ft coupled wheels for hauling trains over the severely-graded Callander and Oban line. Five were built in 1902 and four more in 1905. They were highly successful at their job and favourites with the crews. (NRM)

gauge, and so, when express trains became necessary, a driving wheel diameter of 4 ft—4 ft 1 in with new tyres—was adopted, and that has continued ever since to be the standard size in New Zealand. A few engines with 4 ft 6 in wheels were tried, but that class has not been perpetuated. With 4 ft wheels, however, I have often exceeded 50 miles an hour, several times reaching 57, 58 or 59 miles an hour, and once 64.2. In this last instance a distance of 37½ miles was covered in 44 minutes net, averaging 50.8 miles an hour from start to stop, probably the best run ever made on the 3 ft 6 in gauge, or with six-coupled 4 ft wheels.

On the standard 4 ft 8½ in gauge, however, 5 ft drivers for express engines have been by no means unknown. For a long while that, or 5 ft 6 in, was the normal size in the United States of America. In Britain, so far as I can recollect at

the moment, the only cases of 5 ft wheels being employed for express service have been the 'Stella' class, Nos 3205 etc, and 3502, etc, and their bogie variants Nos 3521–3560, all on the Great Western Railway, and the new Oban express type Nos 55–59, on the Caledonian Railway. Where severe gradients have to be climbed and moderate speeds must be run in the descents there seems to be no valid reason why 5 ft wheels should not be used. Even in point of swiftness they can do very respectably. I have exceeded 65 miles an hour with all three of the classes just mentioned, as I have also with one of the London and North Western Railway's 4 ft 6 in wheeled tanks. When Mr Webb introduced 5 ft 6 in wheels for express work on the same railway—ie in his 'Precursor' class—they were generally regarded as unduly small, but as a matter of experience it was found that they ran to time unpiloted with loads which the 'Precedent' class engines, identical save in having 6 ft 6 in wheels, required pilots, and they were alleged to be proportionately more economical than the larger-wheeled engines. But as a matter of course the piston speed and the motion of the reciprocating and revolving parts were much faster in the smaller-wheeled locomotives, and so they gradually seemed to 'go out of fashion', all forty being in the end rebuilt as tanks. But on the Great Western, London and South Western, London Brighton and South Coast, Great Eastern and Great Northern Railways, engines with 5 ft 6 in to 5 ft 8 in coupled wheels have performed a very large amount of excellent express duty, and I have some schoolday records of extremely smart running on the London Brighton and South Coast, South Eastern, Great Eastern and Great Northern lines with 5 ft 6 in single-wheelers of the 'Little Sharp' type. Even at the present time Mr Churchward's latest class of engine for the South Devon and Cornwall express service on the Great Western has driving wheels 5 ft 8 in in diameter with new tyres, whilst Mr Holden's 5 ft 8 in coupled type, still built, has long proved its all-round efficiency.

But as I have remarked before, other points have to be taken into account than simple theoretical power or swiftness. An engine with 2 ft wheels and 18 in by 26 in cylinders[7], would nominally possess 351 lbs of tractive force for every lb of effective steam pressure, but such an engine would have to make over 14 revolutions per second to run at 60 miles an hour, which would manifestly be undesirable even if feasible. Where speeds exceeding 50 miles an hour are required, 5 ft is the smallest driving wheel diameter that can prudently be employed, if only on the score of the excessive wear and tear involved in the use of a smaller wheel. There seems, however, to be a virtual consensus of opinion nowadays that for ordinary express duty wheels not smaller than 6 ft, and preferably somewhat larger, should be employed as a practical compromise between the 8 ft to 9 ft diameters of some single-wheel 'racers' and the 5 ft to 5 ft 6 in of the sturdy 'hill-climber'. And so we find a very general adoption of 6 ft 6 in,

6 ft 8 in, 6 ft 9 in, and 7 ft in normal British practice. One eminent engineer, Mr Aspinall, has even adopted 7 ft 3 in, but in this choice he stands alone, and a wheel so small as 6 ft is only used nowadays when an exceptionally heavy road has to be travelled at high speed, as in the case of the London and South Western's Salisbury–Exeter services. A diameter of 7 ft is specially favoured on the Great Eastern, London and North Western, Midland and North Eastern lines, but all the other British main lines seem to have come round to 6 ft 6 in–6 ft 9 in, as indeed have the Midland and North Eastern in some of Mr Johnson's and Mr Worsdell's latest designs. That any speed required in modern work can be attained and maintained by a 6 ft 6 in to 6 ft 9 in wheel has been abundantly proved, while a size within those limits seems to be the most useful all-round one from the practical viewpoint. The cases of the Great Western, London and South Western, London Brighton and South Coast, South Eastern and Chatham, Great Northern, London and North Western, Midland, North Eastern, North British and Caledonian lines will at once suggest themselves as in point.

So far as I can ascertain, the experiment of a larger coupled wheel then the Lancashire and Yorkshire's 7 ft 3 in has only been seriously tried in four cases. One was on a French railway many years ago, when the coupled wheels were 7 ft 7 in in diameter. About this class I have very little trustworthy information. Secondly, on the North Eastern, it will be remembered Mr Worsdell had two engines with 7 ft 7¼ in coupled wheels, which were not an unqualified success. Thirdly, a good many years back a certain M Estrade produced a locomotive with six-coupled wheels no less than 8 ft 3 in in diameter, which promptly proved a failure. Lastly came the strange Thuille locomotive shown in the Paris Exhibition of 1900, which had four-coupled 8 ft 3 in wheels, *ten* carrying wheels—in two bogies—and a ten-wheeled double-bogie tender. That also was found to be a mere white elephant. The work it was designed to do was already being done and surpassed by a Nord

---

7 A locomotive with a cylinder stroke larger than the diameter of the driving wheel is a logical impossibility! It would derail every time it came to a set of points.

Caledonian Railway 4–4–0 No 724, one of J. McIntosh's celebrated 'Dunalastair I' class, built in 1896. This picture, taken from an unusual angle, shows the superb light blue livery and the Caledonian practice of numbering the tender at the rear. This engine was also adapted for oil-burning, as the tank on top of the tender indicates. After the first batch of these locomotives three further varieties appeared, each somewhat more powerful than its predecessor, to match the increasing loads of the Anglo-Scottish trains which had to be taken over Beattock summit. (NRM)

engine with only 6 ft 8 in wheels. It may reasonably be anticipated that no more coupled wheels of such magnitude will be employed, even experimentally.

The use of large wheels in six-coupled engines is the latest development. Mr J. G. Robinson in his latest-of-all express type employs six-coupled wheels 6 ft 9 in in diameter, and M Salomon, on the French Eastern Railway, uses wheels as large as 6 ft 10 in in his latest six-coupled type. Mr Churchward, on the Great Western, and Mr Worsdell, on the North Eastern, have adopted 6 ft 8 in—a very convenient and useful size—and Mr M'Intosh and Mr Manson 6 ft 6 in. It would appear as if the ten-wheeled six-coupled 4–6–0 type were to occupy a very prominent place in the British locomotive practice of the future.

DECEMBER 1904

On the new De Glehn 4–4–2 compound locomotive of the Great Western Railway, and on Webb's compounds of the London and North Western Railway, and changes recently made in them

Every candid person will admit that it must have demanded considerable moral courage on the part of the able Locomotive Superintendent of the Great Western Railway to take the novel and important step of recommending the purchase of a French engine for purposes of experiment in comparison with British-built locomotives. A locomotive superintendent could hardly be blamed if he preferred to 'go on his own', to design and build the engines he deemed best suited to the work of the railway over whose mechanical engineering department he ruled,

GWR 4–4–2 No 102 La France, *the de Glehn four-cylinder compound purchased by the Company from its French manufacturers in 1903 and later rebuilt as shown with a coned boiler. Rous-Marten had a high opinion of this engine's ability to run fast with heavy loads, but the GWR Locomotive Superintendent, G.J. Churchward, eventually decided against compounding since simple-expansion locomotives of his own design and similar size could perform as well and as economically.* (NRM)

and hesitated to seek inspiration abroad, however admittedly excellent might be the performances of any particular foreign type of engine.

It is immensely to Mr Churchward's honour and credit that he rose superior to such consideration of mere personal vanity, and that when he might have deemed himself scarcely yet settled in his seat as chief at Swindon, one of his earliest acts in that capacity was to advise his directors to procure for trial a four-cylinder compound express engine of the Atlantic type and of the de Bousquet-de Glehn design, virtually identical with those which for several years had been accomplishing in France work that to British eyes appeared almost phenomenal. *La France* was duly imported, and up to the time I write has just run 30,000 miles on Great Western metals. In that service she has, according to official records, conclusively proved herself more powerful than any other *four-coupled* Great Western engine, but of course, with her limited adhesion weight of only 33 tons on her four-coupled wheels she cannot exercise such large tractive effort as can the six-coupled Swindon-built engines which have 54 tons adhesion weight. One of her achievements, which was not personally recorded by myself, but the full notes of which have been courteously forwarded to me from official quarters, was to haul one of the 'Ocean Specials'—the heavy passenger one, not the relatively light mail special—from Exeter to London *via* Bristol station in 198 minutes inclusive, the load being no fewer than twelve of the heaviest eight-wheeler corridor stock, so that the total load behind her tender, including a crowd of passengers and a vast amount of luggage, could not have fallen far short, if at all, of 350 tons. A stop of 8 minutes was made at Bristol, thus leaving the actual running time from first start to last stop just 190 minutes for the distance of 194 miles. The first stage of $75\frac{1}{2}$ miles[8] from Exeter to Bristol was covered in 72 minutes start to stop, while the climb of 20 miles from Exeter to Whiteball summit, the

last $2\frac{1}{2}$ miles being at 1 in 115, occupied only 22 minutes with that load. The final run in from Bristol to Paddington was done easily in 118 minutes. Moreover the terribly steep South Devon gradients, which include such 'pinches' as 1 in 48, 1 in 43 and even 1 in 40, with $2\frac{1}{2}$ miles' unbroken ascent at 1 in 41, have been ascended by *La France* with remarkable ease and certainty. The time has not yet come to publish all the details of her work and its cost, including that of fuel and repairs. I learn, however, on high authority that the results have been exceedingly favourable.

But the most conclusive testimony to the satisfactoriness of the outcome of this very interesting experiment is that on Mr Churchward's advice the Great Western Railway has ordered two more locomotives of the same type, which are to be built by the same builders, the Société Alsacienne, of which Monsieur de Glehn, the author of the compounding system employed, is the General Manager and Chief Engineer. These two new engines, which are to be ready if possible for next year's heavy summer traffic, will be identical in type with *La France*, but as in the case of the new Paris-Orleans Atlantic engines, of much greater size and power. Practically the Paris-Orleans dimensions will be adhered to in the case of the Great Western newcomers. Thus whereas *La France* has 2,158 square feet of heating surface in her tubes and 167 square feet in the firebox (total 2,325 square feet) and a firegrate area of 29.5 square feet, the new engines will have 2,435 square feet of heating surface in the tubes, 181 square feet in the firebox, or 2,616 square feet in all, while the firegrate will have an area of 33.9 square feet. I may remark here in passing that the dimensions I have given in the case of *La France* were those which I received direct from the Société Alsacienne, her builders. I notice that in another official dimension list her tube heating surface is given as 2,288 square feet, which brings up her total heating surface to 2,455 square feet. I do not pretend to say which set of figures is the more accurate, and at the moment I am unaware if any alterations may have

---

[8] The distance according to the gradient profile is 76 miles.

been made since *La France* was delivered, in the direction of increasing her tube surface. But at any rate the new engines should have a steam-generating capacity in excess of any other locomotive yet seen in Britain with the single exception of Mr Holden's Great Eastern 'Decapod'.

Further, whereas *La France* has $13\frac{3}{8}$ in high-pressure cylinders and 22 in low-pressure, the new engines will have $14\frac{1}{4}$ in high-pressure cylinders and $23\frac{5}{8}$ in low-pressure, the $25\frac{1}{4}$ in piston stroke being adhered to, as also the working steam pressure of 228 lbs per square inch. The four-coupled driving wheels will still be 6 ft $8\frac{1}{2}$ in and the trailing wheels, as in the case of *La France*, 4 ft 8 in, but the diameter of the bogie wheels will be increased by 2 in, namely to 3 ft 2 in. As regards weight, the difference is very striking. *La France* weighs 64 tons 13 cwt in working order; the new engine will weigh 73 tons. *La France* carries 33 tons 7 cwt on her coupled wheels; the new engine will have no less than 39 tons. A most important and highly-interesting feature of next summer's railway work will be a comparison of the results attained by these colossal new engines.

It may fairly be hoped that one outcome of these fresh trials of the compound system may be a further extension of its employment in this country, which at present stands virtually apart from the rest of the world in the general non-recognition of its advantages. It is undoubtedly the fact that the British recognition has been materially delayed through the intrusion of what might be called eccentricities or fads into the designs of the only compound locomotives that have been at all largely used in England. Few engineers, if any, have had the opportunity of making more thorough and extensive observations as to the working of the London and North Western Railway's compounds than, through the courtesy of the authorities of that railway—particularly of the inventor of that system, Mr F. W. Webb—have fallen my way ever since the pioneer of the type came out more than twenty years ago. It has been the fashion in some quarters to shower wholesale condemna-

tion upon Mr Webb's compounds, which have often been declared to be practically worthless. I have always protested against this sort of reckless and wholesale condemnation, on the ground that in a large number of instances I have found these much-abused engines do exceedingly good work, which at least proved that they were able to do this sometimes, but I do not and cannot deny that in other cases, if a minority on the whole, their performances have been distinctly disappointing and sometimes disreputable. Naturally it has been put forward as a serious objection to the engines, that they therefore could not be entirely trustworthy. I am afraid this must be admitted to be in some degree true. But after a large number of observations and most careful study I have found my original impression entirely verified, namely that what faults were to be found with the engines lay not in their principle or general design but in certain vexatious details—the faddy eccentricities to which I have already referred.

In the case of the three-cylinder compounds their gravest fault consisted in the two pairs of driving wheels not being coupled. It was a fad of the designer to believe that in this way he would secure the advantage of single drivers without their drawbacks; the practical result was that only the drawbacks were encountered. As the two sets of wheels and cylinders worked independently there was, every now and then, a failure of synchronism which necessarily caused defective efficiency. When, after building 100 express engines of the three cylinder compound type, Mr Webb took a fresh departure and built four-cylinder compounds, of which eighty are now at work, he very wisely abandoned the fad of uncoupled wheels, and the new engines benefited accordingly. But the 'fatal fad' could not even yet be excluded. The four cylinder compounds were made to drive a single axle with all four cylinders, and the separate cut-off which was so important a feature in the De Glehn compounds was not employed, the two pairs of cylinders being worked with the same cut-off. I am convinced that Mr Webb believed himself to have good reason for thus going in a

Above *LNWR 2–2–2–0 No 66* Experiment *built in 1882 and aptly-named since it was Francis Webb's first essay at building a compound, with two outside high-pressure cylinders and one large inside low-pressure cylinder. Note the unusual siting of the valve motion below the line of the cylinder. The engine was extensively tested but proved inefficient because the high-pressure cylinders were too small. It had a brief life of 12 months, mostly spent working trains on easy schedules between Crewe and Holyhead.* (NRM)

Below *LNWR 2–2–2–0 No 1304* Jeanie Deans, *one of Webb's fourth design of compounds, the 'Teutonic' class, built in 1889. Only ten were constructed, which was rather surprising as they were the only Webb compounds which could be deemed really successful. One of them, Adriatic, made a record run between Euston and Crewe on August 22nd 1895, covering the 158 miles in 148 minutes — though with a load scarcely any heavier than the weight of itself and its tender.* (NRM)

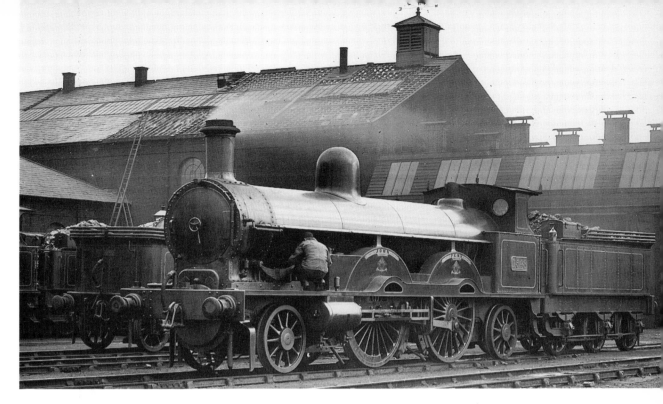

LNWR 2-2-2-2 No 1548 John Penn *one of Webb's last batch of ten three-cylinder compounds built between 1894 and 1898, and similar to his 2-2-2-2 'Greater Britain' class except in having driving wheels 6 ft instead of 7 ft in diameter. The enormous front end of the single low-pressure inside cylinder can be seen just behind the buffer-beam. While the 'Greater Britains' performed on the whole respectably, though often erratically, the 6-footers were no use at all; they were soon taken off main-line trains and as soon as Webb had retired his successor scrapped them.* (NRM)

direction directly opposite to that which the designers of the most successful compounds in other countries had found it expedient to follow. But it is, I think, indisputable that the London and North Western compounds of both the 'Jubilee' and the 'Alfred the Great' classes have been very seriously hampered thereby. That has always been my strong personal opinion, and now has come its entire verification.

Mr George Whale, the new Chief Mechanical Engineer at Crewe, who has already given such striking tokens of his individuality and capacity, almost immediately after his accession to the Crewe chieftaincy determined to try what would be the effect on the four-cylinder compounds of altering their valve gear and giving them a separate cut-off. Several express compounds of the 'Alfred the Great' class have now been fitted with the altered valve gear, and I do not exaggerate when I say that the result has been almost magical. Even the first experiment made by Mr

Whale with No 1952 *Benbow*, the earliest engine thus altered, afforded a tolerably conclusive indication of what was to follow. The engine *Benbow* was put on a train weighing 372 tons behind the tender, and was run a trip each way between Crewe and Stafford. With the original valve gear the engine took $38\frac{1}{2}$ minutes to run from Crewe to Stafford, a distance of $24\frac{1}{2}$ miles, and occupied 22 minutes in the ascent of the bank to Whitmore summit, $10\frac{1}{2}$ miles, including 3 miles at 1 in 177, the remainder being at 1 in 250 to 1 in 330[9] the highest speed attained between these points being 34 miles an hour, and the maximum horse-power exerted 814.8. With the altered valve gear and separate cut-off the

[9] Rous-Marten's figures are not quite correct. Over the $10\frac{1}{2}$ miles from Crewe to Whitmore station the gradients are: first, a mile at 1 in 330; then $3\frac{1}{4}$ miles at 1 in 269; then $3\frac{1}{4}$ miles at 1 in 177; then $1\frac{3}{4}$ miles at 1 in 348; finally, a mile of level and slightly downhill track.

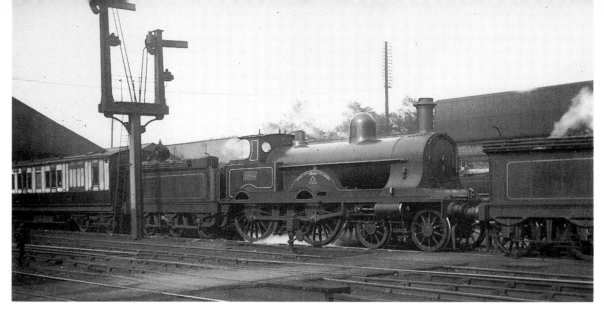

LNWR 4-4-0 No 1905 Black Diamond, *one of Webb's four-cylinder coupled compounds, built in 1897. Even though Webb now discarded his former practice of leaving the driving wheels uncoupled, and achieved a better balance between the high-pressure and low-pressure cylinders, these new engines were still erratic in performance until his successor George Whale provided the inside and outside cylinders with independently-operable valve gears; their performances then improved, and became better still when they were converted from compound to simple-expansion drive.* (NRM, S. Pearce-Higgins Collection)

Crewe-Stafford run was made in 33 minutes—$5\frac{1}{2}$ minutes quicker—and the Whitmore climb was accomplished in $18\frac{1}{4}$ minutes—$3\frac{1}{2}$ minutes quicker; while the highest speed up the bank was 40 miles an hour and the maximum horsepower 940. The average speed between the stations was 37.8 with the old gear and 44.1 with the new. Here again was a sufficiently substantial difference. In the opposite direction the journey time with the new gear was 30 minutes, and the average speed 48.5 miles an hour, as against 34 minutes and 42.9 miles an hour with the old gear, while up the moderate grades from Stafford to Whitmore the new valve gear gave a maximum of 52 miles an hour as against 45 with the old, and the horse-power indicated was 949 as against 756.

Here, then, we have a most remarkable and instructive change. In the one case we have the engine running with the regulator only partly open and the low-pressure valves being notched up similarly with the high-pressure ones. In the other case, with the new apparatus, the regulator was kept fully open and the low-pressure cylinders in full gear, notching up being done entirely in the high-pressure cylinders as required and quite independently of the low-

pressure. To make the matter plainer I may quote the official description of the new gear, which is as follows: 'There is only one reversing screw, which actuates both the high- and low-pressure reversing shafts, either together or independently of each other. The high and low pressure reversing rods are coupled to a short beam pivoted on a central pin which connects it to the main screw operated by the large hand-wheel. To each end of the beam is attached a short rod which slides in a recess in the bracket casting, and this rod can be locked in any position by means of a small hand-wheel and screw. The result of this is that after the engine has started with the high and low pressure reversing shafts in full forward gear, the end of the short beam which carries the low pressure rod can be locked in that position by means of the small hand-wheel and screw, and by revolving the large hand wheel and screw the other end of the beam, to which is attached the high-pressure rod, can be moved back, and thereby the travel of the valve in the high-pressure cylinder is varied while the low-pressure valve is working at its full travel. Studs fixed in the locking bars engage in slots in the bracket casting, and by this means the maximum angle required for each reversing shaft is determined.'

Now let us see how this alteration works in ordinary daily practice. I will not occupy space with lengthened statistics; I will content myself with taking a single casual instance which I personally observed and recorded only a few days ago. The train was the heavy express from Liverpool, Manchester, Carlisle, Holyhead and Birmingham, which finally amalgamates at Rugby into a total of truly portentous dimensions. On this occasion the load was officially computed as '24½ coaches', and in accordance with the weights I have obtained from official sources must have weighed from 460 to 466 tons, including passengers, luggage, staff and stores. I may observe that the train was packed with passengers and loaded up with luggage from end to end, and that when it stopped at Euston it extended from a point near to the buffer stops to a coach-and-a-half in length beyond the extreme end of the platform. Over and over again I have found even two engines unable to keep time over that length with a far smaller load, and I have had the regret to record in the columns of *The Railway Magazine* several such instances. But in the present instance the load was hauled with a surprising degree of ease and efficiency. The engine was No 1941, *Alfred the Great*, which was the earliest-built of the last and largest four-cylinder compounds; this locomotive, I believe, is among the latest to be fitted with the altered valve gear. She had a specially capable driver in B. H. Ward. Getting away well from Rugby, *Alfred the Great* showed full command of the vast train. Up the long ascent at 1 in 365 speed was steadily gathered, and just before the Kilsby tunnel was entered it had reached 40 miles an hour, still with a tendency to rise yet higher. After emerging from the tunnel there was a rapid acceleration down the moderate descent which succeeded; the speed rose quickly to 50 miles an hour, then to 65, 67, 68, 69 and finally to 70, at which rate we passed Weedon, maintaining it half way from that station to Blisworth. The adverse grade of 1 in 350[10]

[10] In fact there are just over 2 miles at 1 in 320.

then brought us down considerably, but our rate had not gone below 52.8 miles an hour when the summit near Roade was attained. Bletchley, 35¾ miles[11], was passed in the quick time of 41 minutes 30 seconds from the Rugby platform, and the 15 miles-long ascent thence to Tring was performed in 17 minutes 58 seconds, the absolute minimum up the final 6 miles of 1 in 330 being 47.4 miles an hour, which was maintained mile after mile to the summit. This, it must be remembered, was with a load behind the tender which would be reckoned as 47 to 48 'coaches' on the South of England railways. The descent from Tring to Willesden was performed at high but not exceptional speed, although in view of the fact that the down gradient was very moderate and the load was enormous, involving 'collar work' all the way, it was perhaps little less remarkable in this way than the preceding ascent. The distance of 26¼ miles from Tring to the Willesden platform was covered in 25 minutes 19 seconds. After full speed was attained near Boxmoor it kept very steadily at 65 to 70 miles an hour. The total run of 77 miles from absolute start to dead stop occupied 85 minutes 42 seconds, and from platform to platform 84 minutes 40 seconds.[12]

This appears to me one of the best performances that I have ever recorded. It was thoroughly good all round. There was very smart uphill work and free running downhill, while from first to last the engine never showed the slightest sign of flagging or sluggishness.[13]

[11] The distance is a full 36 miles.

[12] It is not absolutely clear what Rous-Marten means by *platform to platform*; I assume he means from platform-end at the starting station to platform-beginning at the finishing station. There does not seem much point in recording this detail, which tells one nothing of any importance, and when it appears in subsequent performance accounts I have omitted it.

[13] Was it, one wonders, a performance put on for Rous-Marten's special benefit, the engine being 'thrashed' to produce it? If so, one's sympathies are with the fireman—a functionary whom Rous-Marten seldom deigns to mention.

On speeds attained or attainable by British express locomotives

A naval correspondent, writing from Gibraltar, asks the following three questions: (1) Whether any train running in the British Isles has been known to touch 90 miles an hour? (2) Whether any train habitually touches that speed at any portion of its journey? (3) What are roughly the top speeds attained by trains in their running?

I might content myself with replying briefly as follows: (1) Yes. (2) No. (3) Various. But I do not think that would be treating the matter quite fairly. The querist has asked questions to which I know that numerous readers of *The Railway Magazine* would be glad to have something like an authoritative answer. One reads so much frightful rubbish in the columns of the non-technical Press about alleged 'record speeds', especially in America, that any mere matter-of-fact statement of what is actually done will seem relatively tame to those who are innocent enough to swallow the Penny-a-liners' alleged records to which I have referred. In the very early days of *The Railway Magazine* I dealt in its columns with a number of 'Railway Myths', which had implicit credence among the unenlightened. Even within the last few weeks a preposterous story about an imaginary journey made in America at the 'average rate of 106 miles an hour' found publication. But, I need hardly say, I merely mention these 'yarns' for the purpose of brushing them aside in the most emphatic and contemptuous manner possible. They cannot be wholly ignored because they have imposed and continue to impose upon so many ignorant and credulous people; and, silly as they are, they have done some amount of positive harm by confusing the public ideas about what is and is not feasible in railway work. In what I am now about to say I deal simply with what I myself have personally observed with the most improved methods, the best possible apparatus and the advantage of many years' training and experience . . .

Well, now, dealing with the queries specified above, I may say that had I been answering No 1 only nine years ago I should have been obliged to make my answer 'No', because up to that time there existed no authentic record of a speed of 90 miles an hour being attained, and no authentic figures from which could be deduced any probability that such a speed had been run. But in that year, 1897, I did obtain on one occasion three unquestionable observations at the rate of 90 miles an hour, three successive quarter-miles being run in 10 secs each, with a steady approach on the one hand to that maximum and a gradual recession from it afterwards. The engine, some of my readers will remember, was one of the Midland 7 ft 9 in single-wheelers, and the locality was between Ampthill and Bedford, down a falling grade at 1 in 200. Some years elapsed without my being able, even with the same engine, same driver,

MR 4-2-2 No 2601 Princess of Wales, *built in 1900, one of a final batch of ten 4-2-2 engines constructed by S. W. Johnson at Derby, making a total of 95 in all. The Midland main line is rather steeply graded, so it may seem strange that Johnson should have built single-wheelers for its principal expresses, but the Midland had a policy of keeping loads down and the 4-2-2s were generally able to cope until the introduction of heavier rolling-stock made the trains too difficult for them to haul.* (NRM)

same train, same load, same road and same conditions, to obtain a reproduction of that performance. The most famous single-wheelers of the Midland, Great Northern, Great Western and North Eastern were all tried, but either could not or would not do it. Thus, during all the rest of the nineteenth century I was unable to duplicate this single record.

But then came a perfect cluster of 90 miles an hour speeds, with not a few instances of even higher points being touched. When the 'Atbara' and 'City' classes came out on the Great Western Railway, Mr Drummond's '706' type and the Exeter accelerations on the London and South Western Railway, Mr Billinton's 'Holyroods' and the Brighton record run on the London Brighton and South Coast Railway, Mr Johnson's Belpaires and compounds on the Midland Railway, and Mr Robinson's 'Sir Alexanders' and 'Atlantics' on the Great Central Railway, all of these gave instances of 90 to 91.8 miles an hour, and I also recorded like speeds to the credit of Mr Aspinall's '1093' and '1400' classes, although I accepted these last with some doubt through being unable to secure the contiguous quarter-mile posts at each end of the record length. More recently I have conclusively recorded even higher maxima, including 95.7 and 97.8 miles an hour with 'Atbara' or 'City' engines on the Great Western Railway—neither of these was on the 'Record of Records' Ocean Mail Special run, by the bye—93.7 with one of Mr Whale's new six-coupled express engines on the falling grade approaching Carlisle, and 90 for two miles on end with one of the newest Great Western Railway French compounds. On one occasion a Great Western Railway 7 ft 8 in single-wheeler, which class had as a rule been considerably behind the coupled type in point of maximum rates, accomplished the feat, unparalleled of its kind, of covering a distance of six miles, mostly falling at 1 in 1,320, and the rest level, in exactly four minutes with a light load. I may mention too in passing, that on one special occasion I recorded a maximum rate of 90.2 miles an hour with a compound 'Atlantic' engine of the du Bousquet-de Glehn type on the Northern Railway of France.

The absolute maximum speed that I have ever recorded upon any railway on earth was reached in a special trial which I prefer not to indicate more specifically than by saying that the engine was four-coupled and had 6 ft 8 in driving wheels.[14] On this occasion a series of quarter-miles occupied the following times: 10 seconds, 9.8 seconds, 9.4 seconds, 9.2 seconds, 8.8 seconds—the last of course representing a rate of 102.3 miles an hour. It will be observed that the fastest half-mile was covered in exactly 18 seconds, or at the rate of just 100 miles an hour, and that the speed for the whole mile, taken in successive quarters and also as a whole, was 96.8. The locality was on a somewhat sharply falling gradient, but the road was one of the best in England, and the performance was not attended by the slightest amount of danger, while the travelling was as smooth as any I have ever experienced. I feel sure that these figures, which I have not previously published in England, will be read with much interest.

Coming now to Query No 2, I may say at once and emphatically that no train 'habitually touches that speed at any portion of its journey'. A speed of 90 miles an hour and upward is altogether exceptional. To render it even possible there must be a somewhat abnormal collation of favourable circumstances and conditions. The resistance, both internal and external, at such a speed may easily be augmented by a very slight divergence of the conditions, until so high a velocity is rendered impossible. Thus, with the same Midland engine that first attained a rate of 90 miles an hour I was unable at a second trial to get quite 85, the evident reason being that a slight side wind was blowing. It was a mere gentle zephyr, yet strong enough to press against the lee rail the flanges of every wheel along the train, with the manifest effect of a slight application of brake. But a very small impediment suffices; a trivial change in the mode of firing, in the length of time the engine has been out of the shops, in the state of the atmosphere or of the road, and an

infinity of other seemingly trifling conditions may be quite sufficient, not only in combination but even singly, to render the abnormal hopeless of attainment in respect of extreme speeds.

It has been a noteworthy fact, also, in my experience, that records, or even exceptional maxima, seem rarely to occur in record runs, taking the latter at from start to stop. Thus, in the case of the Great Western Railway's astonishing record from Bristol to London, which averaged 71.5 miles an hour from start to stop, without any allowance being made for delays, the maximum speed was not nearly so high as I have recorded on a different part of the same line on other occasions. It will be remembered that the distance from Swindon to London ($77\frac{1}{4}$ miles) was covered in 59 minutes 40 seconds, with a bridge slow to walking pace, while an average of 80 miles an hour was maintained for 73 miles on end. And yet no record maximum was reached. Again, on the Midland Railway, when the first 90 mile an hour rate was recorded, the complete journey was in no respect exceptional. And when I had that remarkable and, I believe, record run from St Pancras to Leicester, with Selly driving one of the Belpaires, in 95 mins net, we were never going much over 80 miles an hour, while on a second occasion, with an engine of the same type, a rate of 90 was attained, and slightly exceeded, on each of the two stages between St Pancras and Manchester, yet the total from start to stop was not in either instance exceptional. With all the well-deserved fame that the Great Northern Railway so long has enjoyed in respect of high speeds, I have never been able on any occasion even closely to approach a rate of 90, although I have considerably exceeded 80 miles an hour times without number. On the Caledonian Railway I have nearly attained the magic point, yet failed fractionally to touch it. The plain fact is that there is no reckoning definitely upon the speed that any train may reach. So much depends upon varying and uncertain conditions that any definite achievements can never be reckoned upon with anything like certainty, or even probability. Of course some fast running may usually be looked

---

[14] Rous-Marten is of course referring to *City of Truro*'s exploit on 9 May 1904 on the up Ocean Mail Special. It did *not*, however, occur during a special trial; this was perhaps a white lie to mislead the over-curious and avoid the engine and driver being identified.

GWR No 3031 Achilles, *sister-engine to No 3035* Duke of Connaught *which, with a load one van lighter, continued the Ocean mails Special run, previously headed by* City of Truro, *on May 9th 1904 between Bristol and London, making a record time of under 100 minutes and maintaining an average of 80 mph over the 70 miles from Shrivenham to Westbourne Park. See opposite for a reference to this run.* (NRM)

for between Stoke and Tallington on the Great Northern Railway, between Leagrave and Bedford, Aisgill and Carlisle, and Bleamoor and Settle on the Midland Railway, between Whiteball and Taunton on the Great Western Railway, on both sides of Honiton on the London and South Western Railway, and near Haywards Heath on the London Brighton and South Coast Railway, between Shap and Carlisle or Shap and Carnforth on the London and North Western Railway, between Beattock Summit and Carstairs or Beattock and Carlisle on the Caledonian Railway. Yet at the same time it is quite possible that if a train happens to be in extra good time the maximum on any of these tempting lengths may not exceed 65 or even 60 miles an hour. All depends upon circumstances.

To give even 'roughly' what is the 'top speed attained by trains in their running' would require one whole issue of *The Railway Magazine*. A general idea may be gathered from what I have said already. If my querist desires more detailed information than this I do not see how he is to

obtain it, simply because the answer must always depend upon possibilities and conditions and contingencies which may not be known or arise until the last moment before starting, possibly when the journey is half over.

We are really as much in the dark, too, as to what can actually be done in respect of mere speed by various classes of locomotives. The great majority of my highest rates have been attained by coupled engines with moderate-sized wheels. Yet I do not for one moment pretend to assert or imply that the larger-wheeled singles *could* not have done equally well, or even better, in this respect. I see no reason whatever to suppose that they could but I certainly will not assert that they could not. I regret very much that I have never been able to test a single-wheeler at her utmost extension down a long and fairly steep falling grade, such, eg, as the Aisgill–Appleby or Bleamoor–Settle length on the Midland Railway, each of which falls at about 1 in 100 for many miles, and on which speeds of 80 to 90 miles an hour are not infrequently run nowadays. Coupled engines are so essential for the up-climb that it is virtually impracticable to get singles on that road for the downhill runs unless as a special experiment for sheer curiosity's sake, which would not be 'business'. The Wellington bank on the Great Western is a superb 'galloping ground', being specially safe, as well as suitable for extra velocities. I have often had fairly smart runs down that bank with the 7 ft 8 in single 'Amazons', but with them have never yet exceeded 83.7 miles an hour on that length, whereas in like conditions I have over and over again reached much faster speed with engines of the 'Badminton', 'Atbara' and 'City' classes, as well as with the six-coupled bogies and the French compounds. I should conceive *a priori* that the single-wheelers should be able to run at least equally fast, and do it more economically as regards wear and tear. But in my experience they don't do the former, although in the second stage of the 'Record of Records' run 'Duke of Connaught' greatly surpassed anything I have ever seen done on a virtually level road, attaining 90 miles an hour with practically no aid from gravitation. Would she not have been able to do much more down the Wellington bank, whose grade is 1 in 90, or even 1 in 80? I should have thought so. But there is no evidence either way.

What a Great Northern Railway 8 ft single could do from Aisgill to Appleby, or Bleamoor to Settle, or on its own road from Nostell to Doncaster where much of the distance is at 1 in 150 down, it is not easy to estimate. I have often been with one of them over that length but seldom got much more than 80 miles an hour near Hampole. To what extent are they prejudiced by their 28 in stroke, as compared with the Great Western 'Amazons', and the North Eastern Railway's '1517s' which have 24 ins? That is just what nobody can tell us. Even the 30 in stroke of the new Great Western Railway engines does not seem to stand in their way so much as, theoretically, one would have expected. When you find a six-coupled engine with 6 ft 8 in wheels, outside cylinders and 30 in piston stroke attaining a rate of 88.2 miles an hour with over 300 tons behind her tender—as I

have seen—one is forced to realize that neither her 30 in stroke nor the six-coupling of her wheels can have placed her at any very serious disadvantage.

Again, why was it that when, with special credentials, I made my two years' examination of the British railways in 1884 and 1885, with the view of reporting to a Colonial Government, I never found *any* engine able to reach 82 miles an hour, and only thrice reached or exceeded 80? Indeed, when I drew up my report I could not find any instance of a higher rate than 76.3 miles an hour being run. It was only on going through my figures long afterward that I discovered, when working out the speeds, deduced from various irregular lengths—eg $\frac{3}{4}$ mile or $1\frac{1}{4}$ miles or $1\frac{1}{2}$ miles, instead of the regulation mile or $\frac{1}{4}$ mile—that in a very select number of instances 80 miles an hour had been reached or exceeded, one of the Great Western Railway's—formerly Bristol and Exeter's—converted 9 ft single wheelers (No 2002) having touched 81.8 miles an hour down the Wellington bank, and a Great Northern Railway 8 ft single (No 665) 80 near Essendine, a Great Western Railway 'Iron Duke' (*Prometheus*) and a Midland Railway 7 ft coupled (No 1668) doing much the same down Wootton Bassett bank and approaching Bedford, respectively. These, however, were very much below what I have recorded since my last return to England 13 years ago. Whence the difference? That is the puzzle.

No doubt the increased steam pressure accounts for much. Probably, too, even the engines of 1884–1885 have been provided with freer exhaust, back pressure being thus mitigated. But, making every allowance, the difference in performance still lacks full explanation. It is true that the Great Northern Railway 8 ft singles did not run much faster in the 'nineties' than they did in the 'eighties'. But take two justly-famous types that were at their best in the earlier decade—the Midland Railway's '800s' and the London and North Western Railway's 'Precedents'. Innumerable trials with the best trains on their respective roads, and under the most favourable conditions, failed to give me in any case a higher maximum than 75 miles an hour, which indeed was very rarely reached. But ten years later I found all this changed. One of the old '800s' on the Midland Railway reached a fraction over 80 miles an hour with 16 coaches down the bank approaching Chesterfield from the north; and not once, but several times, a 'Precedent' exceeded 88 miles an hour down the banks on each side of the Shap summit. What caused the difference? It may be that the 'Race to Edinburgh' of 1888, and the extensive accelerations which attended or followed that historic development, caused the drivers to 'open their hearts' as well as their regulators, and to undertake performances or attempt feats which in previous years they would have deemed impracticable, if not absolutely dangerous. Also, their superiors may with perfect propriety have given them a freer hand in view of the improvements generally made in the roads, notably in respect of heavier rails. At all events, the fact remains indisputable. Take, for example, the Luton-Bedford run on the Midland Railway; 80 miles an hour and upward may as commonly be noticed now as 70 to 72 then. Also, on those most favourable stretches for high speeds, the Aisgill–Appleby and Bleamoor–Settle lengths, even a dozen years ago the speed was severely restricted, usually to

60 miles an hour and sometimes to 55. Nowadays 80 is common and 90 is not unknown. So, too, on the Wellington bank of the Great Western Railway; it used often to be descended with steam shut off at a maximum of barely 70, often under 65. In these days rates of 80 and even 90 are not seldom met with, and the travelling, as in the other cases instanced, is smoother and safer than ever. And it must be remembered that the improvements of late years in locomotive designing and construction have not been aimed at increased velocity. It has been recognised that the rates feasible and sometimes attained in the 'eighties', and 'seventies', the 'sixties', and even the 'fifties', are still fast enough for all ordinary modern requirements. It has been in respect of haulage power, associated with swiftness, that the advance has been sought and achieved. It has been almost an accidental contingency that enhanced swiftness has come in simultaneously. But it has come, and a run of 2 hrs 44 mins actual travelling time for the 194 miles from Exeter to Paddington, averaging, with an intermediate stop and a bad permanent way slack, 70.6 miles an hour throughout, up and down hill, has demonstrated what is feasible in the present day, when it shall be deemed profitable to utilise the experience thus gained.

SEPTEMBER & OCTOBER 1906

On the Salisbury derailment of July 1st, 1906

Touching the lamentable disaster at Salisbury[15], I desire to express my deep regret that it should have occurred and my sincere sympathy alike with the victims and with the London and South Western Railway Company which, although blameless, has had to suffer for the mishap. As the Company has admitted liability, and declared the cause of the accident to be excessive speed on a too-sharp curve, that causation theory must be accepted *quantum valeat*. But this by no means covers the whole ground or meets the entire issue that has been raised with respect to locomotive practice and performance by the lamentable catastrophe of July 1st.

Now, in the first place, be it observed, the Railway's engineer has officially stated that the curve just east of Salisbury station is of only 8 chains' radius. Several officers declared the speed of the ill-fated train at the point of derailment to have been at least 60 miles an hour, and probably 70 miles an hour. Well, then, it is im-mediately manifest to the merest tyro in engineering that those two factors could not co-exist with safety. It was theoretically impossible for the train to round that curve at that speed without coming to grief. According to the accepting axioms of engineering this is a foregone conclusion. Personally I should say that even a velocity of 30 miles an hour—that sanctioned by the Board of Trade for the passage through Salisbury station—goes very close indeed to the safety limit, and for myself I should be disposed to name 25 miles an hour as the highest rate that ought to be run round an 8-chains curve. It seems to be quite clear that the engine did not leave the rails through the tangential impulse due to what is commonly called centrifugal force, but that through that impulse it was first tilted over towards the outside of the curve until the wheels on the inside rail were actually clear of the metals, and then, the impulse continuing, the locomotive fell right over on its side. So far, then, the cause and its operation would seem to be plain enough. The engine, in colloquial parlance, was top-heavy for the rounding of so sharp a curve at so high a speed, and as a consequence lost its balance and just toppled over. Simple enough, isn't it? And yet how terribly disastrous in its consequences and how disquieting in its suggestiveness. But at any rate we have, up to a certain point, a convincing theory of causation. Very good. But then what follows?

---

[15] The train was a special night express carrying 48 passengers to London from a transatlantic liner which had touched at Plymouth. It had halted at Templecombe to change engines, and here a Drummond large-boilered 'Greyhound' was attached. Its driver failed to reduce speed on the approach to Salisbury, and the train derailed on a reverse curve east of that station, striking another train. 24 passengers and 4 of the Company's employees, including the crew of the locomotive, No 421, lost their lives. No explanation of the failure to slow down was ever forthcoming.

Two years ago the same train ran round that same curve at certainly an equally high speed, probably faster. At all events, at the last quarter-mile post which I took before entering Salisbury station the pace was exactly 75 miles an hour, and although I believe we shut off steam through the station our speed had not been materially checked when we passed round that curve with perfect steadiness and smoothness. But if we accept the conclusion arrived at by the London and South Western Railway's experts, by the Directors and by the Coroner's jury, it is impossible that I should now be alive and writing this article.[16] Yet I cannot doubt that I am alive and writing. Also, several eminent persons who were my fellow-passengers on that occasion, and who independently noted the times and speeds, ought also, as well as myself, to be two-year-old corpses. But we are not. Quite the contrary. How is this discrepancy to be explained? We shall see what the Board of Trade Inspector says when his report comes out, but I really do not see how he is to reconcile these very curious conflicts of fact and theory. For mark, there is, so far as I have been able to discover, only one single difference in detail between the conditions of those two runs, the one on July 1st which killed 29 people, the other two years ago which did not kill me or my companions, and when I mention it I must not be understood for one moment to be implying that the distinction made all the difference, or that the difference caused the accident. It is this: On the occasion of my trip the engine was No 336, of the earliest class that Mr Dugald Drummond designed and built for the

London and South Western Railway. The engine in the Salisbury disaster was No 421, the latest four-coupled express type constructed by him for the same line. Now in some respects these two engines are greatly similar—indeed, almost identical. Both have 6 ft 7 in coupled wheels and 26 in piston stroke. No 336 has $18\frac{1}{2}$ in cylinders, No 421 has $\frac{1}{2}$ in more of cylinder diameter. That is neither here nor there. What is both here and there is that No 421 has a distinctly larger boiler, considerably more highly-pitched than that of the earlier engine. Now the question has to be frankly faced, whether the higher pitch of the latter boiler had or had not anything to do with the upset of the engine. Substantially, this detail is the only relevant one in which No 421 differs from No 336, and anyone thinking superficially might be disposed to conclude at once that this difference afforded the true explanation of the mishap. But, as against that, one has to take into consideration the fact that there are many British engines which have the boiler-axis higher above the rail-level than No 421, and many more Continental engines which stand higher still. Yet these engines run habitually at high speeds round curves, little if at all easier than that of Salisbury.[17] In these circumstances where are we to look for a really sound and exhaustive explanation of the disaster? All that hitherto has been presented seems to me to fail fatally through incompleteness, through not taking into account *every* factor in the whole melancholy affair. For the present I must leave the question an unsolved problem . . .

---

[16] Over-theatricality in making a valid point! He might have been a survivor.

[17] Surely an exaggeration. Rous-Marten does not even hint *where* it was customary for trains to round curves of 8 chains' radius at 60 miles an hour.

* * *

Copious discussion continues to prevail regarding the Salisbury accident and various calculations have been published which, as worked out, would seem to indicate not only that the ill-fated boat train could not possibly have got round that curve without disaster, but also that neither could the record train of April 1904, whose performance I described in *The Railway Magazine* of June 1904.[18] As to that, I express no opinion. But I must reiterate my former conviction that I am not a two-year-old corpse despite the theoretical certainty that I cannot possibly be anything else!

Let there be no mistake, however, on one head. I did not and could not test the exact speed on the 'fatal curve' itself. I could only infer it, but from facts which are indisputable, viz: (1) Each of the last two quarter-miles before entering the Salisbury station from the westward was done in exactly 12 seconds, ie at precisely 75 miles an hour. That was at the foot of a mile at 1 in 115 down. (2) No *material* slackening through the station was perceptible—that, however, is of course a merely subjective estimate. There was undoubtedly a slight reduction when the steam was shut off, and the grinding of the flanges round the curve no doubt produced more, but it was almost inappreciable to one's senses. (3) When we emerged from the Fisherton tunnel just west of Salisbury station[19], that is to say after passing the station with steam off, rounding the curve and threading the tunnel on a rising grade, we were still going 60—ascertained by timing—which speed assuredly did not seem to be higher than that at which we rounded the curve, but rather lower, and which further decreased up the rising grade that contined onward past Porton. Apart from these facts there are other collateral ones, viz: (a) The complete run from Devonport, Stonehouse Junction to Waterloo, was done in 4 hrs 2 mins 51 secs, or in 17 mins 9 secs less than the booked time of the wrecked train; (b) The inclusive time from

Devonport to Salisbury was 10 minutes quicker in any case than that sworn to as made on the occasion of the accident, although the engine, No 399, that ran from Devonport to Templecombe descended the falling grades at a much slower rate than that usually maintained by the ordinary expresses; (c) The time from Templecombe to Salisbury, after changing engines at the former place, was only 27 minutes for the 29 miles. I may add that all these points can be absolutely proved, not merely by my own testimony—for what that may be worth—but also by corroborative evidence. So on the whole I do not see my way to doubt that the train in which I safely rounded that curve must have been going at quite 60 miles an hour. But this, as I have already said, is an inferential deduction from facts absolutely certain.

To those who have been a little 'previous' in jumping to conclusions about this deplorable mishap—which must have and indeed already has a serious influence on British Locomotive Practice and Performance—I should like to offer a word of caution. It is this: All the facts have not yet been disclosed. Some people may be surprised to learn: (1) That the overturning of the locomotive did not take place on the worst curve, but *before* that had been reached; (2) That the engine which fell over on its side stood 9 inches higher above the rails than the one which rounded the curve safely; that is to say, the boiler axis of No 421 was 8 ft 6 in above the rails, and that of No 336 was only 7 ft 9 in. As I have said before, I attach little or no importance to the latter in view of the lessons of actual experience. Still, it is a distinctly relevant factor in the problem. The death of the unfortunate driver removes the evidence that would have been the most valuable of all. But there is much more yet to be learned about the matter before the moral, as regards engineering, can be conclusively deduced. One comfort that travellers on the London and South Western Railway may extract from the lamentable disaster is that they are not likely to be endangered by any over-fast running round curves, more careful slowings than ever being now the rule. One passenger has

---

[18] See page 133.

[19] The tunnel is *east*, not west of Salisbury.

complained of these slowings, even in the case of the very sharp Northam curve. But his objection is absurd. High speed round sharp curves is wholly indefensible. The Salisbury, Preston and Aylesbury mishaps showed this with fatal plainness, but did not demonstrate that there was the slightest risk in the highest possible speeds on suitable roads in good order with rolling-stock to correspond. The slackening on the London and South Western Railway around curves such as those of Northam, Salisbury, Clapham Junction, Yeovil, etc, is undoubtedly proper and should be imperative, but as the superintendent of the London and South Western line quite justly declared in his evidence at the inquest, a rate of 90 might be run with entire safety on the straighter lengths of his railways—indeed, no speed that a locomotive can attain is unsafe under the conditions indicated.

Does the occurrence of July 1st raise any question as to the desirableness or otherwise of high-pitched locomotives? Did No 421 really labour under disadvantage through the axis of her boiler barrel being pitched 9 inches higher than that of No 336? I do not know. But I cannot think so. She ought not. There are crowds of locomotives with boilers standing far higher above the rails than did that of No 421, and yet they get along all right. My readers will note that this, although the commonly-practised way of stating such a case, is utterly fallacious as a mode of statement. No real value can attach to such a comparison unless every minute detail be given and duly appraised. But, speaking quite roughly and generally and empirically, I should say that No 421's high centre of gravity is *not* detrimental and that it did *not* cause the engine's overturn. Indeed, it would never have been noticed or mentioned but for the strangeness—almost uniqueness—of the accident, and the difficulty of satisfactorily explaining *why* the tangential impulse, due to what is commonly (but erroneously) called centrifugal force, should in this particular case have caused the locomotive to fall over on its side.

When the late Mr Stroudley deliberately went in for high-pitched boilers in his 'Devonshires'

and 'Gladstones' some people doubted his wisdom. When Mr Aspinall adopted a still higher pitch in his '1400s' and 'all the world wondered', there were not a few predictions of evil . . . Yet No 1400 and her sisters have gone on for years rounding curves at speed, and never with any ill result. Once, when I was on the footplate of No 1400, I had the opportunity of noting the ease and safety with which she glided round some particularly sharp curves. So, too, with the Great Northern and North Eastern 'Atlantics'; they stand much higher than do Nos 415–434 of the London and South Western, and yet they can round pretty stiff curves without a hint of peril. No, we have something more yet to find out in respect of these matters. What we now know as to the risk and unwisdom of rounding sharp curves at high speed we knew quite well before. Why it *is* done in particular cases we never do know. In the Aylesbury and Salisbury cases the drivers 'being dead speak not', so we cannot tell why they disregarded prudence. In the Preston case the imprudence was inexplicable because, when the train became derailed through rounding at 40 to 50 miles an hour a 7-chain curve which had neither due cant or check rail, there still remained 94 minutes in which to do the distance of 90 miles, which had previously been done by similar engines and loads in $80\frac{1}{2}$ minutes, ie in $13\frac{1}{2}$ minutes less.[20] A speed of 40 to 50 miles an hour proved fatal on the Preston curve; speeds of 80 to 90 have (and had) been run times out of number on other parts of the same journey. It was the far lower speed that proved perilous *owing to the special conditions*, but not otherwise.

---

[20] It is difficult to agree with Rous-Marten here. He is alluding to the accident which occurred at Preston in July 1896, when the night 'Tourist' express, headed by two 'Precedent' 2-4-0s, took a curve at the north end of the station too fast and became derailed. At the enquiry which followed it emerged that not only had neither driver worked this train before but also that neither had ever had to work a train through Preston which was not booked to stop there. Serious misjudgement due to inexperience, rather than imprudence, caused the accident. Rous-Marten appears either not to have known what the enquiry revealed, or to have forgotten it.

On compound locomotives constructed for service on British railways

A week or two ago I had some very interesting runs with Mr J. G. Robinson's earliest three-cylinder compounds . . . I am glad that the compound principle is thus having a fair trial on the Great Central Railway. I hope that more will yet be done in this direction. But please remember one thing: I have never *advocated* compound locomotives. No; what I have advocated has been that compounding should have a *fair trial* in this country, in view of the excellent results it had given abroad. I have not even advocated the adoption of the de Glehn system in this country, notwithstanding the splendid work—in some respects unequalled—which it has given me in France. But I long have contended, and always shall contend, that it ought to be *tried*—on fair and reasonable conditions.

I may of course be promptly assailed with the oft-offered but quite inaccurate assertion that locomotive compounding has already been largely tried in England—for a quarter of a century. And really, when you consider that—taking express engines alone—one English railway (the London and North Western) has had no fewer than 180 of the compound type and, having started building them in 1882, has only recently ceased their production, while another, the North Eastern Railway, has had 47 of another compound type, it would seem to the superficial observers and thinkers that there must be something in the allegation that

locomotive compounding has had an extensive and thorough trial in this country. But, in reality, such a conclusion would be wholly fallacious. For each of these two systems contained within its special feature the fatal germ of predestined failure. In the case of the Webb three-cylinder system, even apart from the self-evident hopeless inadequacy of the boiler power and steam pressure, the lack of wheel-coupling was a fatal flaw, in view of the necessary inter-dependence of the high-pressure and low-pressure action. The two sets of machinery were theoretically independent of one another, and yet each depended on the other. The low-pressure cylinder could not operate until it had received steam from the high-pressure cylinder. The high-pressure cylinder could not operate a second time until the low-pressure cylinder had consented to receive the exhaust of the steam used in the first operation of the high-pressure cylinder. Yet there was no means of absolutely assuring the synchronous working of the two. I pointed this out to Mr Webb so long ago as 1884, but he insisted that there was nothing in the objection. Experience proved that there was *everything* in the objection. The frequent failure in synchronism rendered the three-cylinder compounds untrustworthy and often sluggish. Nevertheless I urged all that time back—23 years ago—as I do still that the plan, in spite of its manifest drawbacks, should have fair treatment and a thorough test. That particular plan has, I think, had a thorough test, and with unsatisfactory results, the outcome being that all of the 100 engines have been condemned and most of them scrapped.

Yet those results were curiously various in detail. There has never been any doubt why the first (or 'Experiment') batch of 30 proved failures. Apart from the non-coupling, the insufficiency of boiler and of steam pressure amply explained this. But the second batch of 40, with larger boilers, had far more promise of success, and indeed in some degree attained it. I have many notes of excellent work with engines of that class. Still, they were not trustworthy, but were always uncertain and often sluggish. The third batch, on the other hand, the 'Teutonic' set, ten in all, were remarkably efficient and very few indeed are their records of failure. It has never been clearly explained *why* this was so, or why the final batch of the three-cylinder compounds—the ten 'John Hicks'—proved the most complete and unadulterated failures of all. That remains a Crewe secret and I shall not attempt to penetrate the mystery. The penultimate, or 'Greater Britain' batch of ten might be classed with the 'Dreadnoughts'. They did much good work and much bad, but like all the rest of the type—excepting perhaps the 'Teutonics'—were untrustworthy. Thus only ten out of the 100 three-cylinder Webb Express compounds could be characterised as fairly successful.

Well, then came the 40 'Jubilee', or four-cylinder compounds, which escaped their predecessors' fault of non-coupling but suffered from two other defects of design—the lack of separate cut-off for the high-pressure and low-pressure cylinders, and the driving of a single axle by all four cylinders—while they shared, albeit in less degree, the weakness of the three-cylinder type in respect of boiler power. And so, while undoubtedly efficient up to a certain point, that is to say so long as the combination of high speed with powerful haulage was not demanded, they proved hopelessly sluggish when rigidly restricted limits had to be passed—as in twen-

tieth century standard express duty, for which they proved wholly inadequate. Finally, the 40 'Alfreds', which though given the advantage of bigger boilers were inefficient in *first class* express service, were rendered distinctly efficient when their originally-defective valve gear was replaced with a separate cut-off by Mr Webb's successor, Mr Whale, although the engines as converted must still be regarded as in the probation stage. Thus we see that this trial of no fewer than 180 express compound engines on the London and North Western Railway, during 25 years from first to last, has been by no means a thorough test of the compound principle, but merely a sort of miscellaneous trial of various plans, all marred by one kind or another of vexatious faddiness.

Again, take the Worsdell-Von Borries two-cylinder compound system. Initiated by Mr T. W. Worsdell on the Great Eastern Railway, in 1884, when he was Locomotive Superintendent of that railway, its application was limited to 11 express engines, all of which were speedily converted by his successor into the single-expansion type. Taking the design with him to the North Eastern Railway in 1885, he promptly turned out 27 four-coupled and 20 single-driver compounds on his system, with which Herr von Borries' name has now been jointly associated. In spite of all that has been ably urged against my view, and notwithstanding also the fact that such eminent engineers as M Mallet, Herr von Borries and Her Görlsdorff long advocated and employed two-cylinder compound locomotives, I have never been able to approve the use of two cylinders of unequal dimensions and working at different pressures for fast running. For goods or slow passenger traffic they may be permissible, although only on the score of relative cheapness. But whatever may be feasible in theory towards approximately equalising the stress, every practical engineer knows that equilibration cannot be achieved, and often cannot even be satisfactorily approximated on such conditions, for reasons which are self-suggestive. This, which appeared to me even in 1884 quite inevitable, has proved in practice to be so, and the system has long been condemned on the North Eastern Railway, while abroad M Mallet, Herr von Borries and Herr Görlsdorff have now gone in for four cylinders in their various compound systems. Here again the system of compounding tried in England was handicapped by an inherent defect, and hence was condemned. But note once more, it was merely a particular *system* of compounding, not *compounding itself*, that was condemned after full trial.

In England, at the present time, five different systems of compounding are on trial. The Great Western Railway is experimenting with three express engines, compounded on the de Glehn four-cylinder system; the Great Northern Railway with two four-cylinder compounds, one of a modified de Glehn type, one on a plan of Mr Ivatt's own; the Midland Railway with some 30 or 40, and the Great Central Railway with four, all compounded on the late Mr W. M. Smith's three-cylinder system; and the North Eastern Railway with two express compounds on the same engineer's four-cylinder plan. Thus, after a quarter of a century of more or less unsatisfactory experimenting, we have now entered upon a new era in England of trials of entirely new methods of compounding as applied to express locomotives. The original departures on the Great Eastern Railway and North Eastern Railway respectively, represented by 58 engines in all, have all suffered condemnation. So have the whole 100 Webb three cylinder engines on the London and North Western Railway, while of his 80 four cylinder express compounds, 40 have been virtually condemned as regards the work for which they were designed and built, and are relegated to service of an inferior order, while the latest 40 are also virtually condemned as regards their original design, all being either converted or about to be converted by Mr Whale into an entirely different type.

But these new designs which are now in course of testing all seem to possess the promise and potentiality of success in a far greater degree than any of their predecessors, whose manifest faults they almost entirely avoid. As to the Great Western Railway de Glehns, I can only say that

on the Hemerdon bank—the severest test that any express engine is put to—they beat in my own experience not only all four-coupled engines but even the six coupled; while I have yet to see *any* other four coupled engines equal the type in such feats of combined speed and load haulage and hill-climbing as I—with other British engineers—have seen them perform in France. I have yet to see any British engine take 309 tons behind the tender up 1 in 200 for 12 miles at a *sustained* speed of 62 miles an hour, or even 300 tons at 60 miles an hour, though I should much like to see it and should rejoice to publish it far and wide. But I have seen sister engines of Great Western Railway locomotives Nos 102, 103 and 104 do it with certainty.

My experience with the two Great Northern Railway compounds I have recorded in the columns of *The Railway Magazine*. It will be remembered that with the modified de Glehn, No 1300 I was at a disadvantage owing to her getting hot bearings, but that the Ivatt compound, No 292, did very good work in spite of her curiously small high-pressure cylinders which, being only 13 by 20, might, one would have thought, have been given with benefit at least an additional inch of cylinder diameter and 4 in more piston stroke, having 2,500 sq ft of heating surface to go upon. However, Mr Ivatt doubtless had good reasons for trying such exceptional dimensions, and the work obtained speaks for itself up to a certain point. But I doubt the probability of the type being multiplied because such good service is being got out of the sister engines, which differ only in being of the single-expansion order, with cylinders $18\frac{3}{4}$ by 24, that there is a strong temptation to 'let well alone'. I suspect too that there is a good deal of this influence at work on the Great Western Railway, where Mr Churchward's single-expansion locomotives are performing so admirably that he may well ask, 'What more do you want?' The two four-cylinder compounds on the North Eastern Railway, Nos 730 and 731, I must leave over for future consideration, for the simple but sufficient reason that when I went north last year specially to try them each

MR No 1000, R.M. Deeley's modification of Johnson's 4–4–0 three-cylinder compound, with a higher working pressure, an improved regulator control and slightly smaller driving wheels. In this form the locomotives proved so successful that, after being superheated, their numbers were greatly multiplied, especially after the Midland was absorbed into the LMS system in 1923. The engine illustrated has been preserved, in the condition shown, at the National Railway Museum, York. (NRM)

had to go into 'hospital' with a 'hot box'—a pure accident which 'will happen in the best-regulated families' of locomotives and humans alike. But I hear good accounts of them.

So I do also of the three-cylinder Smith compounds[21] on both the Midland and the Great Central Railways. I have mentioned in these columns the good work shown me by the pioneer locomotive of this type, No 1619, on the North

Eastern Railway, and by the first five of the same order tried by the Midland Railway, Nos 2631–2635, of Mr Johnson's build. My experiences with the Midland Railway '1000' class, to which Mr Deeley has given the advantage of 25 lbs extra steam pressure, viz, 220 lbs per square inch instead of 195 lbs, have yet to come. But Nos 1000, etc, *ought* to do even better than Nos 2631 and Co. I see no reason why they should not. Finally I come to Mr Robinson's new engines on the Great Central Railway. They have the advantage of being readily and cheaply convertible into the single-expansion type should they prove unsatisfactory as compounds—of which, at present, there seems no likelihood as Mr Robinson has just doubled their number. They are undoubtedly very fine and efficient machines. Personally I prefer the four-cylinder to the three-cylinder design, but I never allow personal preferences to dim my appreciation of good locomotive work by whatever type of engine it is done . . . And thus, while I like four cylinders better than three for express com-

[21] Rous-Marten was to have his knuckles rapped over applying this epithet to the Midland compounds. R. M. Deeley, now Locomotive Superintendent on the Midland after S. W. Johnson's retirement, wrote him a sharp letter to the effect that his railway had no 'Smith' compounds; all had been altered since the Smith reducing valve had shown itself prone to failure, and a simpler starting arrangement had now been fitted. Humble pie was duly consumed; an acknowledgement was made in the May 1908 article that the engines should more properly be described as 'compounded on the Deeley system'. One had to keep on good terms with reigning Locomotive Superintendents! Alas, Rous-Marten was to have no further opportunities of mis-describing anything. When the article appeared he had already breathed his last.

pounds, that liking does not blind me in the least to the efficiency of the Smith three-cylinder type, as employed respectively by Mr Robinson on the Great Central Railway and by Mr Deeley on the Midland Railway. Nor can I refuse to recognise the force of the arguments with which Mr Robinson defends his use of three cylinders instead of four. There are three, viz, (1) Greater cheapness in construction: (2) Diminished external areas exposed to condensation: (3) Greater ability of boiler to maintain steam to the max-imum requirement with heavy loads and long runs. These arguments commend themselves very strongly. Their force cannot be gainsaid. Still, as I have so often had occasion to remark, the question resolves itself into one of 'pro and con', give and take . . . Altogether, then, the new Great Central Railway compounds present themselves as potentially very useful engines, equal to far more arduous duty than as yet they have been called on to perform, upon the main line at any rate.

On the use or non-use of the steam dome on British locomotives

When the nineteenth century closed the steam dome appeared to be all-triumphant, just as did the inside cylinder. No British railway was any longer building domeless engines, just as no British railway was any longer building locomotives of the normal type with outside cylinders. Last month I noted the remarkable revulsion of practice which had occurred in regard to the cylinder position. I am not in a position to assert that a like revulsion has taken place with respect to the use of a steam dome, or even to imply that such a revulsion is impending. But at least I am able to point out that the British railway with the largest mileage has abandoned the steam dome. It remains to be seen whether any other railway will follow the example thus set.

So far as technical readers are concerned, or even those non-technical enthusiasts who through an unhappy and long-repented joke have become permanently branded with the cacophonous designation of *railwayac*, it is of course un-necessary to explain on the one hand the use of the steam dome, or on the other the objections to it, but *The Railway Magazine* is intended for readers among 'all sorts and conditions of men . . .' Therefore I think it well to make it clear that the steam dome is something more than a mere ornament to an engine ('I do like those engines with the pretty brass helmets!' one nice girl remarked to me), and in reality ex-ercises a very important function in the economy of the locomotive. In the first place let me observe that the motive agent of an engine is STEAM. I do not say the motive *power*, you will notice, because the actual power as we know it is heat. But by means of heat the water in the boiler is converted into an agent for the production of power through conversion into the steam which, admitted into the cylinders, forces the piston backward and forward and so, by means of the connecting rods which work on a crank —representing the handle by which a grindstone or a churn is made to revolve—turns the driving wheels. It is hardly necessary for me to say that I am not ignorant of the question that has been raised as to whether the steam really pushes the piston in both directions or whether it does not push the piston one way and the cylinder head the other. That is a very interesting point, but it is not relevant to the subject of my present remarks. I emphasize the fact that the motive agent of a locomotive is *steam* and I repeat that now, with the additional *dictum* that it is not *steam and water*. Yet the latter combination fills the greater part of the boiler's cubic space. But pro-portionately as water mingles with the steam, so is the effective potence of the steam diminish-ed—the more water, the less power. In fact, to put the case in a homely and familiar way, the engine wants her steam 'neat'. The difficulty is, how to extract it in this desirable condition from a boiler which is some three parts full of a ramping, roaring conglomeration of the oxide of hydrogen which we know familiarly in its three forms of ice, water and steam, according to its temperature. Supposing the boiler is filled too full of water, or that any considerable amount of oil or saponified grease should have got into the water, there is often set up that objectionable condition known as 'priming'; that is to say, the water escapes with the steam into and through the cylinders, and is blown out with the exhaust.

I remember one grim experience in this connection. When in 1898 Mr Johnson brought out his No 60 class—7 ft coupled with cylinders $19\frac{1}{2}$ by 26 in—he was good enough to send up Nos 60 and 61 specially to St Pancras in order that I might make observations upon their working on the best expresses between London and Leicester. No 60 took the up train and did very well; No 61 was on the down train. Soon after we started it became evident that, as the driver sadly remarked to me—I was on the footplate—we were going to 'make a mess of it!' We did! The engine primed furiously all the way, spattering the whole length of the train with dirty water and losing time mile after mile. Whenever we got a chance on the down grade we went at it 'eyes out', but whenever we had 'collar work' we fell off again. Up the Sharnbrook bank our pace was quite too awful. If I recollect aright we got down to 18 miles an hour before we struggled to the top, and we wound up by strolling into Leicester more than 20 minutes late on a fine calm day. I remember I had to run the gauntlet through a group of infuriated passengers as I stepped down from the footplate; they had rushed up to the engine to know what had caused the loss of time, and they seemed to persist in holding me somehow personally accountable, which I certainly was not. The explanation was that through accident or trick some oil or grease had got in with the water and caused the tremendous 'priming' which occasioned our heavy loss of time. From which experience we may deduce the moral that it is desirable to have your steam as *dry* as possible.

But how? Well, the preliminary principle is,

of course, that steam should be taken as far above the boiling, bubbling surface of the water as is feasible. This perception naturally suggested the idea of a dome-shaped projection of the upper surface of the boiler barrel, the regulator valve being placed near the top of the dome, and conveying dry steam from thence through the steam-chest into the cylinder. And so we got the steam dome, which is in virtually universal use outside England, and is almost invariably employed in England itself, although at various periods, as I remarked at the outset, there have been departures from this rule. The device itself is so simple and obvious that at first one wonders why it should not be in universal use. But there is a reason for most engineering 'dodges', even if in some cases it may not be a conclusive one. Consider the boiler-barrel itself. Forward of the firebox it is a virtually homogeneous and unbroken cylinder except at one point, and that point is the circular aperture over which the steam dome is placed. And this aperture is essentially and inevitably a point of weakness. It need not be said that so very obvious a fact has never escaped the attention of locomotive engineers, who in various ways have strengthened that part of the boiler so carefully that any risk attaching to the use of the dome has been reduced to a minimum. Nevertheless, if in ever so minute a degree, the structural weakness is there and remains. It is not surprising therefore that some of our greatest locomotive engineers have set themselves to provide some other means of taking the steam from the boiler. I have neither time nor space just now to enter into all the history and details of the various experiments made, but must content myself with saying that the most important of these, which dates from the very early days of railways, was the perforated steam pipe which ran along the top of the barrel inside, and received from numerous perforations along its circumference steam which had been practically dried by filtration, as it were, through these perforations. This, then, was the first and the most extensively employed of the two methods alternative to the dome.

I am not going to discuss any questions as to who invented or first used this plan. It is enough for my present purpose that the most important occasion of its employment was in connection with the introduction of Daniel Gooch's famous standard type of 8 foot single-wheeler express engines of the 'Iron Duke' class. All my readers will doubtless remember that *Iron Duke* was immediately preceded by an engine named *Great Western*, which was in most respects the prototype of the order, having 8 ft drivers, two pairs of leading wheels and a pair of trailers. Originally, like the first batch of the 'Amazon' class of standard gauge 7 ft 8 in singles, *Great Western* had only one pair of leading wheels. But, as in the case of the 'Amazons', designed some 40 years later, it was soon found necessary to supply four leading wheels. There was, however, another and more relevant respect in which *Great Western* differed from *Iron Duke* and the remaining 28 of the 8 ft single-wheelers, and that was in the fact that, unlike all her successors of the type, *Great Western*, like the majority of her predecessors of all types, had a large dome over the firebox. The firebox, in fact, was itself continued upward into a dome of the same longitudinal and lateral measurements. Those who have studied ancient railway history will remember that this form of firebox construction was long a very favourite one, but took two different shapes, the one being that of a strict dome, usually covered with burnished sheet brass or copper, the other being that of a pyramid with four in-curving or tapering sides. The latter was better known as the Stephenson design, the former as the Bury; and I am sorry to say that I am old enough to recollect very well the time when large numbers of these 'Haystack' or 'Gothic' fireboxes, as the two types were often respectively designated, were to be seen on various British railways, notably on the Great Western and Great Eastern lines.

But the Great Western Railway's engine *Iron Duke* was among the earliest locomotives to be fitted with the perforated steam pipe in lieu of a dome. How successful the experiment proved, and how well the device worked, may be deemed to be sufficiently shown by the fact that, in all their long history, the idea of replacing the perforated pipe by a steam dome in the case of any of those celebrated 'Iron Dukes' never seems, so far as I am aware, to have been even mooted. As most of them successively came in for reboilering or rebuilding, and even when several were broken up and replaced by new machines of identical designs, the domeless system was continued. Again, when the invasion and encroachment of the 4 ft 8½ in gauge had become a steady onward march, as against the 7 ft gauge, the domeless design once more prevailed, at any rate as regards the express engines, namely Nos 999, 1000 and 1116–1133, the well-known 7 ft singles. There was another engine of this class, No 55, I believe the first though I am not quite sure as to this. But anyhow, as in the case of the broad-gauge 8-footers, one, this same No 55, unlike all the rest of the class had a steam dome. The ten excellent machines of the 'Cobham' class, Nos 157–166, were also domeless originally and had the perforated steam pipe, and all appeared to steam at least as well as their domed sisters.

All however were subsequently fitted with steam domes, the perforated pipe being abolished by the late Mr W. Dean, and the dome remained a universal institution on the Great Western Railway until shortly before Mr Dean's retirement, when Mr G. J. Churchward had already taken charge of the locomotive department and had become the chief ruler at Swindon. It will be remembered how, in the year 1898, the 'Badminton' class came out, with 6 ft 8 in coupled wheels, inside cylinders 18 by 26 in, and a large brass-covered dome, slightly abaft the middle of the boiler barrel, as in the case of the single-wheeler 'Amazon', and how the engines of this type, albeit distressingly ugly in appearance, proved quite remarkably efficient, and how, when their numbers had been carried from 3292 to 3309, there suddenly occurred what in botany I believe is termed a 'sport'—an abrupt departure from the normal—No 3310, *Waterford*, making her appearance with a big domeless boiler, huge

GWR 4-4-0 No 3310 Waterford *in its original condition — the only member of the 'Badminton' class built during 1898–99 to have carried a domeless boiler from the first; the other domed ones were later rebuilt to match it.* (NRM, F. Burtt Collection)

Belpaire firebox and brass safety-valve column over the middle of the boiler barrel. 'All the world wondered', but the more knowing people abstained from criticism and waited to see. They soon found that they had not waited in vain, for again Mr Churchward sprung a surprise on them with No 3373, *Atbara*, which in many respects resembled No 3310, *Waterford*, but had a still-bigger domeless boiler and a general design in most respects superior. It is familiar history how forty of these splendid 'Atbaras' were turned out in rapid succession, how the same design was applied to the 5 ft 8 in wheeled class for heavy-grade work, the well-known 'Camels' resulting, and finally how the type culminated in the deservedly-famous 'City' class, of which I have always been sorry that only ten were built. Apart from quite exceptional power and swiftness they marked an important epoch in

locomotive engineering, *for they dispensed with both the steam dome and the perforated pipe*, and they introduced for the first time, I believe, on British railways the 'coned' or 'taper' or 'wagon-top' design of boiler; that is to say, the barrel increasing in diameter toward the firebox end. Now this design provided three separate advantages. (1) It gave a valuable increment of steam space at the end where this was most needed and useful, viz, near the firebox; (2) It afforded convenience for the admission of more heating surface, alike in the tubes and in the front of the firebox; and (3) It enabled steam of sufficient dryness to be taken from the highest part of the boiler without the intervention either of dome or perforated pipe. This novel method, which appears to combine the advantages alike of cheapness and of efficiency, does certainly seem so far to have fully justified its own existence. The 'Cities' immediately obtained, and have from the first retained a quite special reputation for swiftness and haulage power. One of that class stands accredited with the highest maximum speed ever authentically recorded, while the second and third authentic maxima also stand accredited respectively to an 'Atbara' and to another engine of the 'City' class; further, the feats they have accomplished in respect alike of load-hauling and hill-climbing are specially noteworthy. It is not at all surprising, therefore, to learn that the two classes of their predecessors, the 'Badmintons' and the 'Atbaras', are being converted into 'Cities' as fast as they come in for reboilering, so that the total number of this admirable class will before long be seventy. Also, all the later 'Camels', with 5 ft 8 in wheels, are being fitted with domeless and pipeless boilers.

Although at this stage Mr Churchward, in order that he might be able to employ a 30-inch piston stroke instead of one of 26 in, adopted outside cylinders for all his new engines of every type and class, he remained firmly adherent to his domeless and pipeless method of 'steam-take'. All his non-compound 'Atlantics', all his six-coupled bogie expresses, his 4-4-0 'Counties', his 'Cardiff' variant of the 'Camel' class, his tanks and his goods engines, take their steam that way. And, judging from results, I should imagine that the method will be of permanent employment on the Great Western Railway, at any rate until some future locomotive superintendent—whose advent, I trust, may be long postponed—may take it into his head to make a change, if only for the sake of change.

So far I have followed out the course of this important feature in locomotive designing as it went its way in the single case of the Great Western Railway, the only one which has yet reached the climax just mentioned. But, as I need hardly tell students of railway history, that railway was by no means the only one which displayed at times a strong preference for the domeless boiler.

Thus Mr J. V. Gooch, of the London and South Western Railway, designed for that line some very fine domeless engines of those days,

including the once-famous 'Snake'—which had outside cylinders $14\frac{1}{4}$ by 21 in with 6 ft 6 in single-driving wheels—and others, and who when he went from Nine Elms to Stratford reproduced much the same type on the Great Eastern Railway—the Eastern Counties Railway as it was then . . . But apart from Mr Gooch's engines the dome was practically universal on the Great Eastern Railway, alike before and after his 'reign' . . .

On the other hand, the domeless boiler was the rule on the Great Northern Railway for more than forty years, the dome being quite the exception. The two great engineers who followed one another at Doncaster, Archibald Sturrock and Patrick Stirling, both favoured the perforated pipe. The curious thing was that in the same class of engines each method was found. Thus the 6 ft single-wheeled 'Hawthorns', Nos 51–70, were virtually identical, save that Nos 51–60 had domes with queer flat-topped covers and Nos 61–70 had none. So with the 6 ft 6 in 'Hawthorn' singles, Nos 203–214, Nos 203 and 214 had the perforated pipe, all the rest flat-topped domes. Nos 1–50, Sharp singles, had domes, Nos 71–90 6 ft coupled and 91–99 6 ft 6 in single Cramptons, perforated pipes—and so on. Mr Patrick Stirling's locomotives all had the perforated pipe and no domes. Mr H. A. Ivatt has now made the dome universal on the Great Northern Railway. The London and North Western Railway many years ago had a few domeless engines, but I do not remember any on the Midland or North Eastern or Great Central Railway. In Scotland the dome has always been the rule, as it has everywhere outside England, but there was one important exception, that of the Glasgow and South Western Railway, under the *régimes* successively of Messrs James Stirling and Hugh Smellie. The former's 7 ft coupled and the latter's 6 ft 9 in coupled expresses have always enjoyed a high character and done good work. On the other hand, when Mr James Stirling migrated to the South Eastern Railway, he brought in the perforated pipe. The device, however, was not previously unknown on that line, although the dome was prevalent. Two very fine single express classes, the Crampton 'Folkstone'[22] class and the Sharp 6 ft single-wheelers, built in the earliest 'fifties' were both domeless. They, too, were very efficient engines, but when Mr Cudworth—Mr J. Stirling's predecessor—built at Ashford about 1856 some express singles with the same chief dimensions he employed the dome. Mr Stirling, in the 'eighties', replaced all, or nearly all his predecessor's domes with the perforated pipe, which he invariably used in the locomotives of his own design, notably the 7 ft and 6 ft coupled expresses, most of which still remain domeless, although his successor, Mr H. S. Wainwright, is a 'dome-ist' and has domed a few of them.

Thus the present outcome of the half-century battle between the 'dome-ists' and the 'pipe-ists' has been the victory of the former all along the line, and it has required the advent of a wholly new method to threaten the universal domination now otherwise enjoyed by the dome. Whether Mr Churchward's coned boiler is destined to prove a permanent mode of dispensing with the dome and its unavoidable concomitant of boiler-weakening—in however small degree—time and experience alone can show. But the special point of wide interest which arises in this connection is the strongly-pronounced illustration which it affords of the principle that . . . engineers may differ from one another in respect of what may seem almost vital points of theory or practice without being either absolutely right or absolutely wrong . . . I should be very sorry to undertake the affirmation that the domeless engines of the Gooches and Stirlings were inferior or superior to the majority of their dome-possessing rivals. Proportionately to nominal power—of course taking into account the weight available for adhesion—I have never known any locomotive do finer work than the 8 ft and 7 ft 6 in domeless single-wheelers of the Great Western Railway (including Bristol and

Exeter) and Great Northern Railway respectively. No rational or educated person would dream of expecting those single-wheelers to do such work as is performed by their more modern and more powerful successors, but at least they would not have failed on account of their domelessness, and supposing it were feasible to match one of Mr Churchward's domeless and perforated-pipeless locomotives with one of Mr Whale's 'Precursors' or Mr M'Intosh's '140s' I am convinced that the question of dome or no dome would have little if any part in determining the result.

Like so many other points in locomotive engineering this is one of necessity largely dependent on circumstances. The provoking thing when one tries to deduce any rule or principle is that one often finds such apparently discrepant behaviour or circumstances in inducing results as to render the task very difficult, if not impossible. Thus for example if you ask any engineer what is the principle benefit that accrues from the use of a dome, the almost invariable reply will be that it prevents 'priming'. Very good. Now for an anecdote in point. One day more than twenty years ago I was standing with Mr Patrick Stirling in front of his office at Doncaster, looking across the railway and sidings at the mixed group of Great Northern and Great Eastern Railway locomotives standing near the shed. All the Great Eastern Railway engines had domes, of course. None of the Great Northern Railway engines possessed one. I happened to remark upon this fact to Mr Stirling, adding that he seemed to be able to manage all right without a dome. Did he find any trouble as regards 'priming'? 'No,' replied Mr Stirling, 'and I will tell you more than that. Worsdell' (Mr T. W. Worsdell, the Great Eastern Railway's locomotive superintendent at that time) 'is always complaining about our Doncaster water. He says it makes his engines ''prime''. Well, our engines use the same water, and they don't ''prime'', although they have no domes, while Worsdell's have domes. So I see no reason why I should put domes on my engines when they do quite as well without.' So that was

---

[22] Not a misprint. This Kent seaside resort only acquired the extra 'E' in its name later in the nineteenth century.

his experience, the experience of an engineer to whom any railway authority would willingly have taken off his hat. But in these days the perforated pipe of the Gooches and Stirlings appears to have gone for ever. The modern interest lies in the problem whether, in the long run, Mr Churchward's method will give equally good or better results, as the outcome of practical experience. That remains for time to show.

* * *

A query has been put to me since the appearance of my previous article: *Why* should the influx of grease or oil into a locomotive's boiler cause 'priming'. I mentioned last month, and indeed most people know, that this is the case, but why does it happen?

Well, I imagine that the explanation is to be found primarily in the principle and action of viscosity or viscidity—whichever you like to call it. When oil or grease gets into the boiler water when the latter is in a state of violent ebullition, the unctuous matter becomes either saponified through combination with the alkaline salts present, or else mechanically mixed with the water, the outcome being to produce a certain viscosity or viscidity. That is to say, the fluid—greasy or oily water—has a sort of glutinous tenacity like that which enables the juvenile experimenter to 'blow soap bubbles'. The water, in fact, is converted into soapsuds. The practical effect is best shown by another illustration: In the course of churning, done in the old-fashioned way, under certain conditions of the cream, a troublesome action is set up which is known as the cream 'going to sleep'. It becomes mechanically impregnated with air to such an extent as to render it a sort of liquid sponge—a mass of innumerable tiny vesicles—the fluid being thus so much expanded as entirely to fill the churn and render the churning process impracticable, because the fluid contents simply revolve with the receptacle without any beating action—such as induces the separation of the butter—being produced.

Now it will be easily understood that if the water in a locomotive boiler be converted into soapsuds and expanded by the innumerable tiny air vessels so as to fill the barrel, much of it will enter the cylinders, and by excluding 'neat' steam will *pro tanto* cause a shortage of power actually exercisable. The action of priming is often induced by inadvertent over-filling of the boiler. I recollect such a case occurring once when I was testing one of the 105 min runs from Leicester to St Pancras. We had on a non-compound Belpaire with a good driver and a moderate load, but through an oversight his boiler was filled too full before starting from Leicester, and so the engine primed furiously all the way until Market Harborough had been passed, after which we did very well, but several minutes had been irrevocably lost, and thus we were late into St Pancras and the run was spoiled. So far, however, I have not come across a single case of serious priming during all my many journeys with the domeless Great Westerns, and I fancy it is of very rare occurrence in the case of those engines, despite the lack of domes.

On the possible establishment of a Railway Museum

Once more the idea of a Railway Museum has come to the front, the match which re-started the flame being apparently the final disappearance of the once-famous 'Problem' engines of the London and North Western Railway, the last of the 60 having recently been broken up. Lamentations are loud and bitter that one of these interesting and excellent locomotives could not have been spared from the scrap-heap and permanently preserved. This has set many people longing again for the establishment of a sort of locomotive Valhalla, where the more celebrated engines of each period might be perpetually enshrined for the worship of succeeding generations. It is, undoubtedly, an admirable and highly attractive proposal—in theory. Unhappily, an impartial analysis reveals several weak points. The matter is so directly germane to my subject that I am about to say a little about it, as circumstances have caused me to occupy a somewhat unique position in connection with it.

In allusion to the matter my friend Mr A. R. Bennett has recently published a letter in the daily papers, recalling in general terms the original movement in this direction. It is therefore advisable that the whole circumstances should be definitely and fully set forth. Some 10 or 12 years ago—I have not my notes at hand to refer to as to the precise date—a movement was definitely set on foot with the object of establishing a 'Railway Museum', where interesting or in-structive relics of railway history might be preserved accessibly for public inspection. As regards this movement I may fairly say—as will appear in the sequel—*quorum pars magna fui*, although I cannot for one moment claim to have been its originator. It was said that many valuable relics of railway history in Britain—the Mother of Railways—were being rapidly and extensively bought up by the United States of America, and also by several European countries, which also were rumoured to have a covetous eye upon certain old British locomotives, notably the Great Western Railway's broad-gauge engines *North Star* and *Lord of the Isles*, and the London and North Western Railway's *Cornwall*. So on a special requisition I attended and presided at a meeting convened in my name in the locomotive department of the South Kensington Museum, on which occasion several notable persons were present, including the venerable and eminent veteran engineer Mr Archibald Sturrock, formerly Locomotive Superintendent of the Great Northern Railway. A Committee was formed which resolved itself into 'The Railway Museum Association', the presidency being accepted by Sir David Salomons who, although he was unable to attend our meetings, took a cordial interest in the object. Many meetings were held, at all of which I had the honour of presiding as Chairman of Council, and many prominent persons whose names are honourably associated with railway and engineering matters, including Mr Sturrock himself, Mr W. M. Ackworth, Mr P. Nursey (Secretary and Past President of the Society of Engineers), Mr A. R. Bennet, CE, Mr Sinclair Fairfax, CE, and others.[23] The Association was formed, with rules, etc, and our subscriptions were regularly paid. But soon we reached a virtual *impasse*. Without going into the multifarious details which occupied during a number of meetings a great deal of the time of several very busy professional men who could ill spare it, and who moreover paid for the privilege (?) of bestowing it with no possible personal object in view, I may say briefly that the leading railway companies displayed no eagerness or even willingness to hand over their respective relics to a self-appointed and virtually irresponsible body, even had we any place in which to stow them safely—which we assuredly had not. No railway official in actual office took any part in our proceedings or gave us any encouragement. On the contrary it was plainly hinted to us in private conversations that while our object might be all right our methods were all wrong; that the railway authorities themselves were the proper people to take the initiative in such a business, and that if they didn't do so it was because they didn't think it was worth doing; and that in any case if the railway companies were disposed to give up the 'relics'—which at that time they weren't—it would be only to such a public institution as the South Kensington Museum they would resign them. 'Even if we gave you our old engines,' said one to me, 'you have nowhere to put them. Get a place first, and then it will be time to talk to us.'

That was sound sense. For, be it observed, what the majority of us had in view was rather a 'Locomotive Museum' than a 'Railway' one. We had noted with deep regret the disappearance of such famous old types as the London and North Western Railway's 'Bloomers', the

Great Northern Railway's No 215, the Great Eastern Railway's Gooch-Sinclair single-wheelers, and the long-boiler Stephensons, and though we knew that the Great Western Railway still preserved at Swindon those venerable celebrities *North Star* and *Lord of the Isles*, and the South Eastern and North Eastern Railways various other antiquities, these were not easily accessible and might at any time be condemned to the scrap heap, as indeed has since happened in the case of the two engines first-named. But while a building and appliances to contain mere drawings and papers might have been found with relative ease, it was quite another thing to provide housing for a number of big locomotives and ground for the rails on which they could stand. Only with Government assistance could this be accomplished. Such assistance there seemed little hope of securing at the period.

Ultimately, after putting the Association into thorough working order so that it could take up work at any moment when the time should seem to have arrived, it adjourned its meetings *sine die*, as there was nothing practical that could then be done, authority being given to me to convene another meeting when there should be anything to be done, but not otherwise, as the members could not really spare any more time for merely formal assemblings. I took prompt steps, 'on my own', to ascertain privately—as I had special means of doing—how our chances really stood. I soon ascertained that the railways were disinclined to part with their old locomotives—at any rate save to some Government public institution such as that at South Kensington; that there was not the remotest probability of the Government, or indeed of any future Government, consenting to appropriate a large sum for the construction and maintenance of a Railway Museum, which was frankly declared to be a matter purely for the railway companies themselves. Here, then, was a *cul de sac*—a 'dead end'. Had it not been final in itself, the shortly-subsequent outbreak of the South African War, with its cost to the nation of 250 millions sterling, would have been utterly fatal to our prospects. Therefore I saw no object in putting the Associa-

[23] A verb, such as 'attended', seems to have disappeared from the sentence.

tion to the needless inconvenience of assembling again for no purpose. But the Association is still in full being, albeit dormant, and could be resuscitated any day if this were worth while. Is it quite true that we did not *officially* approach either the Government or the railway companies. But I am not one who cares to submit himself to an absolutely certain refusal—one which was a foregone conclusion as inevitable as death itself—and as I knew on the best authority that any public application would and must needs be utterly futile, that public application has not been made.

It still could be made at any time, but to what purpose now? It is rather a national characteristic of us 'Britishers' to lock the stable door after the horse has been stolen, and that would emphatically be the nature of any appeal at this date. What old engines remain to be preserved? The 'Bloomers' went more than 20 years ago. The South Eastern Railway's Cudworth singles soon followed. Then went the J. V. Gooch and Sinclair Great Eastern Railway singles, typical machines of their day. Next vanished the last of the Caledonian 8 ft 2 in singles, and only a year or two back the Great Western Railway scrapped *North Star* and *Lord of the Isles* which had so long constituted a museum 'on their own' at Swindon, or rather, to speak more accurately, their outside husks, for both of these historic locomotives had been eviscerated years before. Now the last of the 'Problems' has been cut up, and though *Cornwall* is temporarily saved, as was *Lord of the Isles* on the Great Western Railway, it is without any subsequent guarantee of permanent preservation. Is it 'good enough' to start a museum for *Cornwall* and the few other old engines which stand on pedestals here and there throughout the country now that the really valuable and important and interesting locomotive relics have gone? I hardly think so.

For observe, even *Cornwall* herself is no longer—and has not been for more than forty years—the engine whose special design and construction gave her interest. Her only remaining speciality consists in her having the largest driv-

ing wheels in existence, 8 ft 6 in in diameter. Those wheels *might* well be saved; *they* would not occupy much space. One does regret that one pair of the 9 ft drivers of the old Bristol and Exeter express tanks was not kept as a curiosity. But it wasn't. The boiler of the last 8 ft 2 in Caledonian single is still in use driving a pump or some other humble machine. But the sight of that boiler does not arouse intense enthusiasm. For, let me ask: *What* still existing engines are worth 'museuming' at heavy cost? I really can't think of any that inspire me with a particle of zeal. Could we have retained such epoch-making machines as those I have mentioned above, as also such others as a 'Jenny Lind', a 'Little Sharp', a 'Large Hawthorn', a South Eastern Railway 'Crampton', Mr Sturrock's Great Northern Railway No 215, or one of a very noteworthy class of express tank engine of former days . . . then indeed we might have had a Locomotive Museum of real interest and value. As it is, the opportunity has passed. The Government, with a War Income Tax still in force and huge fresh liabilities looming in the future, is utterly unlikely to do anything, and the railway companies, after long objecting to part with their relics, have suddenly discovered that these occupy too much space and can be profitably realised upon as old metal. And so we must content ourselves with having—thanks to Mr F. Moore and also to many amateur enthusiasts—an abundance of excellent photographs of these old friends which we have lost.

At the same time, while I am constrained to admit that my personal enthusiasm in the matter has in a large degree subsided, I do not wish to throw cold water upon the zeal of others who still see any possibilities in the matter. Indeed I am glad to see a revival of interest and shall always be happy to give any aid that may be feasible to a very busy professional man. I have simply recorded the facts up to date of the inaugural movement so far as it has gone. The two things now lacking are: (1) Funds; (2) Locomotives to preserve. But of the latter, let us hope that at any rate the Great Northern Railway's 8 ft singles will not be allowed wholly to disappear.

PART 2

Performance

GREAT WESTERN RAILWAY

MAY 1903

Four-coupled engines between London and Exeter

Recently I have been making some special observations, through the courtesy of the Superintendent of the Great Western Railway, on the working of the accelerated expresses between London and Cornwall by the newest types of four-coupled engines, viz, those of the 'Atbara' and 'Camel' classes, which have respectively 6 ft 8 in and 5 ft 8 in coupled wheels, both having leading four-wheel bogies, inside cylinders 18 in by 24 in, large domeless boilers with 1,660 sq ft of heating surface, Belpaire fireboxes and 180 lbs steam pressure. It will be remembered that the latest accelerations reduc-

ed the time for the non-stopping runs from Paddington to Exeter and *vice versa* to 3 hours 35 minutes for the 193¾ miles, and from Paddington to Bristol and *vice versa* to 2 hours and 10 minutes for the 118½ miles, the average speeds being respectively 54.1 and 54.7 miles an hour. It will be convenient to deal with the London–Exeter section first, as that is worked by the 'Atbara' engines, the 'Camels' doing the Exeter–Plymouth and Plymouth–Truro services.

Testing first the 2.55 pm ex-Paddington, which makes the non-stopping run to Exeter, I had one of the 'Atbara' class, No 3392

GWR 4-4-0 No 3385 Powerful, *of the 'Atbara' class, constructed in 1900 and named after persons or events prominent in the Boer War of 1899–1902 — in this instance, after a battleship. Rous-Marten clocked a maximum of over 97 mph with one of them. They were later rebuilt with coned boilers and became virtually identical with the 'Cities'.* (NRM)

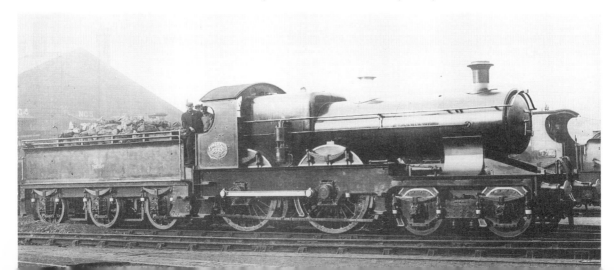

White[1] driven by Burden, who was the driver of the Royal Train which came up from Plymouth to Paddington without an intermediate stop. As the load was six eight-wheelers, or about 150 tons, he and his engine had a relatively simple task to perform; indeed the last 20 miles into Exeter were run under very easy steam. But the journey presented an admirable specimen of even and sustained good work, and some of the details were distinctly interesting. We got through Reading in 38 minutes 55 seconds, but directly after were slowed to 15 miles an hour for permanent way operations, the slack lasting 58 seconds and costing us $1\frac{1}{2}$ minutes. This was followed by a signal check at Moreton Cutting, that dreaded box which has soiled so many fine express runs. Consequently we took 58 minutes 59 seconds to pass Didcot station. But then Burden 'opened out' and soon attained 60 miles an hour up the slight ascent beyond. By the time Uffington was passed we were going at 61.6, at Shrivenham 64.2, at Swindon 65.2, that station being passed in 24 minutes 47 seconds from Didcot—$24\frac{1}{4}$ miles—and in 81 minutes 46 seconds from Paddington, or $79\frac{1}{4}$ minutes net, allowing for the two slacks. The Wootton bank was descended very steadily and Chippenham was passed in 97 minutes 56 seconds for the 94 miles from the London start. Outside Bathampton, however, adverse signals brought us down literally to walking pace for 79 seconds and very nearly to a dead stand. Nevertheless we were in Bath station in 112 minutes 34 seconds inclusive[2] from Paddington, equivalent to 107 minutes net time, allowing for the three delays carefully worked out. This was a very smart performance, but our troubles were not yet over, for just after Bath we had to reduce speed to 4 miles an hour

over a bridge under repair. From this point onward, however, all went well. We were abreast of Bristol[3] in 2 hours 8 minutes 23 seconds inclusive from Paddington, but in 2 hours $0\frac{3}{4}$ minutes net if the delays—other than the regular 'service' slack—be allowed for. The next $44\frac{3}{4}$ miles to Taunton occupied $47\frac{3}{4}$ minutes, the driver taking things very quietly as he was in front of booked time in spite of all delays. Taunton, $163\frac{1}{4}$ miles from London, was passed in 2 hours 56 minutes 10 seconds inclusive, or in 2 hours $48\frac{1}{2}$ minutes net. The $166\frac{1}{4}$ milepost was breasted in exactly 3 hours from the start, notwithstanding delays totalling $7\frac{3}{4}$ minutes and without any extreme speeds been attained. The lowest speed up the Wellington bank was 30 miles an hour excepting for a single quarter of a mile when a length of greasy rail set the engine slipping badly and brought down the rate fractionally lower. From the Whiteball summit to Exeter we ran, as I have already said, under easy steam, taking $20\frac{1}{2}$ minutes for the 20 downhill miles, and yet stopping at Exeter in 3 hours 31 minutes 44 seconds inclusive from Paddington, or in 3 hours 24 minutes net, a result which reflected high credit alike on the engine (*White*) and on her very capable driver, Burden.

Instead of pursuing my onward journey to the far west it will be more convenient if I take next my experimental trip with the corresponding up train, that booked to leave Exeter at 12.5 and reach Paddington at 3.40 pm, the time allowed being thus the same in either direction. But although the booked transit times were identical my return journey was performed under conditions very different from those which attended the down trip. We experienced, it is true, delays to a similar extent by checks, of which there were four: a somewhat severe one to walking pace for bridge repairs near Bath; another to 15 miles an hour, also for repairs, through Box tunnel; one for signals outside Didcot; and a fourth, also for signals, at Acton. But we had a load just 50 per cent heavier than that on the down journey,

---

[1] At the time when the locomotive was given this name no one would have been puzzled. Sir George White, forgotten now, was then a national hero. In the South African War he held Ladysmith against the advancing Boers, and when ordered by his superior to surrender the town to the Boers he refused. In the event Ladysmith was not captured, and his superior was disgraced.

[2] That is, inclusive of all delays: the actual time taken.

[3] The train did not go through Bristol station but passed alongside it, over the avoiding line.

namely nine corridor clerestoried bogies, making up a total weight behind the tender, including passengers and luggage, of approximately 240 tons. Our engine again was of the 'Atbara' type, No 3380 *Ladysmith*, and was driven by the redoubtable Millard, one of the smartest and most careful drivers to be found on any railway. In this instance he ably sustained the high reputation he has deservedly earned by previous work. In climbing the 20 miles from Exeter to the Whiteball summit he had to contend against the formidable disadvantages of a fierce side gale and a rail slippery through persistent drizzling rain. Nevertheless he covered that distance in $27\frac{1}{2}$ minutes from the start, the speed, after *Ladysmith* had got into her full stride, never falling below 50 miles an hour even up the final grade of 1 in 115 for $2\frac{1}{4}$ miles to Whiteball. A brisk descent to Taunton followed, and that station was passed at reduced speed in $36\frac{3}{4}$ minutes from Exeter. The side gale continued very severe across the level country between Taunton and Bristol. Nevertheless the distance of $44\frac{3}{4}$ miles from Taunton to a point abreast of Bristol station was run in 45 minutes 11 seconds. Then came the delays already in-

dicated near Bath and through Box tunnel. A minimum rate of 50 miles an hour was maintained up the Wootton Bassett bank of 1 in 100[4] but owing to the hindrances the $41\frac{1}{4}$ miles from Bristol to Swindon took $47\frac{1}{2}$ minutes. From Swindon to Didcot . . . the distance of $24\frac{1}{4}$ miles of level and slight descent was covered in the very fast time of 20 minutes 29 seconds. After Didcot Millard had to ease down in order to avoid too early an arrival, and as already mentioned we had a nasty check by signals at Acton. Nevertheless we stopped in Paddington just 3 minutes before time, having made the run from Exeter in 3 hours 29 minutes 14 seconds inclusive, or in 3 hours 21 minutes net time. These two samples of the way in which the Great Western Railway carries out its 'Longest non-stopping run in the world' afford conclusive proof that this progressive company does not promise on paper what it is not able and willing to carry out in its ordinary daily practice.

[4] This is misleading. What Rous-Marten obviously means is that speed *fell* to 50 mph up the $1\frac{1}{2}$ miles of Dauntsey bank and was afterwards maintained at that figure on the 1 in 660 that follows past Wootton Bassett Junction and Station.

SEPTEMBER 1903

Paddington to Plymouth with the Royal Train on July 14th, 1903

I had the pleasure of being a passenger on this occasion. The engine, No 3433 *City of Bath* . . . is one of Mr G. J. Churchward's newest and finest type, a development and improvement of the 'Atbara' breed, having like that very efficient class 6 ft 8 in driving wheels, four-coupled, with

outside bearings and leading bogie, inside cylinders 18 in by 26 in, large Belpaire firebox and domeless extended wagon-top boiler spreading out to the area of the vertical cross-section of the firebox, and giving a total heating surface of 1,818 square feet, the steam pressure

GWR 4-4-0 No 3436 City of Chester *at the head of a train leaving Paddington — evidently between 1909 and 1922, during which period GW coaching stock was painted either all-over brown or (after 1912) all-over crimson lake. There were 20 'Cities', which worked the principal expresses of the Company until 'Saint' and 'Star' 4-6-0s took over. The train in the picture is of non-corridor stock but evidently of some importance since the coaches carry destination boards.* (NRM)

being 180 lbs.[5] The engine was driven by Burden, who was in charge of the Royal Train last year over the same road, and he performed his responsible duties with admirable skill and efficiency. Inspector Greenaway, MVO, was on the footplate in general charge of locomotive matters. The train itself was under the care of Mr T. I. Allen, Superintendent of the Line, and Mr J. Vaughan Williams. It consisted of five bogie coaches, including the Royal Car, which was placed in the middle, and together with passengers, staff, luggage and stores, weighed approximately 130 tons behind the tender. All the arrangements were admirably conceived and carried out, everybody travelled in the utmost comfort, the running at all speeds was singularly smooth and steady, and not one single check, either for signals or re-laying, was experienced throughout the whole run of 246 miles. There were of course the inevitable

'service slacks' through the curved station at Bath and round the still more awkwardly curved avoiding line past Bristol, as well as through Exeter station, along the length of single line from Dawlish through the Parsons tunnels, and over Newton Abbot Junction. Also the descents of the steep gradients along the South Devon line were made with invariable care and at quite a moderate speed for the sake of safety in rounding the sharp curves that abound.

As regards the specific figures of the journey, I have deemed it best to supply these in their amplest and plainest form by giving a complete log of the run. But a few remarks may advantageously be added. In the first place, we were doing 60 miles an hour before the third milepost was reached. Slough was passed at 72.2 miles an hour; after Sonning siding, where there is a slight descent of 1 in 1,320, the speed increased to 75 and then to 76.3 miles an hour. On the level near Cholsey our rate had further increased to 77.1; Didcot was passed at exactly 75 miles an hour, and it will be noted that the $24\frac{1}{4}$ miles of

---

[5] A mistake; the boiler pressure was 200 lbs per square inch.

considerably steeper, though still moderate gradients from Didcot to Swindon—the steepest being 1 in 660—occupied only 20 minutes 28 seconds in the running. Then came the downhill stretch, at first moderate and then steep, 2 miles at 1 in 100.[6] Here the speed steadily rose, attaining successively 78, 80, 81.8, 83.7, 85.7 and finally 87.4 miles an hour, two successive half-miles at the foot of Wootton Bassett incline being covered in 20.6 seconds each, and the whole mile in 41.2 seconds.

A rate of 80 miles an hour was then pretty evenly maintained for some little distance, and the Box tunnel, just under 2 miles[7] in length, was threaded in 1 minute 27 seconds. There was a careful slowing as Bath was approached and the station was passed at 15 miles an hour, the Bristol avoiding line being passed over at a still slower rate. Once on the main line again at Pylle Hill we rapidly picked up, and before Yatton were going at 80.3 once more. Then 81.8 was reached near Puxton, 83.7 just afterward. Along the level stretch that extends most of the way from Nailsea to Taunton we seldom were going at much less than 80 miles an hour. The distance of 44¾ miles from a point abreast of Temple Meads station, Bristol, to Taunton station was covered in 37 minutes 57 seconds. Up the Wellington bank, much of which is as steep as 1 in 81, our speed never fell below 50 miles an hour. The 20 downhill miles from Whiteball to Exeter could easily have been run in 15 minutes without any unsteadiness in travelling, but as the Prince and Princess were just then at lunch a signal was made to the driver to ease down, and he took 18 minutes instead; thus, had the train been allowed to run at the same pace that it did

[6] Under 1½ miles, not 2 miles, at 1 in 100.

[7] Just over 1¾ miles would be more correct.

[8] Between Aller Junction and Dainton Summit there are many changes of gradient, but there is no stretch at 1 in 43, though there is a very short one at 1 in 36.

[9] The liberty has been taken, in this and subsequent logs, of simplifying it into the form used by Rous-Marten's successors, and expressing miles decimally instead of giving chainages.

from Bedminster to Taunton, Exeter would have been reached in 2 hours 50 minutes from Paddington.

On the severe South Devon grades Mr Churchward's engine acquitted herself with undiminished satisfactoriness. Up the 1 in 43[8] to Dainton her speed was maintained at a minimum rate of 32 miles an hour, and up the subsequent bank to Rattery it did not go below 36. On the other hand it very rarely exceeded 60 on the downward grades and the whole passage of that difficult bit of road was accomplished with the utmost possible caution and ease. I now give a detailed log of the journey.[9]

Locomotive: **Load:**
No 3433, *City of Bath*   130 tons approx.

Miles	Stations	Min	Sec
00.00	Paddington	00	00
01.27	Westbourne Park	02	47
04.24	Acton	06	05
05.72	Ealing	07	32
07.35	Hanwell	09	02
09.07	Southall	10	35
10.92	Hayes	12	14
13.22	West Drayton	14	13
16.22	Langley	16	42
18.45	Slough	18	32
22.45	Taplow	22	03
24.26	Maidenhead	23	26
31.00	Twyford	29	14
36.00	Reading	33	26
38.64	Tilehurst	35	43
41.54	Pangbourne	38	07
44.79	Goring	40	47
48.46	Cholsey	43	50
53.11	Didcot	47	33
56.52	Steventon	50	24
60.40	Wantage Road	53	40
63.89	Challow	56	42
66.52	Uffington	58	56
71.55	Shrivenham	63	12
77.27	Swindon	68	01
82.90	Wootton Bassett	72	44
87.72	Dauntsey	76	30

Miles	Stations	Min	Sec
93.96	Chippenham	81	10
98.31	Corsham	84	54
101.87	Box	87	41
104.59	Bathampton	89	55
106.87	Bath	92	02
111.32	Saltford	96	42
113.72	Keynsham	98	44
116.97	Bristol East Junc	101	52
118.71	Pylle Hill Junc	104	42
119.09	Bedminster	105	21
123.96	Flax Bourton	110	46
126.10	Nailsea	112	38
130.04	Yatton	115	45
133.64	Puxton	118	34
134.84	Worle	119	38
138.29	Uphill	122	17
142.22	Brent Knoll	125	24
144.97	Highbridge	127	36
148.75	Dunball	130	46
151.27	Bridgwater	132	45
157.05	Durston	137	31
162.84	Taunton	142	39
164.85	Norton Fitzwarren	144	58
169.91	Wellington	150	03

Miles	Stations	Min	Sec
173.69	Whiteball Summit	154	27
178.74	Tiverton Junc	158	58
181.07	Cullompton	160	57
185.22	Hele	164	45
186.45	Silverton	165	44
190.19	Stoke Canon	169	12
193.62	Exeter St David's	172	34
198.37	Exminster	178	32
202.12	Starcross	181	54
205.81	Dawlish	185	32
208.62	Teignmouth	190	15
213.81	Newton Abbot	195	51
217.69	Dainton	201	28
222.50	Totnes	206	46
227.12	Rattery	213	24
229.36	Brent	216	12
231.54	Wrangaton	218	45
234.85	Ivybridge	222	11
237.29	Cornwood	224	49
238.37	Hemerdon	226	24
241.62	Plympton	228	58
242.80	Tavistock Junc	229	54
245.32	Mutley	232	47
245.66	Plymouth	233	35

APRIL 1907

London to Plymouth by way of the newly opened route through Westbury, behind Churchward's recently constructed four-cylinder Atlantic *North Star*[10]

A few days ago I made an experimental trip to Plymouth with Mr Churchward's four-cylinder non-compound Atlantic No 40, *North Star*.

The train was the 10.30 am, which is booked to run from Paddington to Plymouth without a stop, 225¾ miles, in 4 hrs 7 min—247 min, averaging 55.1 miles an hour from start to stop—and to slip a coach at Exeter, 173¾ miles, in the even 3 hrs—180 minutes, averaging

[10] Built as a 4–4–2 in 1906 and rebuilt in 1909 as a 4–6–0 to match the other 4–6–0 'Stars'.

GWR No 40, later named North Star, *built in 1906 as a 4–4–2 and converted to the 4–6–0 wheel-arrangement three years later. It was the first four-cylinder locomotive to be built at Swindon.* (NRM)

57.9 miles an hour. The load was roughly about 250 tons behind the tender at starting, but an eight-wheeled corridor coach was slipped at Westbury (for Weymouth), another at Taunton (for Ilfracombe) and a third at Exeter (for Torquay), these three slips giving a remarkably fine winter express service to those justly popular seaside resorts. From Exeter to Plymouth the load was approximately 160 tons. The weather was perfect, but the road in several places was under repair, so that we had the drawback of four bad permanent way slacks, which Guard Bird estimated as equal to a delay of 10 mins in all. On the other hand, the new road between Castle Cary and Cogload, where the old main line is rejoined, has now become almost entirely consolidated, so that any speed can be run over it with safety . . . I may say briefly that directly after the Patney station, 81 miles from London, is passed, there is a continuous descent for 7 miles, almost all at 1 in 222. An approximately level length then extends to about a mile past Westbury, where a three mile rise at 1 in 222, 1 in 210, 1 in 155 and 1 in 143 begins.[11] It is followed by a drop of 1 in 138 for a mile into Frome. Then come four miles of easy undulations, leading at 105 miles to a sharp rise at 1 in 66 for a quarter of a mile[12] succeeded by $3\frac{1}{4}$ miles of up grade, some easy but a fair portion as steep as 1 in 123, 1 in 119 and 1 in 110 to a summit about 2 miles west of Witham.[13] Then come ten miles of falling gradients, beginning with a mile at 1 in 82; other following down grades are 1 in 93, 1 in 96, 1 in 97, 1 in 113, 1 in 101 for a mile on end, 1 in 81, etc[14], the steepness of the descent gradually decreasing to 1 in 330 at Castle Cary. Then come easy undulations to Somerton; next

[11] The gradient profile shows short pitches of various gradients, none at any of the inclinations stated by Rous-Marten, which culminate in $1\frac{1}{2}$ miles at 1 in 151.

[12] No incline of 1 in 66 is shown hereabouts on the gradient profile. At milepost 105 there is a short rise at 1 in 164.

[13] None of these gradients appears at this point on the profile.

[14] Again, none of these gradients appears on the profile over the 10 miles in question. Either Rous-Marten was referring to an inaccurate gradient diagram, or there have been alterations due to permanent way work since his time.

GWR 4-6-0 'Star' No 4039 Queen Matilda *on an up express between Reading and London. The restored 'chocolate and cream' coach livery shows that the picture was taken after 1922. The 'top-feed' pipes encircling the boiler were fitted to the whole class after 1911, when they were also given superheaters.* (NRM)

5 miles down, nearly all at 1 in 264 past Langport, the rest of the way to Cogload Junction being virtually level. It will readily be seen that on this road plenty of stiff work is laid out for a locomotive hauling a fair load at a booked average speed of 57.9 miles an hour.

Getting away punctually from Paddington the driver, Syme, made no attempt to force the pace at the outset, preferring to allow the big engine to develop herself by degrees. Ealing Broadway was passed in 8 min 21 sec from Paddington, West Drayton in 16 min 3 sec, Slough in 20 min 44 sec, Maidenhead in 25 min 56 sec. But $1\frac{1}{2}$ min after passing the last named station we encountered the beginning of a very bad permanent way slack which lasted nearly 3 minutes, extending past the Waltham siding. Taking into account the loss of time through slowing down, travelling some distance dead slow and then gradually regaining full speed, this slack cost us fully $3\frac{1}{2}$ min or more of delay; consequently we did not pass Reading until 38 min 57 sec from Paddington. Then came the slackening through Reading and round the curve, past the junction of the new line. This slack was observed with

quite exceptional punctiliousness, so that it took us nearly 8 min to cover the first 5 miles after Reading. Then, however, we went ahead steadily and passed Newbury in 11 min 1 sec after Theale, distance $11\frac{3}{4}$ miles. The next $8\frac{1}{2}$ miles, viz, to Hungerford, occupied 8 min 41 sec, and the like distance to Savernake just 2 sec less. Patney, 11 miles beyond Savernake, was passed in 9 min 2 sec from the last-named station, and the $14\frac{1}{2}$ miles thence to Westbury took 12 min 17 sec. At Westbury we slackened and slipped our hindmost eight-wheeler, the run of $95\frac{1}{2}$ miles from Paddington having occupied 95 min 35 sec inclusive, or 92 min net, allowing for the two slacks. There were service slacks through Westbury and through the next station, Frome, but the rising grades between those stations, and again between Frome and Witham—the latter length having one quarter-mile stretch at 1 in 66[15]—did not bring our rate of travel below 55 miles an hour, and a rate of slightly over 60 was as a rule steadily maintained throughout the 13 miles of rising gradient to the

[15] No! See note 12 above.

summit two miles west of Witham.[16] After attaining that point we entered upon the long descent of nearly 12 miles which extends thence almost to Keinton Mandeville, and which I have already described. Here a very high speed was run with remarkable smoothness and steadiness. The distance of $3\frac{1}{2}$ miles from Bruton to Castle Cary was done in 2 min 38 sec.[17] From Castle Cary we eased down carefully over the new line, and until we rejoined the old main line at Cogload Junction, the distance of $22\frac{1}{2}$ miles being allowed to occupy just 24 min, although the grades were extremely favourable for fast running, including the 5 miles at 1 in 264 down from Somerton past Langport. This will show how carefully the restrictions were observed. Taunton, 143 miles from Paddington, was passed in 2 hrs 26 mins 4 secs, inclusive, from the start. The approximate net time would be about 2 hrs 22 mins—142 mins—from London.

Now came the ascent of the Wellington bank which was accomplished with admirable smartness. At Norton Fitzwarren we had not dropped below 64 miles an hour. At Wellington we were still doing 57.6, and as we approached the Whiteball tunnel our speed was yet 45 miles an hour, the absolute minimum in the tunnel being 42.8. Down the subsequent descent we were travelling at high speed when, shortly before Cullompton, we were brought down to dead slow for permanent way repairs. This slow lasted $2\frac{1}{2}$ min—well past Cullompton in fact—and it

cost us quite 3 min delay before we had recovered our full rate. However, Syme was not easily discouraged but 'made the best of a bad job', and so good a 'best' was it that in spite of all the hindrances we were in St David's station, Exeter, 2 hrs 58 min 24 sec, inclusive, from Paddington, equal to a run of 2 hrs 50 min net. As we had slipped a coach each at Westbury, Taunton and Exeter we emerged from the last station a greatly reduced train, about 160 tons behind *North Star*'s tender. Newton Abbot, 20 miles, was passed in 22 min 44 sec from Exeter after yet another re-laying slack, this time between St Thomas and Starcross. Climbing the Dainton bank, our lowest rate up 1 in 43[18] was 23.7 miles an hour and up the similar rise to Rattery our absolute minimum was exactly 25. Over the table-land from Rattery to Hemerdon we ran under easy steam, usually at 60 to 62 miles an hour, then easing carefully down the Hemerdon bank to Plympton and coming to a dead stand for signals just outside Plymouth, 4 hrs 1 min 18 sec from London, but stopping finally in North Road station in 4 hrs 3 min 38 sec from the Paddington start. These times are inclusive; the net times would be about 10 min less; indeed, this was the amount booked in Guard Bird's journal, with which estimate I fully concurred. It will be observed that the travelling time for the 52 miles from Exeter to Plymouth was only 62 min 54 sec, although no high speeds were run down the falling grades. Over such a road this must be recognised to have been a very smart and creditable performance, upon which Mr Churchward and his new *North Star* and Driver Syme may be cordially congratulated.

[16] The first mention of any speeds since leaving Paddington! This is Rous-Marten at his most maddeningly uninformative.

[17] We are not told what the 'very high speed' was, which is a pity as it may well have been the highest attained on the whole journey. The time given between Bruton and Castle Cary indicates an average between those points of $77\frac{1}{2}$ miles an hour, and suggests a maximum of over 80.

[18] See note 8 above.

LONDON AND NORTH WESTERN RAILWAY

DECEMBER 1902

Journeys made behind Webb compounds on an accelerated Birmingham express

The month of October witnessed yet another remarkable acceleration of the Birmingham express service of the London and North Western Railway. There were as a matter of fact two time-shortenings; one of these, however, involved no augmentation of speed, but rather the reverse, the running time remaining as before with a stop taken out . . .

But the other acceleration was much more remarkable as it involved a booked start-to-stop speed of 57.7 miles an hour, the highest ever booked by the London and North Western Railway. Previously to October 1st the 9.20 am express had been allowed 2 hours 20 minutes from Euston to Birmingham, with two stops, one of 2 minutes at Willesden and another of 4 minutes at Coventry. What was done was to reduce the journey time by 10 minutes 'at one fell swoop', while still retaining the Willesden and Coventry stops and the slip at Blisworth. This was effected by reducing the Willesden–Coventry time from 101 to 92 minutes for the $88\frac{1}{2}$ miles, the remaining minute being saved between Coventry and Birmingham. To cover $88\frac{1}{2}$ miles in 92 minutes means to average 57.7 miles an hour the whole way from start to stop, uphill and downhill. This has never before been undertaken in London and North Western time bills, the nearest approach to it being 57.2 miles an hour when the 8 pm from Euston was booked to run from

Crewe to Carlisle, $141\frac{1}{4}$ miles, in 2 hours 28 minutes.

So the promise was a somewhat remarkable one, and it became very interesting to see how it would be performed in actual practice. True, the road is relatively a fairly easy one; still, the 22 miles of up-grade, mostly at about 1 in 330, to Tring, and the 7 similar miles approaching Roade form obstacles to be reckoned with in attempting an average of nearly 58 miles an hour throughout. There was no question at all as to the exceptional character of the booking. The only question was: How would the promise be fulfilled?

At the courteous invitation of the London and North Western authorities I made several experimental trips to test this point. Some experienced drivers expressed the opinion that the timing was 'too fast' in view of the long slack past Rugby and Trent Valley junction, in addition to the temporary slowing for repairs through Kilsby tunnel, and that time would only be kept with light loads in fine and calm weather. I travelled by the inaugural trip of the accelerated train, when, unfortunately, the conditions were adverse, a strong side wind being experienced all the way. The load, however, was not heavy, consisting of eight bogie coaches, two of them being slipped at Blisworth, when, however, two-thirds of the journey had been done including all the hardest part. That is to say, the load was reckoned as twelve coaches to Blisworth and nine thence. The engine was No 1923 *Agamemnon*, one of Mr Webb's 'Jubilee' four-cylinder compounds, with a very good driver. Unluckily the locomotive for some reason would not steam well; indeed, I noticed that shortness of steam on two separate occasions compelled the driver to 'shut off' and 'blow up'. What with this and the side wind combined, we dropped more than 9 minutes on the Willesden–Coventry run, taking 101 minutes 24 seconds instead of the prescribed 92 minutes. This of course was disappointing but purely accidental. So I tried again.

Next time I had No 1921 *Ismay* (another 'Jubilee') as train engine and No 363 *Aurania* as pilot. The latter is a three-cylinder compound of the earliest or 'Experiment' class, not so well suited to fast running. Still, she did very creditably on the whole, the two engines taking the load of nine bogies and one six-wheeler—reckoned as '14$\frac{1}{2}$ coaches'—from the Willesden start to passing Tring in 29 minutes 45 seconds, with the speed never falling below 55 miles an hour; in fact it actually increased from that minimum to 58.4 during the last 3$\frac{3}{4}$ miles from Berkhamsted to the summit. This was excellent uphill work and did credit to both locomotives. But down the following descent to Bletchley the running was not smart enough to fulfil the requirements of the sharp booking in case any check should happen to be encountered. And this did happen, adverse signals being met with near Roade, when the 7-mile bank at 1 in 330 had been ascended to that point at a minimum speed of 56 miles an hour. Speed was reduced to 20 miles an hour and this slowing lasted 66 seconds. That cost us fully 2 minutes delay, and on the level and falling grades after Roade the deficient speed of *Aurania* was very noticeable; indeed, at times *Ismay* was perceptibly 'shoving along' the engine which was supposed to be assisting her. Nevertheless the run as a whole was a very fair one, although we lost 95 seconds, for in addition to the delay of 2 minutes by signals there was another of 1 minute, slowing for repairs in Kilsby tunnel.

Thus the net time may be put down as 90$\frac{1}{2}$ minutes, and the load after the Blisworth slip was 130 tons. So the work altogether was not bad.

But my third trip had the traditional good fortune of third attempts and produced a distinctly brilliant performance, notwithstanding that the final arrival in New Street, Birmingham, was 9 minutes late. For in the first place there were two signal stops through fog before Willesden was reached. Next, there was again a bad repairing slack in Kilsby tunnel. Then there was a dead stop for 1$\frac{1}{2}$ minutes for signals immediately outside Coventry station. Lastly we were stopped dead for more than 5 minutes outside Birmingham. How this important express came to be thus negligently blocked outside each of the stations at which it stopped was not explained but it certainly implied some great carelessness on the part of subordinates. However, so far as affording a test of locomotive work was concerned, the result was admirable. For the run of just under 88$\frac{1}{2}$ miles from the Willesden start to the stop just outside Coventry station was actually done in the splendid time of 87 minutes 58 seconds inclusive, 4 minutes 2 seconds being thus gained on the very fast timing, in spite of more than a minute being lost by the Kilsby relaying slack. Thus the net run was little more than 85 minutes for the 88$\frac{1}{2}$ miles.

The train engine was No 1927 *Goliath*, a four-cylinder compound, and the pilot was No 1430 *Pandora*, a 7 ft 6 in single-wheeler. The load consisted of ten eight-wheeled vehicles, reckoned as '15 coaches', two vehicles of which were slipped at Blisworth. Tring was passed in 28 minutes 42 seconds from the Willesden start, the pace never falling below 60 miles an hour after full speed was attained—indeed, only dropping so low as that during the last mile before the summit. Similarly, up the Roade bank we were never going less than 60, but the downhill rate, although high, was never extreme or exceptional. It was in fact a case of good even work all the way. Steam was shut off at Hillmorton, 2 miles before Rugby, that station and the Trent Valley junction being passed with due caution.

LOGS OF THE THREE RUNS DESCRIBED ABOVE:

Miles	Stations	Run No 1		Run No 2		Run No 3	
		Min	Sec	Min	Sec	Min	Sec
0.0	Euston	00	00	00	00	00	00
						2 sig. stops	
5.4	Willesden Junc	08	43	08	42	13	12
0.0	do	00	00	00	00	00	00
2.7	Wembley	04	46	04	00	04	13
6.0	Harrow...	08	47	07	41	07	42
7.9	Pinner	11	11	09	49	10	06
10.6	Bushey	14	22	12	47	12	54
12.1	Watford	15	55	14	18	14	20
15.6	Kings Langley	19	52	17	59	17	50
19.1	Boxmoor	24	00	21	50	21	27
22.6	Berkhamsted	28	06	25	39	24	57
26.3	Tring	32	39	29	45	28	42
30.7	Cheddington	37	38	33	59	32	49
34.8	Leighton Buzzard	41	48	37	34	36	13
41.3	Bletchley	48	48	43	40	41	47
47.0	Wolverton	54	48	49	07	46	50
49.4	Castlethorpe	57	32	51	20	48	56
				Sigs			
54.5	Roade	63	43	57	45	54	11
57.4	Blisworth (SLIP)[19]	67	08	61	28	57	09
64.3	Weedon	74	33	68	21	63	23
69.9	Welton	81	06	74	11	68	48
		PW slack		PW slack		PW slack	
77.2	Rugby	89	26	81	23	76	08
83.8	Brandon	95	50	88	18	83	30
88.7	Coventry	102	24	93	35	87	58[20]
0.0	do	00	00	00	00	00	00
		Sigs				Sig	
						stop	
18.9	Birmingham	23	04	22	04	29	51

[19] Two bogie coaches slipped at Blisworth on runs 1 and 3, one on run 2.
[20] Time to a stop just outside Coventry station.

It may give an idea of the smartness of the performance if I mention that Rugby was passed in 76 minutes 8 seconds *inclusive* time from the Willesden start, and 91 minutes 14 seconds from Euston, in spite of *three* separate stoppages with their respective additional startings and slackenings. This run emphatically corroborates the evidence of some of my previous experiences with Mr Webb's four-cylinder compounds, that they have abundant speed capacity as well as large haulage power.[21] Certainly on this occasion *Goliath* was remarkably well-handled by her skilful driver, nor must a due share of praise be with-held from the pilot *Pandora* and *her* driver, who contributed materially to the success of the trip.

[21] Taken together, these three runs might well serve to demonstrate how unsatisfactory these latest four-cylinder Webb compounds were before George Whale altered their valve gear. They could not keep time with light loads unless piloted. Rous-Marten was much more critical of their capacities later on, after Webb had retired as Locomotive Superintendent on the LNWR and there was no need any longer to placate the 'powers that be'.

DECEMBER 1904

Journeys made behind Mr Whale's 4–4–0 'Precursors'

The new locomotives of Mr Whale's own particular design, those of the 'Precursor' class, have already covered themselves with honour and glory. A few instances of what occurred under my own personal observation may fairly be left to speak for themselves. I had a very smart run with one of these engines recently on the 3½-hour up morning express from Manchester to Euston. The engine was the second-built of the type, No 1395 *Harbinger*, driven as usual by Austin. Both engine and driver have given me several good performances. In this case the load was not heavy—barely 200 tons—but the running was very brisk and at the same time uniform. Stafford, 55¼ miles, the first stop, was reached in 60 minutes 22 seconds in spite of a relaying check before Stockport was passed. The final run of 133½ miles from Stafford into London was done in the fast time of 2 hours 18 minutes 34 seconds, and that from Rugby (passing) to Euston (stop) in 84 minutes 16 seconds, Willesden being passed in 77 minutes 58 seconds from Rugby, 77 miles.[22] Up the 6 miles at 1 in 330 to Tring the speed never fell below 56 miles

an hour except momentarily at the summit, when the quarter-mile took 17 seconds, indicating a rate of 52.8 miles an hour. That drop I suspect, however, to have been due, as in so many other cases, to a slight 'previousness' in notching up. But, taking it all round, it was an excellent run, especially as the downhill speed was consistently moderate throughout.

A still finer performance—finer because the load was so much heavier—was shown me by No 1419 *Tamerlane* on the 10.45 am down 3¾-hour express to Liverpool. The train was reckoned as '18½ coaches', equivalent to about 350 tons behind the tender, including passengers, luggage, etc. It was booked to make its first stop at Stafford, 133½ miles, in 2 hours 22 minutes from Euston, involving an average speed of 56.4 miles an hour. The actual inclusive time occupied from dead start to dead stop was 2 hours 18 minutes 25 seconds, 3½ minutes being thus gained . . .

[22] Actually 77.2 miles, or nearer 77¼ if one is reckoning in fractions.

LNWR 4-4-0 No 1419 Tamerlane, *one of Whale's 'Precursors', which began to appear in 1904. Handsome yet straightforward in design, with two simple-expansion inside cylinders, these 'no nonsense' locomotives were popular with the footplate staff and enabled the Company not only to dispense with the double-heading which had been necessary with even moderate loads when Webb compounds had been employed, but also to accelerate some of its expresses, so that Birmingham could be reached from Euston in 2 hours and Manchester in 3½.* (NRM, S. Pearce-Higgins Collection)

minutes 25 seconds, 3½ minutes being thus gained . . .

The first mile out of Euston was somewhat slow through permanent way alterations, and so was the last mile into Stafford owing to a signal check approaching the junction with the line from Birmingham. This left just 130½ minutes for the remaining 131½ miles, so that the entire journey between the first and last miles was performed with that heavy load at an average rate of over 60 miles an hour. Up the bank from Watford to Tring the speed never fell below

54.8 miles an hour, and that minimum point was reached only for a single quarter-mile, the lowest otherwise being 56.2, and as the Tring summit was approached the speed actually rose along the final stretch of 1 in 330, reaching 56.9, with a still-rising tendency until the summit was attained. Up the 7 miles at 1 in 350 passing Roade[23] a minimum rate of 55.5 miles an hour

[23] Actually the distance up the bank is under 6¾ miles and no 1 in 350 gradient features on it, though it may average that figure.

was maintained. Tring was passed in 38 minutes 20 seconds . . . Bletchley, 51 minutes 36 seconds; Rugby 86 minutes 20 seconds; Tamworth, 113 minutes 26 seconds; Lichfield, 119 minutes 19 seconds; Stafford being reached as above-mentioned. Deducting the delay caused by the check approaching Stafford, the net time for the $133\frac{1}{2}$ miles was 135 minutes—certainly a very remarkable performance with that heavy load. I may add that the same engine went on to Liverpool, but with a train reduced to '$14\frac{1}{2}$ coaches'. The running continued to be extremely smart. Crewe was passed dead slow in 26 minutes 44 seconds . . . or in 2 hours $44\frac{3}{4}$ minutes from Euston with an intermediate stop. The Liverpool suburban station at Edgehill was reached 6 minutes in advance of booked time, but as the train was delayed until the advertised time of departure she could not get into Lime Street terminus more than 2 minutes before time. But for that tiresome and archaic stop she would have been in easily 6 minutes early. Such a run, had it stood alone, would have been sufficient to stamp Mr Whale's 'Precursors' as possessing exceptional merit alike in fleetness and haulage power.

On another occasion No 2 *Simoom* simply played with a train of '17 coaches' due in London at 3.30 pm, finding the booked time, although averaging $51\frac{1}{2}$ miles an hour from Rugby to Willesden, a great deal more than she could easily fill up. And in spite of every effort on the part of her driver to 'spin out' things we finally stopped at Euston 5 minutes before time. Another day No 412 *Paget* gained 2 minutes with the same train between Crewe and Rugby, the load being estimated as '$22\frac{1}{2}$ coaches', or 430 tons behind the tender; and again, with the same train, No 7 *Titan*, running from Crewe to Euston with a load reckoned as $23\frac{1}{2}$ coaches, gained 1 minute on booked time at each stage.

One more illustration of the work of these engines may be interesting as showing the notable swiftness they possess in addition to such vast pulling power. When the 9.20 am from Euston to Birmingham was accelerated two years ago, so as to run from Willesden to Coventry, $88\frac{1}{2}$ miles, in 92 minutes, averaging 57.7 miles an hour, it was taken on the opening day by a 'Jubilee' compound which lost 8 minutes in the running; subsequently it was worked by two engines, generally both of the 'Precedent' 6 ft 6 in class, but sometimes by a compound and a 7 ft 6 in single-wheeler. The pilot generally came on stealthily at the last moment before starting and ran off instantly on arrival at Coventry; the load was usually eight eight-wheelers, occasionally nine but seldom more—not a creditable load for two engines. But the advent of the 'Precursors' has 'changed all that' too. Travelling by that train recently, No 2 *Simoom* was the engine, the load was eight eight-wheelers, or '12 coaches', one of which was slipped at Blisworth. The outcome constituted an astonishing metamorphosis as regarded former experiences. Our speed up the bank to Tring never fell so low as 60 miles an hour, and the summit was passed in 27 minutes 27 seconds from the Willesden platform.[24] The final $14\frac{1}{2}$ miles from passing Watford, all uphill, chiefly at 1 in 330, was covered in 13 minutes 46 seconds. Similar work was done up the Roade bank; Rugby was passed in 73 minutes 29 seconds from the Willesden platform[25] . . . and Coventry was reached in 85 minutes 5 seconds . . . This was distinctly brilliant, reflecting high credit on Mr Whale's engine and on George Ward, her driver.

[24] Does Rous-Marten mean 'from the start at Willesden' or 'from passing the platform end?' His habit of mentioning 'platforms' turns intended exactness into unnecessary vagueness.

[25] See previous note.

JULY   1905

Journeys behind a new 'Precursor' 4-4-0 and an old 'Precedent' 2-4-0

Since my last article was penned I have had several interesting experiences on the metals, notably on the London and North Western. One of these was so remarkable as to be almost phenomenal. I had travelled down to Birmingham one day by the 11.50 am two hours' express. The journey was characterised only by uniform excellence of travel. Speaking roundly, we left Euston about a minute late and reached Birmingham about 2 minutes early. The engine was a 'Precursor', No 685 *Cossack*, and the load was officially reckoned as '11½ coaches' weighing approximately 220 tons behind the tender. There was a long and bad relaying slack near Brandon which cost us a couple of minutes or so. I do not go into details more minutely because there is no occasion; the run was simply performed so easily and uniformly well that it was uneventful . . . The net time from London to Birmingham was 1 hour 55 minutes. The driver, Willis, managed his fine engine extremely well, but Inspector Davis, who was on the engine, was by no means satisfied with the result, because we took over 35 minutes to pass Tring, which he had hoped to do in 32 minutes, the explanation being that the engine was not steaming so freely as usual owing to her fire not being well burned through at the start. In the circumstances, however, there seemed remarkably little to complain of, and personally I thought the run a most creditable one even though it might

be lacking in sensational interest. No such lack was to be complained of in the return journey which, although there was a loss of 2 minutes between Birmingham and London, was one of the most remarkable in all my London and North Western experience. The train was the 2.45 pm from New Street, which is allowed 2 hours to Euston; the engine was again a 'Precursor', No 310 *Achilles*, driven by Forrester, with Inspector Davis once more on the footplate. The load, unfortunately in a sense, was a relatively light one, being estimated as 'equal to nine coaches' which were packed from end to end with passengers and luggage, and represented a total inclusive weight of close upon 170 tons behind the tender. I have termed that a 'relatively light load', because it would still be reckoned on the South of England railways as '17 coaches'. Now came the performance to which I have referred. *Achilles* went away almost with a bound and got through Stechford, 3¾ miles, in 4 minutes 49 seconds from New Street. By this time we had already attained a speed of 70 miles an hour, which increased to 77.4 passing Marston and was maintained at the same rate past Hampton. The rate dropped a little past Berkswell, but we regained the same point approaching Coventry and did not go below 75 miles an hour until we slowed for the Trent Valley junction, approaching Rugby. Here, unluckily, we encountered adverse signals which brought us practically to a dead stand at the northern entrance to the station. Up to this time we had covered the distance of $30\frac{1}{4}$ miles from Birmingham, virtually from start to stop, in 27 minutes 19 seconds. We crawled slowly through Rugby station, and when the starting signal at last dropped took a fresh departure from the southern end of the platform, having spent 2 minutes 8 seconds in the station. We went so smartly up the grade of 1 in 364 to Kilsby tunnel that we had attained 60 miles an hour before its darkness put a temporary stop to speed-timing. After emerging from the tunnel we soon attained a rate of 80.3 miles an hour, which we kept up nearly to Blisworth, dropping to 71 up the 1 in 326[26] to Roade summit. Down the subsequent descent we glided again at 80, which we should have sustained all the way to Bletchley but for the signal check at the Denbigh Hall Box, so often the terror of expresses. We got through Bletchley station at speed, only to be checked at Stoke Hammond. Nevertheless we quickly recovered to 72.6 miles an hour up the slightly rising grade, and we never once wavered or fell afterward from that rate all the way up the ascent to Tring. Up the final 6 miles of continuous rise at 1 in 330[27] this speed was persistently and unchangeably maintained, and we passed the summit at that rate—a performance which stands alone in my London and North Western experience.

At this point all the interest of the journey ceased, for directly after passing Tring we encountered the first of a series of signal delays which in the end continued right through to Euston, so that the descent of $31\frac{3}{4}$ miles actually occupied more than 48 minutes, but what had gone before atoned for all that followed.[28] Our

total time from Birmingham to Tring, including the 2 minutes 8 seconds spent in Rugby station, was 74 minutes 56 seconds, and the net time, allowing for the delays at Rugby, Denbigh Hall and Stoke Hammond, could not have been more than 68 minutes. Coventry, 19 miles from Birmingham, was passed in 17 minutes 45 seconds; Rugby, $30\frac{1}{2}$ miles, in 27 minutes 19 seconds; Bletchley was passed in 32 minutes 13 seconds inclusive—31 minutes net—from the Rugby start[29], distance $35\frac{3}{4}$ miles; Tring summit was passed in 13 minutes 16 seconds inclusive from Bletchley, without allowing for the signal check at Stoke Hammond, or in $12\frac{1}{4}$ minutes net . . . It is hardly necessary for me to point out how very remarkable was this uphill achievement by Mr Whale's new engine, of which I think he may justly be proud. One more detail I may add, that the time for the 51 minutes from the Rugby start[30] to Tring was only 45 minutes 29 seconds inclusive, or $43\frac{1}{2}$ minutes net, allowing for the two intermediate signal slacks. I have dwelt at some length upon this performance, because even from the viewpoint of swiftness with a somewhat light load it is very exceptional, and deserves to be classed among the finest locomotive feats yet accomplished in this country. I desire to offer my cordial congratulations to Mr Whale who, I am glad to say, continues to turn out these splendid 'Precursors' in gratifyingly large numbers.

It seems rather a step backward to turn now to the work of an engine whose nameplate[31] bears the remote date, 1873; but, as it happened, only a few days after I had recorded such brilliant work with Mr Whale's engine bearing the date 1905 I had the pleasure of observing another very smart London and North Western performance, of which the locomotive hero was an

---

[26] The gradient is actually 1 in 320.

[27] The gradient is actually 1 in 333.

[28] If, as Rous-Marten says earlier, the train was 2 minutes late at Euston, the figures show it must have been about 15 minutes early at Tring; no wonder it ran into signal delays.

[29] But, as Rous-Marten explains earlier, the train never actually stopped in Rugby station, but crawled slowly through it.

[30] See previous note.

[31] More accurately, *number-plate*.

engine which bore the date 1873[32], and in whose construction Mr Whale's two successive predecessors, Mr James Ramsbottom and Mr F. W. Webb, had a share. It was one of Mr Ramsbottom's well-known and always efficient 6 ft 6 in coupled 'Newton' class which had subsequently been rebuilt by Mr Webb as one of *his* always useful and efficient 'Precedent' class. The locomotive bore the number 1141 and the very grim and gloomy name *Graves*. The train was the American Boat Special, leaving Euston at mid-day, and was, for a wonder, a comparatively light one, reckoned at 11 coaches, the total weight behind the tender being about 212 tons. Several Americans were returning to the States by this train as far as Liverpool and one of them had a good deal to say about the engine. 'I guess you don't use very big locomotives on this line,' he remarked, 'but if that's the sort of trains she has to pull it's no wonder.' I suggested that usually the trains were much heavier and that the London and North Western Railway owned a large number of much bigger engines. The American smiled. 'I surmise that those figures on the name-plate mean the year she was built, don't they?' he enquired, indicating the year 1873. I assented, but observed that she had been converted into a 'Precedent' some years ago and was now as good as new. 'Well, sir,' said the American, 'I calculate that in my country if we converted an engine built 32 years ago it would be into scraps. I see she's called *Graves*. Is that considered a kind of cheerful name in this country? Perhaps it's meant to encourage the passengers?' But at that point I had to jump into my compartment and so the interesting conversation was nipped in the bud.

But the despised little engine with the funereal name soon showed its pace with such briskness as to make it very clear that an exceedingly useful machine would have been sacrificed had it been scrapped at the date that commended itself to the American. Let it be borne in mind that the load, although light for the London and North Western, would have been counted as '21 coaches' on the South of England railways. Rather more than a 'hand-cart', that![33] But *Graves* pulled it merrily up the bank to Tring, keeping up a steady rate of 53 to 56 miles an hour. Tring was passed in 37 minutes 48 seconds from the Euston start; Bletchley in 51 minutes 50 seconds; the first 55 miles from London were covered in exactly 6 seconds under the even hour. Rugby was passed at reduced speed in 89 minutes 40 seconds from Euston; Tamworth, 110 miles, in 1 hour 58 minutes 54 seconds; the 111th milepost was passed in just 8 seconds under the 2 hours; Stafford in 2 hours 23 minutes 55 seconds from London; Crewe in 2 hours 51 minutes 29 seconds . . . and we had reached a point only 10 miles short of Liverpool, Edge Hill, which was to be our first stop, in 3 hours 18 minutes from London, so as this left us 27 minutes to do the last 10 miles we had, of course, to ease down, and even so reached Edge Hill, 192¼ miles from Euston, in 3 hours 33 minutes 7 seconds. We could have got there easily 5 minutes earlier, but as it was we were 12 minutes in advance of booked time. The run of 192¼ miles without any intermediate halt is, of course, the longest non-stopping run done regularly on the London and North Western. But it now has a counterpart in the up run of the evening dining-car train from Liverpool to Euston, which stops nowhere after Edge Hill. Formerly it was joined on to the 5.30 pm from Manchester, due to reach Euston at 9.15. Since May 1st, however, as the combined train has become too heavy even for the 'Precursors', it has been booked to run separately without stopping at Crewe, and to gain 10 minutes thereby, making the total journey from Liverpool (Edge

---

[32] The same information twice within a few lines! This rather suggests that Rous-Marten wrote his articles in a hurry and sent them off for publication without reading them through and making corrections.

[33] The allusion is to a jibe bandied around by East Coast route champions during the Race to Aberdeen in 1895, that the record-making *Hardwicke* 2-4-0, when it made its record time of 126 minutes between Crewe and Carlisle on August 21-22, was so lightly loaded that it amounted to no more than an 'engine and a hand-cart'. Actually the train weighed 70 tons.

Hill) to Euston in 3 hours 40 minutes. I came back from Liverpool by this train. The engine was No 1419 *Tamerlane* of the 'Precursor' class, but the load was only '8½', viz, two 12-wheeled dining cars and three corridor eight-wheelers, about 160 tons in all behind the tender. In such circumstances *Tamerlane* obviously could only 'play with' the train, and this was done. We ambled along quietly all the way, leaving about a minute late and reaching Euston punctually to the very second. A most even and uniform and precise performance, but by no means exciting or very interesting as a specimen of locomotive work. Yet who could complain? Rather, one was constrained to admire such steady travelling and extreme punctuality.

OCTOBER   1907

Journeys from Crewe to Carlisle and back behind a newly-built 'Experiment' 4–6–0

On my way to make my special 'Diamond Jubilee' locomotive trips on the Caledonian Railway . . . I travelled to Carlisle by the 10 am West Coast 'Day Scotch' from Euston on one of the last days before its daily duplication began . . .

At Crewe the interest of the trip was considerably discounted, first by the division of the train, my own part, the Glasgow one, becoming only '9½ coaches' or barely 190 tons; and secondly by the fact that the Birmingham, Liverpool and Manchester joint 'Day Scotch' express had left Crewe late just before our arrival, that it consisted of '19½ coaches', and that the driver had proclaimed his determination to take it up Shap without assistance. We at once realised that this meant serious delay for us, and wondered why such a risk should be daily run, of blocking and discrediting the best West Coast day train from London to Scotland when, as it seemed to an outsider, the timing of the train might well be altered so as to avert this disadvantage. However, we duly started with one engine,

No 2052 *Stephenson*, 4–6–0 class. We got away brilliantly and were soon doing 71.4 miles an hour. We passed Warrington (24¼ miles) in 24 min 53 sec, Wigan (36 miles) in 37 min 21 sec, and Preston—dead slow—in 54 min 34 sec from Crewe, distance 51 miles. Oxenholme (40 miles) was passed in 44 minutes 13 seconds from Preston. By this time our speed, ascending the Grayrigg bank at 1 in 120, etc[34], had fallen to 45 miles an hour, and just before Grayrigg the minimum was exactly 40. Here we caught up the Birmingham–Scotch express and had to slow down almost to walking pace, and before we had recovered from the check we were stopped dead by signal at Tebay after covering the 104¼ miles from Crewe[35] —start to stop—in 1 hour 58 minutes 31 se-

[34] There is no such gradient on Grayrigg bank. From Oxenholme onwards it varies between 1 in 178 and 1 in 124 for 2½ miles, 2¼ miles at 1 in 131 follow, and then come 2 miles at 1 in 106 to Grayrigg station.
[35] Actually, just over 104 miles.

LNWR 4–6–0 No 66 Experiment *(not to be confused with Webb's previously-built compound of the same name!), built in 1905 and here seen in unlined wartime black. This was the first of a series of what were in effect enlarged 'Precursors', with six-coupled wheels in place of four-coupled. They were principally intended for coping with the severe gradients of the Lancaster-Carlisle road, and did this with success, showing a surprising turn of speed when running downhill.* (NRM, S. Pearce-Higgins Collection)

conds, in spite of the Grayrigg slack, which in-volved a loss of fully 2½ min. After being kept at Tebay nearly 7 minutes by the Birmingham train in front we got away at last with a bank engine pushing in our rear, so we climbed the 4½ miles of 1 in 75[36] easily at 36 miles an hour, dropping the pusher at the summit. The follow-ing descent was made at a generally cautious speed, although we touched 80 miles an hour near Clifton and 78.2 miles an hour near Wreay. In spite of an exceptionally long and careful slow-in we were again stopped by signal by that pestilent 'Birmingham Scotch' at the en-trance to Carlisle, our engine buffers being abreast of the platform-end, having come from Crewe in 2 hrs 45 min 21 sec, inclusive, or 2 hrs 38 min 52 sec actual travelling time, 2 hrs 33 min net. This too was distinctly smart work,

although of course the load was a comparatively light one. Still, it should be remembered that it would be reckoned on certain English railways as '18 coaches' and would have been regarded as at least '15', even on the London and North Western, not so many years ago.

On the return journey the load was estimated as 'equal to 17½ coaches'. The weight behind the tender was approximately 350 tons, and the locomotive was again one of the 4–6–0 type, viz; No 1991 *Palmerston*. In this case, as an absolutely punctual start was made from Carlisle, the engine was hampered by the extremely liberal time-allowance to Crewe, viz, 2 hrs 55 mins for the 141 miles, involving an average speed of on-ly 48.3 miles an hour. Still, some troublesome banks had to be faced, so the locomotive's task was not a light one, hauling 350 tons. Up the as-cent toward Shap a speed of 41–43 miles an hour was pretty steadily maintained until we got on

[36] Only 4 miles at that gradient.

the last and steepest length, where the gradient is 1 in 100.[37] Here we gradually dropped to 34.6 miles an hour, but recovered to 37 before the summit was reached. Down the bank to Tebay we ran without steam and with a frequent touch of the brakes, the same experience being repeated down the less-steep Grayrigg bank, and we only once touched 70 miles an hour, the driver having his time well in hand. We passed Penrith in 26 min 48 sec from Carlisle (17¾ miles), Shap summit (31½ miles) in 46 min 51 sec, Preston (90 miles) in 109 min 48 sec. Then we eased down persistently to avoid too early an arrival, apart from the fact that the Edinburgh portion of the train was in front of us. We reached Crewe in 2 hrs 50 min 39 sec from Carlisle (141 miles), or 4 min 21 sec under booked time, thus averaging only a minute fraction below 50 miles an hour; this, with a load of 350 tons, can-

[37] In fact there is no gradient as steep as this anywhere to the north of Shap. The last 2 miles after Shap station going southwards are ¼ mile on the level, ¾ mile at 1 in 106 and ½ mile at 1 in 130.

not be regarded as otherwise than a creditable performance, and yet everywhere, except on the ascending grades, the running was made under easy steam, while on the up grades the locomotive was never at all pressed. No doubt could exist that, had it been desired, the run from Carlisle could easily have been made with that load in 10 or perhaps 20 minutes shorter time. As, however, the train was so early there would have been no object in doing this; and, on the other hand, it would have caused considerable disarrangement of the traffic. Viewing critically these performances by Mr Whale's 'Experiments', it is impossible to resist the conclusion that they are distinctly efficient machines. It may quite reasonably be held that they would be better still with 6 ft 6 in wheels combined with somewhat larger boilers and cylinders. But it appears sound policy to design an engine proportionate to the work it is to be called on to do, and so far as my personal experience goes I feel constrained to recognise that this is what Mr Whale has done successfully.

MIDLAND RAILWAY

NOVEMBER 1903

Performances of newly-built 4–4–0 compounds on the Settle and Carlisle line

In *The Railway Magazine*, Vol xi, on pages 170 and 349, I described and illustrated the three-cylinder compound engines designed and built for the Midland Railway by Mr S. W. Johnson, Chief Mechanical Engineer of that line. Recently . . . I have had some highly favourable opportunities of testing the work done by the new engines . . .

One was with the 11.50 am Midland Scottish express from Carlisle to Leeds. The load was approximately 240 tons behind the double-bogie tender. We got away punctually from the Citadel station, but immediately outside we were stopped by signal, so that we did not make our actual start until 2½ minutes later. The compound soon got to work, and at the end of the second mile from the start we had attained 40 miles an hour, although the whole distance was on a rising grade of 1 in 132.[38] After full speed had once been reached we never afterwards fell below 47.4 miles an hour until after Appleby was passed. Our time from Carlisle to Appleby was 34 minutes 33 seconds for the 30¾ miles—extremely smart work with a 240 ton load and no pilot. On the moderately-falling gradient near Lazonby the speed rose to 72.4 miles an hour. But it was after Appleby that the crux had to come—those dozen miles of

almost continuous 1 in 100 up between Ormside and Aisgill summit. Here the compound did some most excellent pulling and climbing. Up to Crosby Garrett the speed never fell below 45 miles an hour—indeed only went so low as that for a single quarter-mile, otherwise keeping to 47.4. After Crosby Garrett it rose steadily to 48, 50, 51.1 and even 53.6, then gradually sank to 51.1, 50 and 47.4 near Kirkby Stephen. Up the final length to Aisgill summit our rate dropped to 45, and finally to 43 miles an hour, that being maintained as an absolute minimum mile after mile to the top of the bank. I had no previous experience of equal merit up that severe incline. The time for the 18 miles from Appleby to Aisgill was only 23 minutes 5 seconds. Thus the 48½-mile climb of over 1,100 feet from Carlisle to Aisgill was accomplished in 57 minutes 38 seconds. Along the table-land, which has a slight downward grade from Aisgill to Bleamoor, we were generally doing about 65 to 67 miles an hour.

But next was to come the test whether the new compound engine could develop swiftness sufficient to cope with the modern Midland accelerations. One would have expected Mr Johnson's engine to exert immense power of haulage and climbing, but it might have done that and yet failed to prove fast enough for the easier portions of the road where time has often to be gained. The trial was now to be made. The descent of

---

[38] Not the whole distance. The 1 in 132 is not reached until 1.1 miles from Carlisle.

some 15 miles, nearly all at 1 in 100 or even steeper[39], which extends from Bleamoor tunnel to Settle Junction, affords a superb 'galloping ground', there being a perfect road without curves sharp enough to render the highest speeds dangerous. Along this length we made some splendid running, breaking all my Midland records, and coming very near to lowering all my records of mere speed, either in this country or abroad. A rate of 75 miles an hour was soon reached; then 80 and 85. But still the speed rose steadily; quarter-miles were done successively in 10.8, 10.6, 10.4, 10.2 and 10 seconds; 90 miles an hour had been reached and my Midland's record with No 117, 7 ft 9 in single-wheeler, had been equalled. It was immediately broken. The next quarter-mile was done in 9.8 seconds, and several successive quarter-miles each in the same time. That represented a speed of 91.8 miles an hour and consequently beats my record maximum with one of the du Bousquet-de Glehn 'Atlantics' on the French Northern Railway, which once gave me a rate of 145.2 kilometres or 90.3 miles an hour. As regards British speed records, I have mentioned in these articles that I recorded a single quarter-mile at 90 and another next day at 91.8, on the Lancashire and Yorkshire[40], but that being unable to get the adjacent posts I could not accept these reports as conclusive, because they *might* have been due to the accidental misplacement of a quarter-mile post, as happened on the London and North Western with post 38¾ from Euston, which has been responsible for many 'fancy' speeds supposed to have been recorded at that spot. But in this latest Midland case—as in that of the former Midland record of 90 miles an hour—no doubt whatever exists, as the register of speeds was continuous and consistent. I may be asked whether even this 91.8 miles an hour is my present 'record', and if so I must reply, 'No'. But as yet I am not authorised to publish my highest. It is my rule, as my readers are aware, never to

publish any exceptional speeds noted by me until I shall first have received a written assurance that such publication will not be prejudicial to the interests of the driver, the engineer or the railway concerned. Such assurance I have received in the case of Mr Johnson's engine, and therefore I am able to publish the remarkable figures, which I do with very great pleasure.

As we had got considerably in front of our booked time we eased down near Settle, and merely strolled along the rest of the way. Yet we passed Hellifield in 83 minutes 12 seconds from Carlisle, and Skipton in 93 minutes 18 seconds. The remaining 26 very easy miles to the Leeds stop occupied no less than 44 minutes 29 seconds, owing to the fact that we were stopped by signal twice and slackened to walking pace no fewer than *eleven* times through slow trains having been deliberately turned on to our road in front of us. Nevertheless we more than kept our booked time—viz, 2 hours 18 minutes—between Carlisle and Leeds, our actual time from start to stop being 2 hours 16 minutes 47 seconds for the 112¾ miles[41] in spite of delays totalling over 17 minutes. It does not need much demonstration that this was a very fine piece of locomotive work. I may also add that it reflects much credit upon the driving of the engine by Killan.

In the second case my trip was from Hellifield to Carlisle by the afternoon express, which is allowed 88 minutes for the 76¾ miles. On this occasion the load was slightly heavier, totalling 250 tons . . . With this load the run was accomplished in 80 minutes 57 seconds from start to stop. The Settle bank, 15 miles of 1 in 92 to 1 in 100[42], was ascended at a steady rate of 36 to 40 miles an hour. On one bit, at 1 in 92[42], the speed for a single quarter-mile dropped to 35, the absolute minimum. During the descent after Aisgill a speed of 88.2 miles an hour was attained. The run in from Appleby to Carlisle,

[39] According to the gradient profile there are *no* steeper gradients than 1 in 100 on this descent.

[40] See page 130.

[41] According to the gradient profile it is slightly above 113 miles.

[42] There is no pitch steeper than 1 in 100 anywhere on the ascent in question, according to the gradient profile.

30¾ miles, was done under relatively easy steam but was performed in 28 minutes 2 seconds to the stop . . . There was a strong side wind blow-ing during the latter half of this run, which will be recognised as perhaps equally meritorious with that in the opposite direction.

SEPTEMBER   1904

Journeys on the main line from St Pancras behind non-compound 4–4–0s with Belpaire fireboxes, recently built by Mr S. W. Johnson

With all my experiences as to what the Midland could do between St Pancras and Manchester Central if really put to it, I could not but deem a booking of 3 hours 35 minutes over such a road a very formidable locomotive undertaking, even with loads well under 200 tons behind the ten-der. Yet I recollected that just twenty years ago, when the Midland Railway, like the London and North Western and Great Northern–Great Central Railways, undertook to perform the London–Manchester and Manchester–London journeys in 4 hours 15 minutes, I once travelled from Manchester Central to St Pancras in 3 hours 47 minutes actual running time. But I should explain that I accomplished this by changing trains at Leicester and proceeding thence to London by the Scotch express, then the only train that did not stop at either Bedford or Kettering. No stop was booked between Manchester and Leicester, and that stage was accomplished by one of Mr Johnson's 6 ft 9 in coupled engines of the 1657–1666 lot, in 115 minutes, but with a load of only four eight-wheelers. In the opposite direction my best time was a little longer. But these figures were suffi-cient to show, evey twenty years back, that the Midland Railway had a great deal in hand as regarded the competition for the London–Man-

chester trains, and that a booking of 3 hours 45 minutes could be faced with perfect equanimity and a virtual certainty of being able to keep time under normal conditions. Still, just as at sea it is the last knot that counts, so on the Midland Railway it was the last 10 minutes struck off that fast timing, over a road that among other in-teresting features has a single bank at 1 in 90 for 9 miles[43], and with a double load as compared with that of 1884, that combined to place the strain upon the Midland engines. That the Lon-don–Leicester and Leicester–London stages could and would be run to time with the utmost ease I was perfectly well aware. It was the stage between Leicester and Manchester that imposed the most serious difficulty in the way of timekeeping. There was no doubt as to the capacity of several different classes of Midland express engines to do good work even up the steep banks that abound. But it is one of the drawbacks of the Peak route that sharp reverse curves are frequent along the steeper lengths, and these not only enhance the difficulty of the

---

[43] The ascent to Peak Forest summit from the south is for 3 miles at 1 in 90, before which the grades are easier. In the opposite direction there are indeed 9 miles at 1 in 90 or even steeper, but here and there are short lengths of somewhat easier grading.

upward climb, but also present a check upon the needful swiftness of the downhill running with the old rolling-stock, and there used to be frequent complaints of the uncomfortable riding over that part of the line. Thus, keeping all these points in view, it should be said that I approached the actual test of performance with considerable curiosity and interest.

Here let me clear the gound by saying in general terms that the newest rolling-stock of which some of the accelerated trains are composed afforded admirably smooth and easy running even over the worst parts of the steep and sinuous road. No reasonable ground of complaint could be found on the score of any roughness. Secondly, Mr Johnson's Belpaire engines showed themselves entirely capable of grappling successfully with all the difficulties in respect of gradients, while with the aid of water troughs at Oakley and Loughborough, and by means of extra-large double-bogie tenders, it became practicable to run the same engine right through from London to Manchester without incurring

the delay of changing at Leicester as had previously been necessary. It is perhaps hardly necessary that I should mention that the trains in question are the 10 am down from St Pancras, which is due at Manchester at 1.35, and the 4.15 pm from Manchester, due at St Pancras at 7.50 pm.

On the occasion when I made my experimental trip the load was approximately 170 tons behind the tender. The engine was No 2788 of the Belpaire class, which was driven by Selly, who had given me so many excellent performances . . . Our start from St Pancras was an exceptionally good one, Hendon being passed in 8 minutes 55 seconds, quite my best experience between those points. Elstree summit, $12\frac{1}{2}$ miles, was attained in 14 minutes 28 seconds from the London start and St Albans was passed in 20 minutes 59 seconds from St Pancras, both of these also being my best on record. But then we encountered misfortune. That wretched 9.33 am from London, which had brought me disaster on a previous occasion, once more lagg-

MR No 2788, built in 1901, one of Johnson's 4–4–0 'Belpaires'. Next to his three-cylinder compounds they were the Midland's most powerful express engines. This picture shows the superb crimson lake livery and its elaborate lining-out to perfection. The large tender, on eight wheels, is a sign that this line did not have many water-troughs at the turn of the century. (NRM, F. Burtt Collection)

ed in the way, first slowing us just beyond St Albans and then stopping us for nearly a minute at Sandridge Box. This of course involved an actual delay of more than 3 minutes and inspired a fear that the result of my experiment would be unfavourable. Happily, as matters turned out, this hindrance only went to accentuate the brilliance of the performance accomplished. Stimulated by this vexatious obstruction, Selly lost no time in setting himself to make up what had been lost. We ran through Luton in 33 minutes 29 seconds inclusive from St Pancras—or in barely 30 minutes net—and then came the quickest run I have ever had from Luton to passing Bedford, although curiously enough the maximum speed did not come anywhere near what I have often recorded between those points. The time for the distance of $19\frac{3}{4}$ miles, 16 miles of which is mostly down at 1 in 200, was only 15 minutes 21 seconds, and so Bedford station was passed in the splendid time of 48 minutes 50 seconds from the London start, or in $45\frac{1}{2}$ minutes net.

Although by this time we had got distinctly in front of schedule, notwithstanding the delay at Sandridge, there was no flagging on the part of either the engine or her driver. They went up the Sharnbrook bank of 1 in 100 to 1 in 119 with striking swiftness, and our speed had never dropped below 55 miles an hour when the summit was attained. Milepost 61 was passed in exactly 60 minutes from the St Pancras start. There was a slight but noticeable easing down as Kettering was approached, but we ran through that station in 69 minutes 50 seconds from St Pancras, distance 72 miles. The 22 miles from Bedford over the Sharnbrook 'gable' had been covered in precisely 21 minutes. On the steepest bit of the bank approaching Desborough we dropped momentarily to 50 miles an hour; the rest of the ascent was made at a minimum of 52. Down the Desborough bank and past Market Harborough Selly ran very cautiously, and the speed round the last-named station and round the adjacent curve barely reached 50 miles an hour. By this time it became manifest that if full speed were maintained an unduly early arrival

at Leicester would ensue. Accordingly the remainder of the journey was performed under very easy steam. Nevertheless we stopped in Leicester station in 99 minutes 9 seconds inclusive from St Pancras. Making due allowance for the stoppage and delay at Sandridge, the net time was $95\frac{1}{2}$ minutes . . .

Having arrived at Leicester well in front of booked time, we had of course to wait for several minutes so as not to start before we were due. We got away to the second. No 2788 and Selly still headed the train. Very soon we proceeded to do some further remarkable things. Trent, $20\frac{3}{4}$ miles, was breasted in 19 minutes 7 seconds from Leicester, and Derby in 29 minutes. The subsequent run through the beautiful but difficult Derbyshire route was done with admirable smartness and without any exceptional speed being attained, while the uphill work was extremely fine. Ascending the final 6 miles at 1 in 90 continuously[44] to Peak Forest, the speed never dropped below 36 miles an hour, at which point it kept uninterruptedly quarter-mile after quarter-mile. This brisk ascent enabled the following downhill stretch to be descended at a relatively easy pace. We did not get to Manchester without encountering three signal checks in the outskirts of the Cotton City. Nevertheless in spite of all hindrances we stopped in the Central Station, Manchester, 3 minutes before time, having run from London in 3 hours 31 minutes 48 seconds inclusive of all stoppages and delays, or in 3 hours $20\frac{1}{2}$ minutes actual travelling time without any allowance for signal or other delays. If these were taken into account the net time would be left at $3\frac{1}{4}$ hours. So clearly the Midland Railway had effectually vindicated the feasibility of what had at first appeared an almost audaciously bold London–Manchester booking.

My experience on the return journey by the 4.10 pm train ex-Manchester, which was booked to be done in the same time with practically

---

[44] Only the last 3 miles are at this inclination; the previous three are slightly easier. 'Continuously', therefore, is incorrect.

the same load, was of a very similar character. The engine, No 830, was the first of the latest batch yet built of the Belpaires, and virtually identical with No 2788. The load was the same as that of the morning train. Once more there was an experience of very smart uphill running, the 9 miles at 1 in 90 approaching Peak Forest being ascended at a minimum rate of 36 miles an hour, as on the down journey, while similarly the downhill travelling was particularly steady and cautious. That is to say, instead of flying along for considerable distances at speeds exceeding 80 miles an hour, we hardly ever approached 70 very closely. Nevertheless we covered the distance from Manchester to Leicester in 103 minutes 45 seconds notwithstanding two bad checks near Loughborough and another outside Leicester. The same engine went through to London and accomplished that run in exactly one minute longer time than the down journey, namely, 100 minutes 9 seconds, St Pancras being reached more than 5 minutes in advance of booked time in spite of a bad signal check being encountered near Carlton Road. Once again I had occasion to notice the moderate rate of speed on the downhill lengths, the smartness with which the banks were ascended—although this last did not equal the work on the down journey—and the admirable smoothness and steadiness of the travelling all the way. The inclusive time from Manchester Central was 3 hours 29 minutes 16 seconds and the actual travelling time 3 hours 23 minutes 54 seconds; the net time was barely 3 hours 20 minutes. I am therefore fully justified in characterising this double journey as a brilliant vindication by the Midland Railway of its paper timing.

Next I took occasion to try the Midland Railway's new long non-stop runs, namely the 9.45 am which runs from St Pancras to Sheffield, 158 miles, without a halt, and the 3.45 pm up from Leeds, which makes the entire journey of 196 miles to St Pancras without any pause by the way.[45] Here again the very excellent Johnson Belpaires were the heroes of the day. I had No 821 on the down journey and No 822 on the up.

The load was substantially the same both ways and may be taken as approximately 180 tons behind the tender. It may be remarked at the outset that each run, although in itself very creditable, represents in reality a comparatively small task for the Midland engines to perform . . . Such proved to be the case. On the down journey we got through Hendon in 10 minutes 36 seconds, breasted Elstree summit in 16 minutes 35 seconds, passed St Albans in 23 minutes 53 seconds and Luton in 34 minutes 19 seconds. Down the long descent thence to Bedford we simply strolled, our speed keeping very little over 60 miles an hour. Bedford was passed in 53 minutes 6 seconds from the London start, and then the driver carried his easygoing tactics to such an extent that in ascending the Sharnbrook bank we had dropped to 27 miles an hour before the summit was reached—rather a contrast to the minimum of 55 miles an hour maintained by another engine of the same class only a few days previously up the same bank with a similar load; nor did we in the subsequent descent improve on our very easy Luton–Bedford pace, 65.2 miles an hour being our maximum along 4 miles of 1 in 120 down.[46] Nevertheless we got through Kettering in 79 minutes 13 seconds from St Pancras. Our lowest rate at Desborough was 39.5 and Kibworth 40.6, the corresponding descents being a mere saunter. Still, in spite of all this apparent loitering we got through Leicester station, slackening almost to a walk, in 110 minutes 51 seconds from St Pancras. Trent was passed 20 minutes 50 seconds later, and it is noteworthy that the highest speed of the entire journey was run during this length, which is nearly level although with a slight downward tendency. Up the Dronfield bank, 5 miles at 1 in 100[47] to the

---

[45] Rous-Marten's account of the up journey from Leeds is so brief and lacking in detail that it has been omitted.

[46] According to the gradient profile less than 3 miles are at that inclination.

[47] Only $4\frac{1}{4}$ miles are at that inclination.

Bradway tunnel, we went at a steady 30 miles an hour, and after a very long slow in we stopped at Sheffield in 3 hours 2 minutes 7 seconds, getting in more than 2 minutes before time . . . A comparison with my previous journey as far as Trent will show immediately that the time between St Pancras and Sheffield might be greatly reduced.

GREAT NORTHERN RAILWAY

NOVEMBER 1903

Performances of an Ivatt 4–2–2, a small-boilered 'Atlantic' and a large-boilered 'Atlantic'

In my August article I promised to give full details of my 'record' run by the Great Northern from Kings Cross to Leeds, made in July . . . The down journey was made by the 9.45 am express from Kings Cross. The engine was No 261, 7 ft 7 in single-wheeler (designed by Mr H. A. Ivatt), with cylinders 19 in by 26 in. The load was estimated at well over 250 tons inclusive behind the tender, consisting as it did of six twelve-wheeled vehicles, one eight-wheeled and one six-wheeled. The train was booked to run without stop from Kings Cross to Doncaster, 156 miles, in 2 hours 49 minutes. Our actual time taken was 2 hours 47 minutes 11 seconds. The single-wheeler slipped rather

badly on the 1 in 105 in Maiden Lane tunnel and we had a serious permanent way slack at Finsbury Park. Consequently we took 19 minutes 42 seconds to reach the Potters Bar summit, our lowest speed up the 8¼ miles at 1 in 200 being 38.8 miles an hour. Hatfield was passed in 25 minutes 13 seconds from the start, and the 4¼ miles thence to Welwyn, mostly up 1 in

GNR 4–2–2 No 267, one of 12 single-wheelers built during 1898–1901 by H.A. Ivatt, Stirling's successor. They were intended for the more lightly-loaded Great Northern expresses of that time, and were able to keep time on fast schedules with up to 150 tons. (NRM)

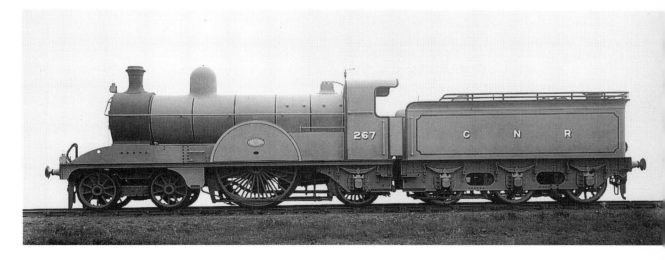

GNR 4–4–2 No 271, the only one of Ivatt's 'Atlantics' not to have outside cylinders. It was first built in 1902 as a four-cylinder compound and ran in this state for some years before being reconstructed as a two-cylinder simple engine, as shown. Photographs of it in this condition are rare. (NRM)

200, occupied only 4 minutes 1 second. Hitchin was passed in 39 minutes from Kings Cross, and then came a somewhat remarkable bit of downhill running, the times from Hitchin to Three Counties, $3\frac{3}{4}$ miles, and thence to Arlesey, 1.3 miles, being only 2 minutes 53 seconds and exactly 1 minute respectively. From Kings Cross to Huntingdon, just under 59 miles, our time was $62\frac{1}{2}$ minutes precisely, the time for the 27 minutes from Hitchin being only 23 minutes 29 seconds. Peterborough was passed dead slow in 79 minutes 39 seconds from London. Up the final 3 miles at 1 in 178 to Stoke summit our rate fell off to 39.1 miles an hour, and a bad check was encountered at the top, followed by a second at Grantham. Consequently we took 116 minutes from London to pass that station, a somewhat disappointing result after so much good running. However, we then picked up; we passed Newark in 13 minutes 49 seconds from Grantham, Retford in 33 minutes 32 seconds from the same point, maintained 55.8 miles an hour up the 1 in 198 to Pipers Wood and completed the journey of 156 miles from London to Doncaster in 2 hours 47 minutes 11 seconds start to stop . . . or 2 hours 45 minutes

net. From Doncaster to Leeds (Holbeck station) No 1309—'400' class—took the train, reduced to 170 tons, notwithstanding two bad slacks, in 34 minutes 53 seconds, and our total time from London was 3 hours 27 minutes—a record.

The return journey was still faster, but with a lighter load, viz, three twelve-wheelers from Leeds to Wakefield and four thence to London, or about 145 tons, including passengers, luggage, staff and stores. The engine was No 253, the newest of Mr Ivatt's 'Atlantic' or '990' class, which has 6 ft 6 in coupled wheels[48] and outside cylinders $18\frac{3}{4}$ in by 24 in. Up the bank at 1 in 150 approaching Nostell a minimum rate of 53 miles an hour was sustained. The subsequent descent was made at quite a moderate speed but Doncaster was passed in 20 minutes 25 seconds from the start, the distance being only a small fraction under 20 miles. Very steady running was kept up, no exceptional speed being attained until after Grantham was passed in 52 minutes 29 seconds from Doncaster. We slowed down below 40 miles an hour taking in water from the track-trough near Newark. In the Stoke tunnel

---

[48] The diameter was actually 6 ft 7 in.

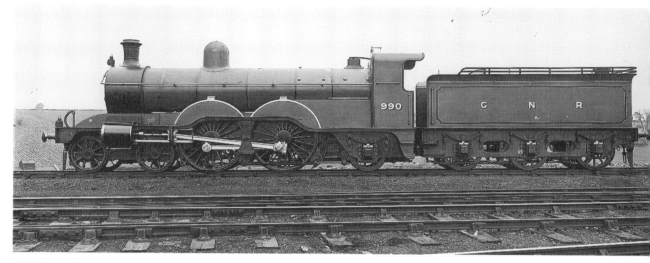

GNR 4–4–2 No 990, later named Henry Oakley *after the then General Manager of the Company. Built in 1898, it was the first of the long sequence of 'Atlantics' built to Ivatt's designs. Its relatively small boiler was necessitated by the state of the track on the main line, which was largely of light-section rail and badly needed relaying.* (NRM)

we again had a bad relaying slack which brought us down to 10 miles an hour, but down the subsequent bank we soon recovered speed and shortly after Bytham we were going at 85 miles an hour when we found the Monkswood signals against us, the result being that we were brought to a dead stand for 73 seconds. This of course was a severe disappointment, as we were booked to make the run of 176 miles from Wakefield to Kings Cross without any intermediate halt. However, when we again got under way, although we had passed the best of the down grade, we soon got up successfully to 70, 75, 76 and finally 77.4 miles an hour near Helpston, when adverse signals once more brought us down to quite a slow pace. We passed Peterborough dead slow in 33 min 22 sec from Grantham, having lost fully 6 minutes by the delays . . . But from Peterborough to the finish we made a remarkably fine run, although even then we encountered two annoying signal checks—one midway down the Abbots Ripton bank which spoiled our descent, and the other shortly before Hatfield which impaired our subsequent climb of the up grade to Potters Bar. We also had the usual engineering slack through

Finsbury Park. Nevertheless, from passing Peterborough dead slow we ran to the Kings Cross stop in 75 minutes 13 seconds. Our time from Wakefield to London was 3 hours 1 minute 10 seconds inclusive, 3 hours 0 minutes 27 seconds actual travelling time, 2 hours 53 minutes net. Our inclusive time from Leeds (Holbeck) to Kings Cross was 3 hours 20 minutes 5 seconds . . . actual travelling time 3 hours 13 minutes 34 seconds; net time 3 hours 3 minutes 4 seconds. It will be observed that the actual travelling time from Wakefield to London was only $180\frac{1}{2}$ minutes for the 176 miles, and that the net time, 173 minutes, was well in excess of the 'mile-a-minute' standard, as also was our time, 75 minutes 13 seconds, for the $76\frac{1}{4}$[49] miles from Peterborough to Kings Cross. Thus the double journey was a distinctly interesting one, which showed to much advantage the capabilities of three of Mr Ivatt's locomotive types. It also showed conclusively that whenever the Great Northern Railway shall see fit to cut down the London–Leeds time to the even 3 hours, and do the journey without a stop, that

[49] Nearer $76\frac{1}{2}$, actually 76.4 miles.

will be an entirely feasible undertaking.

At this stage it may perhaps be convenient that I should deal with yet another Great Northern Railway experience, my first with the newest of Great Northern Railway new engine types, namely No 251. This is one of Mr Ivatt's latest batch of 'Atlantics', or '990s', but like No 990 herself it stands apart from the rest as a 'sample' engine. The other ten of this newest lot, namely Nos 250 and 252–260, are practically the same as '990' excepting that they are framed to carry a much larger boiler than No 990, while this, again, is the special feature differentiating No 251 from her sisters. No 251 is a most massive and imposing engine in aspect. Her huge boiler, 5 ft 6 in in diameter, spreads out on both sides over the 6 ft 6 in coupled wheels[50], and rises so high as to leave but little room for chimney, dome or safety-valve column. It is understood that as the other engines of the class come in for rebuilding or re-boilering, all will be

fitted with boilers of this vast size, which gives 2,500 square feet of total heating surface, and will have a working pressure of 175 lbs per square inch . . .

On the occasion with which I am about to deal No 251 worked the 1.30 pm fast dining-car express from London to Doncaster. Hitherto the practice has been to change engines at Peterborough, but in the present case No 251 ran throughout. The load was reckoned as 250 tons behind the tender. Again there was the vexatious engineering slack at Finsbury Park which, I fear, will remain chronic for some time to come. Nevertheless, so rapidly did No 251 gather speed that the distance of 76 chains from passing Hornsey to passing Wood Green was covered in the quick time of 54 seconds. About

50 Their diameter was 6 ft 8 ins.

GNR 4-4-2 No 251, the first of Ivatt's large-boilered 'Atlantics', built in 1904 when the track on the main line had been re-laid so as to bear their extra weight. The engine created something of a stir when it first appeared because it looked so enormous. (NRM)

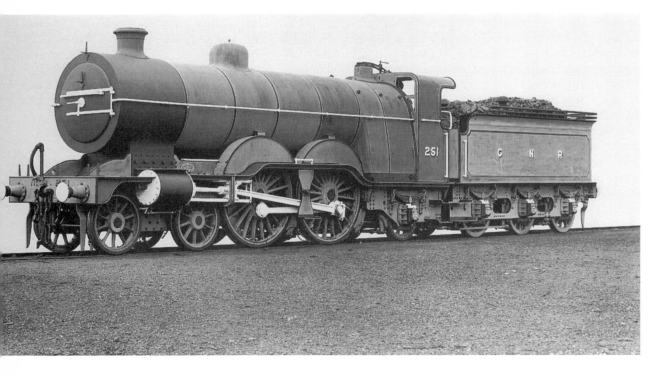

half way up the 8 miles at 1 in 200 to Potters Bar our speed had settled down to 53 miles an hour. which thenceforward was maintained unwaveringly to the summit, and Potters Bar was passed in exactly 18 minutes from the start, Hatfield in 23 minutes and Hitchin in 37 minutes 32 seconds. As there was no intention to attempt any 'record-breaking', but only to make the very fast booked journey at a speed as nearly uniform as might be, the pace was carefully kept down on the falling grades, and so instead of passing Huntingdon in 23 minutes 29 seconds, as in the former instance when the single-driver was employed, No 251 took 25 minutes 29 seconds for the 27 miles, exactly 2 minutes longer, and Huntingdon was passed in 63 minutes 1 second from Kings Cross. Up the bank of 1 in 200 approaching Abbots Ripton our speed never went below 55 miles an hour, nor did it exceed 70 down the subsequent descent. Peterborough was reached 2 minutes before time, the run from London having occupied 81 minutes 3 seconds from start to stop.

Making a fresh start from Peterborough the big engine, running on the level and slight rise, attained a rate of 60 miles an hour in $3\frac{1}{2}$ miles from the dead start. Passing Tallington the speed was 65, and after Essendine it was still as high as 64.2. Up the 3 miles at 1 in 178 immediately preceding Stoke summit a minimum of 56 was maintained. But just after the summit had been reached we encountered a bad signal check. This was followed by a still worse signal check at Ponton and then by a dead stop for 2 minutes 40 seconds at Saltersford Box. These hindrances delayed us altogether for fully $7\frac{1}{4}$ minutes and we did not pass Grantham until we were 38 minutes 16 seconds from Peterborough, in spite of all our fine running, and a late arrival at our destination seemed imminent. But the resources of No 251 were not yet exhausted. We passed Newark in 13 minutes

3 seconds from Grantham, Retford at greatly reduced speed, and after another relaying slack, in 31 minutes 11 seconds, having sustained a steady and unswerving rate of 60 miles an hour up the ascent of 1 in 200 to Askham. Up the length of nearly 3 miles at 1 in 198 to Pipers Wood summit our rate never went below 60.8 miles an hour, and we finally stopped at Doncaster more than a minute before time, having run the $79\frac{1}{2}$ miles from Grantham[51] in 86 minutes 33 seconds inclusive, start to stop . . . and 83 minutes 23 seconds travelling time, and $78\frac{1}{2}$ minutes net—that is to say, after deducting the delays caused by a signal stop of 2 minutes 40 seconds and three bad slacks. Clearly this represents excellent locomotive work, and it should be added that, so far from the engine being in any way 'extended', the speed was persistently kept under on all the downward grades, and at other points where a considerable gain in time could have been accomplished. As a matter of fact the rate seldom was allowed to exceed 70 miles an hour. Once or twice it reached 72, and twice just touched 73.8 for a single quarter-mile. No 251 was undoubtedly running well within her means, and could have 'cut time' very materially on each of the two stages had this been desired. Her large boiler supplied abundance of steam throughout; in fact during the greater part of the journey she was blowing off vigorously. Mr Ivatt's newest departure is an unquestionable success, and I was not surprised to hear during a recent visit to the Doncaster workshops that an order had been given to construct no fewer than twenty of the '251' class, which is evidently to be the standard express type henceforward on the Great Northern.

---

[51] An obvious mistake for Peterborough—and a sign that Rous-Marten was not in the habit of reading his articles through to correct them before sending them in for publication.

Performance by a Stirling 8-footer single-wheeler contrasted with that of a large-boilered Ivatt 'Atlantic', on the same train out of Kings Cross

Rous-Marten is here dealing with a contention, made in certain engineering circles, that it was a waste of money to build such heavy engines as the Great Northern 'Atlantics' when their tractive power appeared to be no greater than those of Patrick Stirling's 8-foot singles. He agrees that the relations between wheels and cylinders suggest on the face of it that the latter engines have a larger tractive force than the former, but points out that what also matters is the ability continuously to supply steam to the cylinders, and that the extra adhesion weight on the two pairs of coupled wheels makes it possible to exert the tractive effort without slipping taking place. He then goes on to describe similar runs with different engines to emphasize his point.

The single-wheeler often does splendid work. To this day you may see this on the Midland, Great Northern, Great Western and North Eastern, and even on the London and North Western with those 'tiny tots', Mr Ramsbottom's 'Problems', which date from the 'fifties'. But they are not trustworthy as servants of all work. They are essentially racers and will not do for cart-horse service. And yet we do see them performing work which seems impossible—which *is* impossible according to certain old-fashioned theories made in the seventies. Once, travelling north by the 1.30 pm Great Northern Railway express from Kings Cross I had from Peterborough to Doncaster No 667, one of the smaller class of 8 ft single-wheelers with cylinders 18 in by 28 in. The load was reckoned as '20 coaches' weighing 276 tons behind the tender, and the booked average speed from start to stop was 51.8 miles an hour, the time allowed for the $79\frac{1}{2}$ miles being 92 minutes while there were the respective banks to Stoke, Askham and Pipers Wood at 1 in 178, 1 in 200 and 1 in 198 respec-

tively. Moreover there was a strong side wind blowing most of the way. Well, we didn't do it in 92 minutes, but we *did* do it in $93\frac{1}{2}$ minutes—93 minutes 32 seconds to be quite exact, average 51 miles an hour. The distance of $23\frac{3}{4}$ miles from the Peterborough start to Stoke summit occupied 32 minutes 59 seconds, and the minimum rate up the final 3 miles of 1 in 178 was 37.8 miles an hour. Up the 1 in 200 approaching Askham it was 40.9 miles an hour. Grantham was passed in 38 minutes 51 seconds from the Peterborough start, Retford in 35 minutes 32 seconds from Grantham—distance 33 miles—and Doncaster in 54 minutes 41 seconds from Grantham, $50\frac{1}{2}$ miles. Now this was surely very excellent work, especially as the side wind constituted a serious hindrance. On the same occasion No 98, another of the class, ran from Kings Cross to Peterborough, hauling 246 tons, in 87 mins 29 secs inclusive, or 85 mins net, a relaying slack to 10 miles an hour being experienced *en route*. In this case Potters Bar was passed in 19 mins 58 secs from Kings Cross, at a minimum speed of 41 miles an hour. and a distance of $52\frac{1}{4}$ miles was covered in the first hour from the London start. Here again the work was clearly good, and other instances might be given of equal or nearly equal merit. But assuredly each locomotive was being 'flogged' to her utmost.

Here we have two remarkable specimens of what the old 8 ft singles of the 1870 design could do. But now let us see what one of the new Atlantics could do, and did, on that same train, only with 60 tons heavier load. In the first place, No 294, with 306 tons, went up the bank to Potters Bar at a sustained minimum speed of 52.8 miles an hour, as against the single-wheeler's 41 miles an hour with the smaller load, 246 tons. Secondly the Atlantic got past Potters Bar . . . in 16 mins 23 secs from the Kings Cross start, as compared with No 98's 19 mins 58 secs. Thirdly, No 294 passed Hitchin in 34 mins 33 secs, and No 98 took 40 mins 48 secs. Fourthly, No 294 covered the $5\frac{1}{2}$ miles from Huntingdon to Abbots Ripton[52], which includes 3 miles' rise at 1 in 200, in 4 mins 37 secs, the speed never going below 60 miles an hour; No 98 took 6 mins 48 secs over the same length. Fifthly, the maximum speed attained down 1 in 200 was 77.5 miles an hour by No 294, 70.6 miles an hour by No 98. So at all points the Atlantic did vastly better work of the two.

But let us compare also the second stage of the same journey, that from Peterborough to Doncaster. The same Atlantic went through with unchanged load. The single-wheeler, No 98, went off at Peterborough, another of the same class,

No 667, coming on with 30 tons additional load. The Atlantic engine with 306 tons performed the journey of $79\frac{1}{2}$ miles at 83 mins 3 secs with a very bad relaying slack, or in 81 mins net. The 8 ft single took 93 mins 32 secs without any intermediate check. No 294 got through Grantham in 31 mins 34 secs from Peterborough, the minimum rate up the 1 in 178 to Stoke Summit being 52.4 miles an hour. No 667 took 38 mins 51 secs . . . and dropped to 37.8 miles an hour up the 1 in 178. Up the 1 in 200 to Askham No 294 maintained 53 miles an hour; No 667 fell to 40.9 with 30 tons less load.

Here then is a perfectly fair comparison between the performances of two typical locomotives, each 'on its best behaviour', in practically identical circumstances and under the same conditions[53], the case moreover being one in which the work of the single-wheeler was so fine as to be almost impossible under the old theories . . . eg sustaining 60 miles an hour on the dead level with 276 tons behind her tender, although her nominal tractive force for each lb of effective cylinder pressure was only $94\frac{1}{2}$ lbs instead of the 100 lbs supposed to be needed to maintain that speed on the level with only 150 tons. Nobody can pretend that this was other than good work. Yet we find an Atlantic beating it 'hands down' on every point—even in maximum downhill speed.

[52] The distance is $4\frac{1}{2}$, not $5\frac{1}{2}$ miles.

[53] It does not appear that the circumstances and conditions *were* identical. Rous-Marten makes it plain that the single-wheeler No 667 had to cope with the effect of a stiff side wind, with its consequent braking effect on all the train's lee-side wheels as they were pressed against the rail. Nothing is said about the Atlantic having to overcome that sort of disadvantage.

GREAT CENTRAL RAILWAY

JUNE 1904

Performances of Robinson 4–6–0s between Marylebone and Leicester

My May article concluded with a brief account of an experience with one of the new Atlantics designed and built for the Great Central Railway by Mr J. G. Robinson. My June article must begin with a still more remarkable experience with one of the other new types, . . . that constructed on the 4–6–0 plan . . . which differs from the Atlantics solely in having a third pair of coupled 6 ft 9 in wheels instead of a small pair of carrying wheels behind the firebox. It was so entirely obvious that a locomotive having six-coupled 6 ft 9 in wheels, cylinders 19½ by 26 inches, 1,911 square feet of heating surface and 180 pounds of steam pressure would be able almost to haul, at slow speed, the Marylebone station itself, were the building placed upon wheels, that my chief interest was in ascertaining the capacity in respect of sheer speed of the new engine whose hauling power was manifestly indisputable.[54] So Mr Robinson very courteously put No 196 of this class to work the 4.30 pm Manchester express from Marylebone to Leicester, which has the fastest booked time on the Great Central system, viz, Finmere to Leicester, 48 miles 50 chains, in 50 minutes—58.6 miles an hour from start to stop. The load, as on the occasion of my run with the new Atlantic, was approximately 150 tons behind the tender, and manifestly a very inadequate one for an engine of such enormous power. I need not devote much space to the first stage, namely Marylebone to Finmere, as the time allowance for the 54 miles 37 chains was 69 minutes, representing an average of 47.4 miles an hour, expect to remark that, travelling as I did on the footplate, I found the engine 'ride' very well and steadily, especially for a six-coupled on a roughish road, distinctly not so well suited as it might be for express running.[55] When we got on to the Great Central proper at Quainton Road the difference was strongly marked on the favourable side. As a matter of fact, however, we covered the 54 miles 37 chains in 65 minutes 44 seconds, or in 59¾ minutes net, notwithstanding that we had a bad relaying slack near Pinner and were stopped dead by signal at Wendover for 1 minute 1 second, while as usual we were slowed down severely past Aylesbury

---

[54] Robinson, when ordering his first 'Jersey Lily' 'Atlantics', asked for two of the batch to be built as 4–6–0s, identical in all respects with the rest except in the wheel arrangement, for purposes of comparison. Nos 195 and 196 were the only ones so built, Robinson evidently concluding that the Atlantic wheel arrangement was adequate for the light express trains on his line, though others resembling the 4–6–0s but with smaller wheels were later built for freight traffic.

[55] The 'roughish road' was the Metropolitan Country extension, which was not intended for express running when it was built. Great Central trains used it from Harrow to Quainton Road.

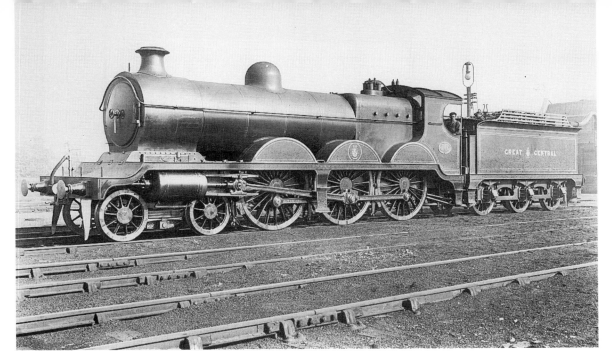

GCR 4–6–0 No 196, built by Robinson in 1904 as one of a pair similar in all respects to the two-cylinder 'Atlantics' except in having six-coupled wheels in place of four-coupled and trailing wheels. They were built for comparison with the 'Atlantics', but were evidently not regarded as significantly better performers as no more were constructed. An astonishing piece of work performed by No 196 is logged by Rous-Marten in the accompanying extract. (NRM)

and round the Rickmansworth curve. Our actual average rate, from start to stop, was 54 miles an hour.

But obviously the interest of the run centred in the second stage, that from Finmere to Leicester, and this run proved to be an exceedingly remarkable one, albeit not in a way that I had hoped and expected. Unfortunately another express leaves Marylebone at 4 pm, just half an hour in front of the 4.30 pm, and this train stops at several stations, including Woodford, where it picks up traffic from Bournemouth, Portsmouth, Southampton, Reading, etc. On the occasion under notice it happened to be delayed at Woodford for these connections; consequently it left only just before we rushed through Woodford station, our train being somewhat in advance of booked time. And then came trouble. Approaching Charwelton, 2 miles beyond Woodford[56], we had overtaken the

4 pm train and were slowed to walking pace. We were then allowed to proceed, but only to be brought to a dead stand at Charwelton station. However, we had done the distance of 17 miles 3 chains from the Finmere start in 17 minutes 36 seconds, or in $16\frac{1}{2}$ minutes net. At Charwelton we were stopped for 84 seconds. When we were allowed to go on again, the driver (Johnson), a particularly smart man, made immediate effort to recover the lost time. The rapidity with which he regained full speed may be gauged from the fact that when we were again stopped by signal at the next station, Willoughby, we had run the distance of 7 miles 3 chains in the extraordinary time of 7 minutes 39 seconds—a start-to-stop performance for so short a distance absolutely unique in my experience. It is true that the line falls at 1 in 176 practically the whole way, but even allowing for that, the run will I think be admitted to be almost marvellous, keeping in view the fact that the start had to be made, full speed reached and the slowing to a stop effected all within that brief time. At Rugby we were slowed once more by signal, and about 2 miles beyond

[56] Charwelton station is $2\frac{1}{2}$ miles from Woodford. The '2 miles' is evidently the distance from Woodford to the point where Rous-Marten's train was stopped.

we were for a third time stopped dead, this time at Shawell Box, where we remained at a dead stand for 2 minutes 2 seconds. The slower train still kept in our way and checked us very badly both at Lutterworth and Ashby. Now when it is remembered that we had been stopped dead three times in this run, for 4 minutes 10 seconds altogether, and badly slowed four times in addition, it will easily be perceived that there was not much margin left for doing the distance of 48 miles 50 chains in 50 minutes. In fact this had manifestly become impossible, and the inclusive time taken was 56 minutes 3 seconds—or, deducting the time at an actual dead stand, 51 minutes 53 seconds, with three extra startings and stoppings and four different slowings. In ordinary experience 3 minutes would be allowed for each of the three extra startings and stoppings, and 2 minutes for each of the four slowings. That would make 17 minutes altogether. But I do not suggest for one moment that this was the time actually lost, because that would leave a manifest impossibility, implying that the net time for the $48\frac{1}{2}$ miles was less than 36 minutes. Still, it certainly could not have much, if at all, exceeded 40 minutes, and this seems to me to illustrate very strikingly the singular quickness with which the new engines start and gather speed. But a notable illustration and proof of this was furnished by what I may call our last stage before Leicester, namely the final length of 9 miles 10 chains from Ashby station, where we slowed to 10 miles an hour, to the dead stop just outside the Leicester platform. That distance was covered in the very extraordinary time of 7 minutes 49 seconds from the slow pass to the final stop.[57] Once more this was done on an almost continuously falling grade of 1 in 176[58],

but it still wholly eclipses any performance of the sort that has ever come under my notice, and I offer my cordial congratulations to Mr Robinson on what I cannot but think a marvellous achievement by his splendid engine. The engine never reached her full limit of maximum speed, but still attained a faster rate than I have ever before recorded to the credit of a six-coupled locomotive.

I returned with No 195 . . . which is identical with No 196 save in having $\frac{1}{2}$-inch more cylinder diameter. This train of 175 tons was simply played with by the fine engine. The driver (Turner) handled her in all respects excellently, but as we got away from Leicester with absolute punctuality no opportunity offered for really 'extending' the engine. The run from Leicester to Woodford, 34 miles 1 chain, was done in 36 minutes 15 seconds, steaming very easily, and the 69 miles 6 chains from Woodford to Marylebone took 79 minutes 11 seconds, done also under very easy steaming. Even so the actual running time from Leicester to Marylebone, 103 miles 7 chains, where we arrived 3 minutes early, was only 115 minutes 26 seconds, allowing nothing for the starting and stopping at Woodford or for the service slows at Quainton Road, Aylesbury, Rickmansworth and Pinner. We had a strong side wind during each journey, so that the conditions were by no means so favourable as they might have been. All the more credit is due to the new giants.

[57] The time is so extraordinary as to verge on the impossible and one wonders if Mr Rous-Marten did not misread his watch.

[58] Not 'almost continuously'; it falls at that grade for 5 miles and then levels out.

MAY 1907

Runs behind compound 'Atlantics' between Marylebone and Leicester

Apart from his multiplication of the compounds, Mr Robinson continues to multiply his non-compound Atlantics. I had No 1088 on the 10 am down express the other day, and No 363 on the up express from Manchester as far as Leicester. Both did all right but the former was badly handicapped by permanent way delays on the new road *via* Wycombe, and hence was late into Leicester after, however, some capital running. She was driven by Dulson, who gave me my record run of 2 hours 48 minutes from Marylebone to Sheffield.

As for the compounds, I had No 258 on the 3.25 ex Marylebone, which on this occasion was sent *via* Aylesbury, owing to the condition of the Wycombe route. The load to Leicester consisted of a dining car and four eight-wheelers, or approximately 150 tons behind the tender. Chapman was the driver. Carefully observing the prescribed slacks, we got through Aylesbury in 45 min 21 sec and passed Quainton Road Junction in 52 min 49 sec from the London start. Clear now of the Metropolitan Railway, we began to go ahead, maintaining 60 miles an

GCR 4-4-2 No 264, built by Robinson in 1904, one of a class of 31 which was arguably the most graceful 'Atlantic' ever to be built for any railway anywhere. All but four were two-cylindered; the exceptions were three-cylinder compounds. The picture shows the beautiful livery — Brunswick green with red framing — with the GCR coat of arms on each splasher and on each tender side. These engines were popularly known as 'Jersey Lilies', a reference to the celebrated actress Lily Langtry. (NRM)

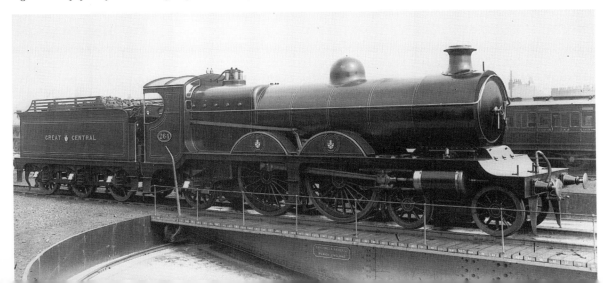

GCR 4-4-2 No 258 Rt. Hon. Viscount Cross, G.C.B., G.C.S.I. *(surely one of the longest names ever to be carried on any locomotive). Comparison of this with the previous illustration shows almost no difference in appearance; in fact, the compound's outside cylinders were 1½ inches greater in diameter.* (NRM)

hour up the bank of 1 in 176 and attaining 81.8 down the corresponding descents. The train passed through Leicester in exactly 108 min from Marylebone, having averaged 57.2 miles an hour, and the slip coach in which I travelled came to a stand there a few seconds later. Our time for the 60 miles[59] from Quainton Road Junction to Leicester was 55 min 20 sec, with a slack at each end - decidedly smart work. Who said that compounds cannot attain high speeds?

In the opposite direction I had No 259 *King Edward VII* as my engine, and a load of about 120 tons behind the tender. The train was the 1.45 pm up ex Leicester, which is booked to run thence to High Wycombe, 79½ miles[60], in 81 minutes, averaging 58.9 miles an hour.[61] Bell was the driver. We started brilliantly from Leicester on an up grade[62] and we were doing 60 miles an hour when only 3 minutes had elapsed. Once more the uphill work was excellent and the downhill running remarkably free. The engine was never pushed, and was not allowed to exceed 82 miles an hour, which she could very easily have done. When we had run 57½ miles from the Leicester start, in 52 minutes, we were brought to a dead stand by adverse signals near Grendon Underwood. Nevertheless, although we were detained 3 minutes there, and lost fully 5½ minutes by the stop, we reached High Wycombe in 79 min 26 sec inclusive from Leicester, 1 min 34 secs under booked time. Our actual travelling time was only 76 min 24 secs for the 79½ miles, and our net time 74 min, certainly a capital run. Thenceforward to London the permanent way delays rendered it futile even to time the journey. But the Leicester–High Wycombe spurt entirely sufficed to show what the compounds could do in the way of smart travelling. Both were excellently managed by the drivers, Chapman and Bell respectively.

Another run that I made on the Great Central

[59] It is in fact only 59 miles.

[60] The distance is actually 79.8 miles . . .

[61] . . . and so the average speed was higher, 59.1 mph.

[62] Incorrect. The start from Leicester is on a level grade for ¼ mile, then follows ¼ mile down at 1 in 140 and another short level stretch. The line does not begin to rise until a mile out of Leicester, and the grades are fairly easy until the 1 in 176 is reached 3 miles further on.

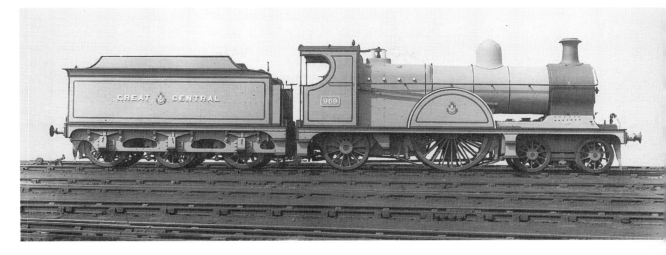

Above *GCR 4-2-2 No 969, built in 1899 by H. Pollitt, for running lightly-loaded expresses on the newly-opened London extension. It was the only single-wheeler type to be built with a Belpaire firebox. Increasing loads on the London main line eventually caused all these single-wheelers to be relegated to the Cheshire Lines Committee's route from Manchester to Liverpool (locomotive power for which was provided by the GCR) where they continued to provide an efficient and punctual service until the 'twenties.* (NRM)

Below *GCR 4-4-0 No 1035, of class '11B', climbing Whetstone bank with a train from Nottingham to Marylebone. It was built in 1902 by the Locomotive Superintendent, J.G. Robinson, who succeeded Pollitt and remained in charge of the locomotive department until the end of the GCR's separate existence in 1923. A run behind a sister-engine is described by Rous-Marten in the accompanying extract.* (Ken Nunn Collection, Locomotive Club of Great Britain)

Railway was by the 6.18 pm express from Leicester to Marylebone, which is booked to perform the journey of 103 miles in 2 hrs 4 min inclusive, with three intermediate stops, viz, at Woodford, Aylesbury and Northwood, and to do the 34 miles from Leicester to Woodford in 35 min, start to stop, averaging 58.3 miles an hour, this being the second fastest booked run on the Great Central Railway. The engine was No 1021[63] . . . The load comprised five eight-wheelers, six fish wagons and one van, 12 vehicles, reckoned on that line as '17 coaches'

but on most other railways as '$14\frac{1}{2}$'.[64] This load proved too much for the locomotive at such a fast timing. We lost no less than 7 minutes from Leicester to Woodford, taking 42 minutes instead of 35 minutes, and continued to lose time all along, ultimately reaching Maryleborne 20 minutes late. This was disappointing, but in view of what I have seen sister engines do I cannot think that any fault lay with the locomotive. Nor can I attribute any sluggishness to the driver, for he certainly seemed to be pushing his engine 'for all he was worth'. I must leave the riddle unsolved.

[63] Not an 'Atlantic' but one of an earlier class of 4–4–0 built by Robinson soon after he became Locomotive Superintendent on the GCR, with 6 ft 9 in coupled wheels.

[64] Probably well over 200 tons—a considerable weight for the GC line's London Extension.

NORTH EASTERN RAILWAY

JUNE 1902

Journeys from Leeds to Scarborough and back behind 'I' class 4–2–2s, from Darlington to York behind 'R' class 4–4–0s, and from Darlington to York and Newcastle to Berwick behind an 'S1' class 4–6–0

I find among my notes of 1901 some . . . very interesting performances, both by the newest North Eastern and by some of the older locomotive types. Beginning with the earlier-built, I may mention that whereas all the ten latest and largest of Mr T. W. Worsdell's two-cylinder compound single-wheelers, Nos 1517–1526, have long been converted by Mr Wilson Worsdell into simple high-pressure engines, all of the earlier and smaller ten, Nos 1326–1330 and 1527–1531, have remained until a comparatively recent date in their original shape as compounds. It has been the fashion to speak somewhat disparagingly of the earlier batch as altogether feeble and incapable machines. My own experience of them has not supported that unfavourable view. I have always found them do well even with very considerable loads. But I understand that the fiat has gone forth for their conversion into the non-compound type, and one day, not long since, I had No 1330 on the 'Leeds–Scarborough Special', the fast express which leaves Leeds every evening at 5.5 and runs to Scarborough, 67¾ miles, passing through York without halting. The load was the usual light one, of five bogie coaches, weighing in all 126 tons . . . No 1330 made a very fine run, doing the journey from Leeds to Scarborough start to stop in 72 minutes 14 seconds inclusive, with a bad relaying slack at Waterloo Junction and a worse

signal check at Huttons Ambo, the latter very nearly a stop. The net time from Leeds to Scarborough was only 69¼ minutes, making no allowance for the regular service slacks at Church Fenton Junction, at York station and round the Kirkham curves. This was one of the best runs I have had with that splendid train. A speed of 80.3 miles an hour was attained down the Micklefield bank, and the final stage of 42 miles from York (passing) to Scarborough (stop) was covered in 41 minutes 44 seconds net. The last 21 miles from Malton to the Scarborough stop occupied 20 minutes 40 seconds. All the prescribed service slacks were most strictly observed. I should add that No 1330, which is a 7 ft single-wheeler, with leading bogie, and which formerly had one 18 in high-pressure cylinder and one 26-in low pressure cylinder, with 24 in piston stroke, now as converted by Mr Wilson Worsdell has two 18 in high-pressure cylinders. Those ten engines in their rebuilt shape ought to be very efficient when used on duty that suits them, such as the working of these special seaside expresses. Indeed, No 1330's performance on the occasion under notice proved her to be an ideal locomotive for that class of service.

Equally suitable, and of course more powerful, are the engines more commonly employed on that duty, the ten 7 ft 6 in single-wheelers already referred to which, formerly compounds,

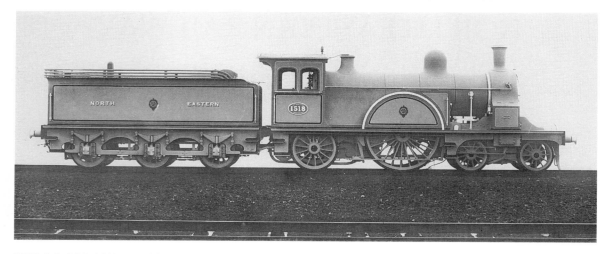

NER 4–2–2 No 1518, one of the Worsdell-von Borries type of two-cylinder compounds built by Thomas Worsdell in 1888. In these locomotives a smaller high-pressure cylinder passed steam into a larger adjacent low-pressure cylinder, and there was some difficulty getting an even torque. Thomas Worsdell's successor, his nephew Wilson Worsdell, did not share his uncle's enthusiasm for compounding, and converted all these single-wheelers into simple-expansion engines. (NRM)

had also been rebuilt as non-compounds. On my return trip from Scarborough to Leeds by the corresponding morning train leaving Scarborough at 8.35 am, I had No 1518, which en-

joys a special individual celebrity among the ten of her class as having made several particularly swift runs. It was No 1518, in fact, which ran the first of the 'racing' trains in 1895 on the

NER 4–4–0 No 1621, one of a batch built by Wilson Worsdell in 1892–1893 and which took part in the 'Race to Aberdeen' in 1895, hauling the racing train between York and Newcastle on the final night of the race, August 21st–22nd. The locomotive illustrated made a fast run, 80½ miles in 78½ minutes, but its sister-engine No 1620 put this performance completely in the shade by running the 124½ miles from Newcastle to Edinburgh in 113 minutes. The latter engine, restored to its original condition, is preserved at the National Railway Museum, York. (NRM)

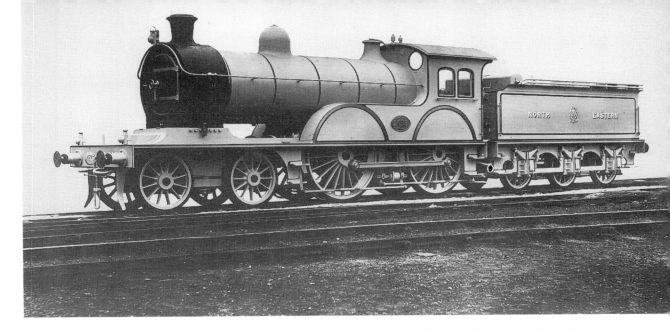

NER 4-4-0 No 2019, of the 'R' class, the largest type of 4-4-0 to appear on this railway, built by Wilson Worsdell during 1899–1902. The 'fastest train in the British Empire', the mid-day express from Newcastle to Sheffield, was regularly hauled by one of these engines between Darlington and York, 44.1 miles in 43 minutes, for many years. (NRM)

York–Newcastle stage, when, hauling a train of 180 tons, she made the journey in 92 minutes in spite of 6 minutes delay at the Durham viaduct reconstruction, the operations involving single-line working, with two dead stops and a double cross-over for the down trains. Thus the net time for the $80\frac{1}{2}$ miles was 86 minutes, which a sister engine, No 1522, with 50 tons less load, succeeded in cutting down to 79 minutes 54 seconds inclusive, or 76 min net. On this more recent occasion No 1518, with the normal train load of 126 tons, ran from the Scarborough start to passing York in 44 minutes 59 seconds, slackening considerably through Malton and round the Kirkham curves. At the next station, Copmanhurst[65], the train was stopped for a hot axle, the 46 miles from Scarborough having been done in 50 minutes 41 seconds.

With the newest North Easterns I had some experiences far more striking. For several days in succession I experimented with the 'fastest train in England', that booked to do the $44\frac{1}{4}$ miles from Darlington to York in 45 minutes, or at an average start-to-stop speed of 58.9 miles an hour. The engine in each case

65 The station is actually called Copmanthorpe.

was No 2020, one of Mr Worsdell's latest type of four-coupled express engines, which have 6 ft 9 in wheels . . . and cylinders 19 in by 26 in, which are in my humble opinion not only the best four-coupled locomotives yet seen on the North Eastern Railway metals, but also among the finest express engines in the whole kingdom. As a matter of fact No 2020 was greatly underloaded with this train, which is usually a light one. During my tests its weight was generally about 140 to 150 tons.

On the first occasion we were stopped by signal at Danby Wiske and again just outside Northallerton, but on making a fresh start we ran the 30 miles from Northallerton to the York stop in 26 minutes 18 seconds, very brilliant work. The highest velocity attained was 76.6 miles an hour. Next time we were again stopped by signal, but nevertheless did the run of $44\frac{1}{4}$ miles from Darlington to York in 43 minutes 8 seconds, or 41 minutes net. On another day we made the run in the fast time of 42 minutes 29 seconds inclusive, with a long and bad slack at Wiske Moor over the place where new water-troughs are being laid down along the track. The actual net time was $39\frac{1}{2}$ minutes, being an average rate of 67.2 miles an hour.

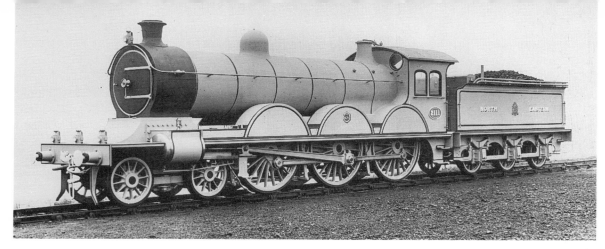

NER 4–6–0 No 2111, of the 'S1' class, built by Wilson Worsdell in 1900 for express passenger trains. Like their contemporaries, the Great Western 'Saints', they proved very fast runners. (NRM)

Another day an effort was made to run at the same timing the first portion of the Anglo-Scottish East Coast afternoon corridor dining-car train, which weighed 260 tons behind the tender. The engine was one of Mr Worsdell's magnificent six-coupled ten-wheelers of the '2111' class, with 6 ft 8 in drivers and cylinders 20 in by 26 in. The run from Darlington to a signal stop just outside York was made with this 260 ton load in 40 minutes 51 seconds start to stop. The highest speed attained was 72 miles an hour, but as a rule a steady 70 was persistently maintained mile after mile. Indeed, after full speed had been reached it never fell below 68 or rose above 72.

In a trial between Newcastle and Berwick, with twelve bogie coaches weighing approximately 300 tons, another engine of the same class, 6 ft 8 in six-coupled, accomplished the journey of 67 miles in 66 minutes 24 seconds inclusive. Two bad checks, one for signals and one for relaying, lost us 3½ minutes, so that the net time did not exceed 63 minutes. A rate of 52.6 miles an hour was maintained up the Longhoughton bank of 1 in 150, and on slightly falling gradients speeds of 80, 81 and 82 miles an hour were several times attained, the engine travelling with notable ease and freedom. With a light train of six bogies another of these splendid engines ran from York to Newcastle in 78 minutes 54 seconds net, easing down for a considerable distance so as not to arrive too early.

DECEMBER   1907

A return journey between York and Newcastle behind a Smith 4–4–2 compound

I have been unable until now to fulfil my promise that I would give some information as to the work performed by Mr Wilson Worsdell's newest North Eastern Railway compounds constructed on the four-cylinder balanced system of the late Mr Walter Smith. Mr Worsdell courteously put No 730, the pioneer of the class, on the down 'Day Scotch' from York to Newcastle. The load behind the tender, including passengers (a crowd) and their luggage (very heavy), staff and stores, was just 300 tons; not a great load as modern loads go, but a good substantial one. We started 2 min late from York and took things very easily at first, not attaining a speed of 60 miles an hour until 10 miles had been covered, or exceeding that rate until Thirsk was passed, the distance of 22 miles from York to that point occupying 25 min 2 sec. Then we went ahead a little more and passed Northallerton at 65.2 miles an hour, 32 min 58 sec from York, distance 30 miles. A bad slack approaching Darlington cost us quite a couple of minutes delay, so we did not pass that station until 45 minutes 18 seconds after leaving York. But for the check we should certainly have done the distance in 1½ minutes less, notwithstanding the very moderate pace at which we had generally travelled. We were only going at 25 miles an hour when we passed Darlington,

and this of course made us later than we should have been through the next important station, Ferryhill. Down the subsequent falling gradient towards Durham speed rapidly improved until we were doing 70 miles an hour, when compelled to slow very badly for permanent way repairs close to Durham station, from which we emerged at a bare walking pace. There is always a bad slack through Durham, but this one was much worse than bad and certainly must have cost us not far short of another 2 min delay. After that we spun along cheerfully, attaining 74 miles an hour near Chester-le-Street and Birtley, and stopping in Newcastle Central station at 3.25 . . . We had got in 8 minutes before time and had gained 10 minutes on the booked travelling allowance.[66] This will be admitted to be distinctly creditable work, equivalent to a run of 83½ minutes net time . . .

[66] Rous-Marten fails to say what the actual time taken was between York and Newcastle, but if, as he says, the delays cost about 4 minutes, it would have been about 87½ minutes.

NER 4-4-2 No 730, one of two four-cylinder compound Atlantics nominally designed by Wilson Worsdell but actually the work of his Chief Draughtsman, Walter Smith. It appeared from Darlington Works just before the latter's early death in 1906. The illustration is a posed shot at the head of a stationary train. (NRM)

A few days later I travelled from Newcastle to York by the corresponding train in the opposite direction. No 730 was again the engine, through the courteous arrangement of Mr Worsdell. Of this journey also I am compelled to say that it calls for no special comment. Everything was really too propitious to afford the engine sufficient difficulty to enable her to put forth her powers without arriving unduly in advance of booked time. The load, too, was slightly less than on the down journey, approximately 280 tons behind the tender. We ascended the stiffish bank of 1 in 150 to 1 in 120 past Chester-le-Street[67] at a minimum rate of 52.5 miles an hour which, however, dropped to 47.4 at the summit near Plawsworth.[68] At Durham we again had the same dread permanent way slack to walking pace as on the down journey and, as in that case, we were slowed by signal through Darlington. However, we gained more than

3½ minutes on the booked time from Newcastle to York, performing the run in 92 minutes 24 seconds, and we ran into York from passing Darlington in 45 min 53 sec. The same engine continued on to Doncaster but, the road and the booking both being easy, the latter 40 minutes for the 32¼ miles, no scope was offered for locomotive brilliance. However we had a relaying slack about 2 miles out of York, which cost us fully a minute, and we service-slowed past Selby to 15 miles an hour. So we did very respectably to get to Doncaster in 38 min 34 sec from the York start.

These performances, while in no way sensational or spectacular, represent good solid locomotive work and reflect distinct credit upon this latest type of English compound locomotive. Whether the type will be deemed, as the result of experience, to perform work sufficiently superior to that accomplished by the less costly simple-expansion engines to warrant the additional cost of compounding remains yet to be seen. It would be premature at the present time to pronounce a decided opinion. It is however very satisfactory to find, at any rate, one British system of compounding is having a fairly extensive trial.

---

[67] There is *no* gradient of steeper pitch than 1 in 150 until Durham.

[68] It is difficult to see what Rous-Marten means. You cannot have two minimum speeds on the same ascent unless there is a speed-up between them, and he does not say there was one.

LANCASHIRE AND YORKSHIRE RAILWAY

JULY 1902

Journeys behind Aspinall inside-cylindered 4–4–2 'Highflyers' and an Aspinall 4–4–0, with light loads, between Manchester and Liverpool

So far I am not aware that any public record has appeared of work by the huge ten-wheeled Lancashire and Yorkshire Railway engines with which Mr J. A. F. Aspinall startled the railway world some four years or so ago. It is true that certain penny-a-lining 'yarns' have been spun about imaginary 100-miles-an-hour runs between Manchester and Southport, but these were promptly contradicted and apparently the fictionists became discouraged, for no more romances on that subject have come out of late. The performances of these engines are however sufficiently fine to need no mendacious embellishment. The engines themselves have . . . four 7 ft 3 in coupled wheels, leading bogie and trailing pair of carrying wheels, vast boilers with 2,052 square feet of heating surface, a large Belpaire firebox, 175 lbs steam pressure and a weight of $58\frac{3}{4}$ tons in working order, exclusive of tender. It would at once be assumed from the mere aspect of these locomotive giants, or even from a recital of their dimensions, that they could pull anything in the way of loads that could be accommodated by stations and sidings. But at the first glance a casual observer is apt to wonder whether these great ponderous machines can really be swift. They offer so striking a contrast to the slender and graceful Midland single-wheelers and Great Northern eight-footers and London and North Western 'Problems'—each of which is the ideal type of railway

greyhound—or to the small-boilered Midland '2600' coupled class, which are also famed for their swiftness, that at first glance it seems absurd to think of such giants as flyers. But just as Dr W. G. Grace's immense height and bulk have not prevented his being the smartest of cricketers, so the apparent lumberingness of the Aspinall '1400s' in no way militates against their capacity for high speed, which I may say is not surpassed by that of any locomotive running in Britain at the present day.

Of this I give some proofs on the strength of my personal observations. I had one of these mighty engines on a train from York which had to run through from Manchester to Liverpool. The load was a light one—a 'featherweight' for such a big engine—as it did not weigh more than about 100 tons behind the tender. Starting from Manchester Victoria station, the locomotive, which was very smartly driven and well handled, gathered speed with such remarkable rapidity that we passed Pendleton, $2\frac{1}{4}$ miles from the start, in 2 minutes 51 seconds . . . Up the rise at 1 in 92 to 1 in 94 which immediately follows and extends for nearly 5 miles[69] we maintained a steady 59 miles an hour, never once dropping below that point except when checked by fog. Down the following descent we flew as if we had

---

[69] Incorrect. The rise is only 2 miles long, pitches of 1 in 99 and 1 in 80 being separated by $\frac{1}{4}$ mile at 1 in 132.

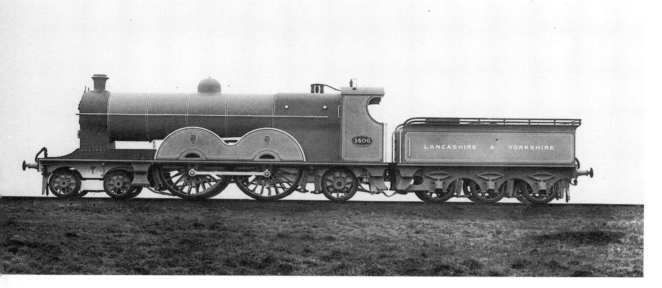

LYR 4–4–2 No 1406, one of a second batch of 20, out of 40 in all, built by Sir John Aspinall for express haulage. Like their 4–4–0 predecessors, these 'Highflyers', as they were called, had 7 ft 3 in driving wheels. With light loads they kept the sharp 40–minute timings between Manchester Victoria and Liverpool Exchange, 36½ miles, with ease, despite the steep gradients en route. (NRM)

been any sort of single-wheeler, the length of 14 miles after Walkden being covered in 11 minutes 41 seconds, while the speed reached 80 miles an hour for a short distance. The last 4 miles of those 14 are on an up grade at 1 in 91[70], up which the speed never went below 61 miles an hour. This was a splendid piece of hill-climbing, even though the load was light. Unluckily, a little before the summit, just outside Orrell station in fact, we were stopped by signal, although only momentarily. So we had then to start afresh on that rising gradient of 1 in 91 with rail rendered very slippery by the mist. The distance of 21 miles from Manchester to the signal stop, which included 8 miles of rising grades at 1 in 91, 1 in 92 and 1 in 94, was run in 20 minutes 13 seconds start to stop.[71]

[70] Incorrect again. Only the last 2 miles are so graded, at 1 in 92.

[71] The distance includes only *4* miles pitched at this sort of gradient.

Again, we made a good start, getting quickly over the summit and then bowling along merrily down the subsequent falling gradient. Some very high speeds were attained, several miles being run at over 83 miles an hour. One quarter-mile was done in exactly ten seconds, most carefully taken by chronograph, but as I did not get the adjacent quarter-mile on either side I am unable to accept it implicitly as a trustworthy record. Even allowing, however, for the ever-present possibility of error when only a single post can be noted, it is certain from the quarter-mile times near at hand on each side of that one which was apparently done in 10 seconds, that the speed could not have been very far, if at all, short of that indicated by the record, viz, 90 miles an hour. Still, it is subject to doubt as standing alone, and so I only give it with that qualification. I may observe, however, that on the following day the same quarter-mile gave me the same record, but again the adjacent posts could not be caught. But the fact that the engine certainly attained a speed of over 87 miles an

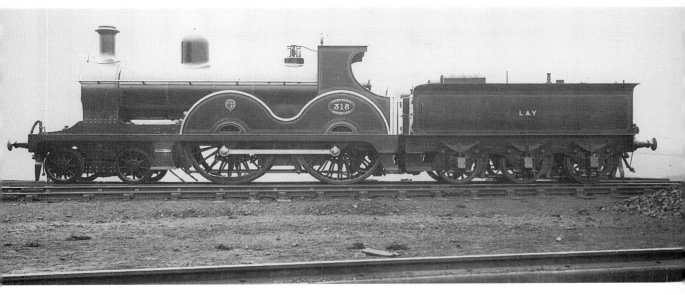

LYR 4–4–0 No 318, built in 1894 by Sir John Aspinall, this line's Locomotive Superintendent; it was one of a class with coupled wheels with the unusually large diameter of 7 ft 3 in. They were intended for hauling lightly-loaded trains west of Manchester, and could certainly travel fast downhill. (NRM)

hour shows how exceedingly swift are these big and seemingly lumbering locomotives.

Outside Sandhills another signal stop was experienced, this one lasting 2 min 38 secs. Nevertheless the whole journey of 36 miles 47 chains from Manchester to Liverpool[72] was done in 40 minutes 44 seconds inclusive of all delays. These comprised two dead stops, one of 2 minutes 38 seconds duration, and a slack. Thus the actual travelling time, start to stop, was only 38 minutes 6 seconds, and if all the delays be deducted the actual net time comes out as 33 minutes 21 seconds. The run from Manchester to Sandhills, 35 miles 2 chains, was done in 34 minutes 33 seconds, with a stop in the middle.

On the following day I repeated the run, but had one of Mr Aspinall's '1093' class of 7 ft 3 in

coupled, cylinders 18 in in diameter—formerly 19 in—and 26 in piston stroke. The load was approximately 120 tons behind the tender, slightly heavier than on the previous day. The run was much impeded by fog and by signal checks, two very bad slacks bringing down the speed to a walking pace, while there was a dead stop just outside the Liverpool Exchange station. The net running time was 39 minutes 27 seconds. Again there was some very fast running after Upholland, and again as I have already mentioned my stop-watch showed a particular quarter-mile to be covered in 10 seconds, a record which, however, in the absence of seconds for the adjacent quarter-miles I can only receive with serious qualification. Still, as on the previous occasion, several miles were certainly run at a speed of well over 83 miles an hour.

These engines have always been a very successful type since their cylinders were lined up from 19 in to 18 in. One of them, No 1112, has been converted into an experimental four-cylinder compound by Mr H. A. Hoy, who succeeded Mr Aspinall as Chief Mechanical

[72] Decimalised, this comes to 36.59 miles, but the gradient profile suggests that it was just about 36.4 miles, which is the distance given in a log of a journey over the same line timed by Mr Cecil J. Allen. It is possible that the typesetter misread 47 for 41.

Engineer at Horwich, on Mr Aspinall accepting the General Managership of the Lancashire and Yorkshire Railway. This engine as converted is still in its stage of trial, and it would be premature to express any opinion as to the likelihood or otherwise of the type being perpetuated or multiplied.

In the opposite direction, viz, Liverpool to Manchester, the maximum speeds were not in my experience nearly so high, never exceeding 75 miles an hour. One of the large '1400' class, with 120 tons, ran from Liverpool (Exchange) to Manchester (Victoria), 36 miles 47 chains[73], in 40 minutes 19 seconds, notwithstanding signal delays that lost us three minutes, leaving a net

time of only $37\frac{1}{4}$ minutes. On a second occasion with the same engine and 140 tons load the time for the $36\frac{1}{2}$ miles was 40 minutes 48 seconds, with three slacks for signals or relaying, leaving the net time 38 minutes. All these are very good performances, even allowing for the lightness of the loads, for the fact that grades of 1 in 91, 1 in 92, 1 in 94, 1 in 100 and 1 in 110 have to be faced for 10 miles one way[74], and 1 in 96, 1 in 111 and 1 in 150 for 9 miles in the opposite direction[74], implies that some stiff climbing has to be done by the locomotives when running trains booked at an average speed of 54.9 miles an hour from start to stop.

[73] See above, note 72.

[74] Incorrect—for $5\frac{1}{2}$ miles at most, in both instances.

LONDON AND SOUTH WESTERN RAILWAY

JUNE 1904

A record run between Plymouth and Waterloo behind a small-wheeled and a large-wheeled Drummond 'Greyhound' on April 23rd 1904

On April 23rd the London and South Western Railway not only broke but utterly demolished all its own records and also all Great Western Railway records up to that date between Plymouth and Exeter and London. The occasion was . . . the third special trip for the conveyance to London of the passengers from an American steamer. The special train consisted of four corridor bogies, including a dining and kitchen car, the total weight including passengers and baggage being about 105 tons. The engine . . . was No 399, one of the new and larger class which has 6 foot driving wheels, four coupled, 19 in cylinders and a bigger boiler than the class to which No 336 belonged, which worked the latter half of the journey, No 336 having 6 ft 7 in coupled wheels, 18½ inch cylinders and a smaller boiler.

The departure point whence we started at 3.59.21 pm was the Stonehouse Pool Junction, a little more than a quarter of a mile west of Devonport station, from which we emerged at 4.0.42. Very quickly picking up speed along the level length which extends to a point near St Budeaux, we entered at a speed of 65.2 miles an hour upon the long climb to the Dartmoor summit, up which for something like 25 miles there is an almost unbroken series of gradients such as 1 in 73, 1 in 75, etc. Up these severe grades No 399 did some excellent work, our speed generally being maintained at well over 40 miles an

hour, only once falling so low as 36, from which minimum we speedily recovered to 40.6 and 41.9. During the final stretch of 1 in 73 to the summit[75] our rate was almost exactly 40 miles an hour, and the last 22½ miles to the absolute summit occupied only 30 minutes 58 seconds, which completely distances all my former experiences over that length. The corresponding down grades to Exeter were descended almost continuously without steam at very moderate speeds, it being desired to keep our rate over the hilly portions of the road as approximately uniform as possible. Thus the last 31¾ miles to the Exeter stop occupied 32 minutes 42 seconds, or distinctly under 60 miles an hour. Our time for the 57¼ miles from Devonport to Exeter was 66 minutes 7 seconds.

Once more the Great Western Railway authorities, whose territory the London and South Western Railway crosses at Exeter, exercised the right they claim of stopping all trains at St David's station. But practically the delay was nominal as in any case the speed must not exceed a walking pace through that station, and as a consequence we were able to accomplish a record start-to-stop run from Exeter to London. Getting away from St David's at 5.7.24 and Exeter (Queen Street Station) at 5.9.49, we repeated thence to the end of our first stage, a

---

[75] The final gradient is actually 1 in 78.

LSWR 4–4–0 No 708, built in 1899, one of Dugald Drummond's highly-successful 'T9' 'Greyhounds'. Note the casing covering access to the cross-water-tubes in the firebox, a feature of Drummond's later practice, which increased the heating surface. (NRM)

point about a quarter of a mile west of Templecombe, the same tactics as those which were exercised on the Plymouth–Exeter length; that is to say, we went up the steep grades of 1 in 80, etc, at a great pace, our rate only dropping so low as 47.4 miles an hour up the steepest grade of 1 in 80, and keeping up to 55.5 miles an hour on another grade of 1 in 90, while on the falling gradients we never, except momentarily, exceeded a maximum of 70. Yeovil Junction, 49 miles[76], was passed in 54 minutes 24 seconds from Exeter[77] and No 399 finally stopped dead west of Templecombe at 6.14.14, having run the 117½ miles from Devonport in 2 hours 13 minutes 32 seconds, averaging 52.7 miles an hour, or in 2 hours 14 minutes 53 seconds from the actual starting point a quarter of a mile west of Devonport station.

At Templecombe West No 336 . . . replaced No 399, and the driver, F. Gare, from the first evidently had set his heart upon record-making. We ran through Salisbury station at full speed[78], and after attaining a very high maximum down the descent at 1 in 165 near Porton[79], and also between Worting Junction and Woking, while we were never going at less than 64.2 miles an hour up the bank at 1 in 178 near Whitchurch[80], we finally stopped in the Waterloo terminus at 8.12.12 pm, having run the 112½ miles from Templecombe West to Waterloo in 104 minutes 33 seconds . . . equivalent to an average rate of 65 miles an hour from start to stop. From pass-

---

[76] This is the distance from Queen Street, Exeter, not from St David's. It is actually 48.9 miles.

[77] This was the time from St David's station. Rous-Marten has confused the two. The distance from St David's station to Yeovil Junction is 49.3 miles.

[78] There was a 30 mph limit through Salisbury station, so Driver Gare was a lucky man. See page 60 'On the Salisbury derailment', dealing with the fatal accident that occurred when another boat train tried to negotiate Salisbury station at full speed.

[79] Not 'near Porton' but 'beyond Grateley'. Rous-Marten is getting his stations mixed up.

[80] There is no such gradient near Whitchurch; it occurs further to the west between Andover and Hurstbourne.

ing Salisbury to arriving at Waterloo (83¾ miles) we ran in 76 minutes 30 seconds; from Basingstoke to Waterloo (48 miles) we took 42 minutes 33 seconds, and from Woking to Waterloo (24½ miles) 22 minutes 44 seconds, while in the last hour's running we covered 67 miles. Our running time from Plymouth to London, that is to say deducting the stoppages at Exeter and Templecombe, was 3 hours 58 minutes 17 seconds; our inclusive time from St David's (Exeter) to London was 2 hours 53 minutes 48 seconds; travelling time from St David's to London was 2 hours 52 minutes 4 seconds; and from Exeter (London and South Western station) to London (Waterloo) our running time from passing to stop was 2 hours 49 minutes 39 seconds. The performance throughout was very fine.

The following is a condensed log of this remarkable journey:

Miles	Stations, etc	Mins	Secs
00.00	Plymouth (Stonehouse Junction)	00	00
00.29	Devonport	01	21
02.76	St Budeaux	03	48[81]
16.16	Tavistock	21	27
32.49	Okehampton	42	44
46.86	Yeoford　　　　(SLACK)	56	13
50.54	Crediton　　　(SIG SLACK)	59	47
	(SLACK AT COWLEY BR JUNCTION)		
57.61	Exeter St David's　Arr	67	28
00.00	Dep	00	00
00.34	Exeter Queen Street	02	25
12.87	Sidmouth Junction	16	12
24.11	Seaton Junction	28	55
49.24	Yeovil Junction　　(SLACK)	54	24
60.01	Templecombe　Arr	66	50
00.00	Dep	00	00
26.56	Salisbury	28	03
46.00	Andover Junction	45	09
64.56	Basingstoke	62	00
79.12	Farnborough	74	13
88.02	Woking	81	49
100.37	Surbiton	92	30
108.49	Clapham Junction	99	39
112.44	Waterloo	104	33

Great credit is due to the Traffic Department for the way in which the line was kept clear throughout the whole 230 miles, not one single check being experienced, while the express due at Waterloo at 8.7, which might otherwise have impeded the special, was brought in well in advance of booked time so as to leave a clear road. The performance was most creditable, alike to the Traffic and Locomotive departments.

[81] According to Rous-Marten's log the distance between Devonport and St Budeaux was covered at an average of slightly more than 60 mph. The former station would have been passed at slow speed, and immediately afterwards there follows an adverse gradient of 1 in 132 for a whole mile. The thing seems impossible, and one can only suppose that he either mis-read his watch or his notes.

JULY 1906

Performances of large-boilered Drummond 'Greyhounds' on the main line between Waterloo and Exeter

I have something to say about . . . Mr D. Drummond's newest standard four-coupled express engines on the London and South Western Railway, of which twenty have been built and which are numbered 415-434 . . . They are of the 4–4–0 type and have four coupled driving wheels 6 ft 7 in in diameter, two inside cylinders 19 ins by 26 ins, 1,550 sq ft of heating surface and 175 lbs of steam pressure. I selected for my experiments the fastest trains running regularly on the London and South Western Railway, viz, the 11 am from Waterloo to Exeter and the corresponding up train. The engine on the down train was No 415, the first of the class, and the train was made up of new corridor bogies and a dining car, the whole weighing approximately 200 tons behind the tender. The running was remarkably steady and uniform throughout, the driver aiming rather at even-ness of speed than at anything at all sensational. There was a bad relaying slack near Andover Junction which seriously marred the running on the best length of 'galloping ground' between Waterloo and Salisbury. Nevertheless the engine kept time from start to stop. Surbiton (12 miles) was passed in 15 min 21 sec from Waterloo, Woking (24½ miles) in 29 min 4 sec, Basingstoke (48 miles) in 54 min 48 sec. The minimum rate up the 11 miles of about 1 in 300 approaching Sturt Lane Junction was 56.3 miles an hour and a rate of 60 was steadily maintained up the slight as-

cent from Brookwood to Basingstoke.[82] At Andover Junction the relaying slack already mentioned was encountered, and then came the bank at 1 in 165 near Grateley, near the top of which the speed was 45 miles an hour. Down the final descent towards Salisbury the driver contented himself with a very moderate rate, slightly under 65 miles an hour, and Salisbury was reached in the prescribed time of 92 minutes, from which 1½ minutes should be deducted on account of the delay caused by the relaying check.

At Salisbury No 415 went off and No 399 came on, the load remaining the same. It may perhaps be recollected that this engine was the one which ran the first stage of the London and South Western's 'Record' trip from Plymouth to London on the 23rd April 1904[83] . . . On the present occasion the load of course was very much heavier, in fact nearly double, and in view of this fact the performances of No 399 were in

---

[82] The average speed from Woking to Basingstoke was 54.8 miles an hour. Since the *minimum* speed up the gradient beyond Woking was 56.3 mph and presumably quickened up afterwards, how could the engine have taken so long from Woking to Basingstoke? It seems more likely that 60 miles an hour was maintained for a *part* of that way, on the level through Farnborough and Fleet, but fell off afterwards—unless Rous-Marten was a minute out with his time at Basingstoke.

[83] See the extract immediately preceding this one.

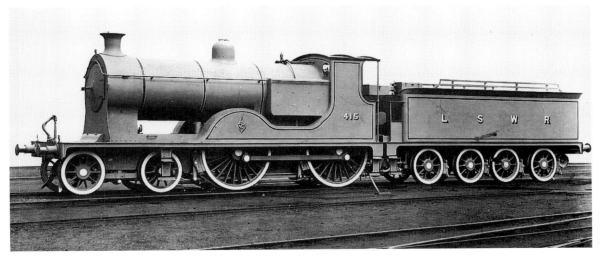

LSWR 4-4-0 No 415, a large-boilered 'Greyhound' of the 'L12' class, built in 1904. A sister-engine, No 421, headed the Ocean Liner Express which was derailed at Salisbury on July 1st 1906 with considerable consequent loss of life; Rous-Marten discusses this incident on pages 60–63. (NRM)

no respect inferior. Getting away from Salisbury very smartly, we passed Dinton, after $8\frac{1}{2}$ miles of continuous ascent[84], in 10 mins 24 secs, and breasted Semley summit, 18 miles[85], in 22 min 43 sec. Then came some very fast running down the falling grades past Templecombe[86] and Sherborne, a speed of 88 miles an hour being attained at one point, when the travelling was perhaps the smoothest of the whole journey. There was a careful slowing past Yeovil Junction, and then came the severe Crewkerne bank, 3 miles at 1 in 80, preceded by 4 miles at 1 in 150.[87] The steeper grade was ascended at a steady minimum pace of 36 miles an hour. Down the

14-mile descent on moderate grades past Axminster a high but not specially great speed was maintained; the maximum was 77.5 miles an hour. Then came the hardest strain of all, the steep ascent approaching Honiton tunnel, where the rise is continually at 1 in 80 for 5 miles on end[88], with $\frac{1}{2}$-mile at 1 in 70 in the middle. This was climbed very steadily, the minimum rate up 1 in 70 being 31 miles an hour. Then succeeded a swift spin down the Honiton bank, where a maximum rate of 86.1 miles an hour was reached, with the usual effect of rendering the running as smooth as if we were sliding over ice. A bad relaying slack near Whimple, which lasted for $1\frac{1}{2}$ miles, delayed us about 1 minute. But the entire run of 88 miles from Salisbury to Exeter was completed from start to stop in 96 min 57 sec inclusive, or in 96 minutes net—very satisfactory work over so exceptionally severe a road.

For the return journey I selected the fast express from Ilfracombe which is booked at practically the same speed as the 12 noon Plymouth express from Exeter to Waterloo, but stops at Sidmouth Junction to pick up two corridor

[84] The ascent is not continuous; there are two marked downhill stretches, $1\frac{1}{2}$ and 2 miles long respectively, and $\frac{1}{2}$ mile of level.

[85] From Salisbury to Semley is actually under $17\frac{1}{2}$ miles.

[86] Not *past* Templecombe, but *before* Templecombe; the latter is in the middle of a steep 3-mile rise.

[87] Rous-Marten's gradient indications are quite incorrect. The alleged '4 miles at 1 in 150' are in fact 4 miles of almost continuous downhill from a minor summit at milepost $126\frac{1}{4}$. Then follow $2\frac{3}{4}$ miles at 1 in 80 past Crewkerne.

[88] Not 5 but $4\frac{1}{2}$ miles, including the half-mile at 1 in 70.

coaches from Sidmouth and Exmouth. The engine was No 399 once more, but the load included an additional corridor coach, the total being approximately 225 to 230 tons behind the tender. On such a road, with an average start-to-stop booking of over 54 miles an hour, this represented a distinctly hard task for the locomotive to perform. The 12 miles run from Exeter to Sidmouth Junction had to be done under easy steam in order to avoid being too much before booked time, the allowance being perhaps a little over-generous. But after starting afresh from Sidmouth Junction with the full load above mentioned, a stiff task had to be faced, beginning with the climb of the Honiton bank, which has grades as steep as 1 in 90 to 1 in 80. Notwithstanding the increased load No 399 went up those steep grades quite as quickly as it had done on the down journey with a somewhat lighter train, the minimum rate up 1 in 80 being again 36 miles an hour. After emerging from the Honiton tunnel a very rapid descent followed past Seaton and Axminster, the distance of 3¼ miles between those stations being covered in 2 mins 26 secs. Past Yeovil Junction we slackened to 10 miles an hour, and then after passing Sherborne we ascended the subsequent bank of 1 in 80 again at a minimum rate of 36, while up the rise of 1 in 90 to 1 in 100 near Templecombe the lowest point touched was exactly 45 miles an hour, and up the subsequent length of 1 in 100 to Semley the minimum was 44. The booked time allowance from Sidmouth to Salisbury was exceeded by a few seconds due to a slight check for relaying.[89] But the performance of the engine with such a load on grades so severe was undoubtedly very creditable.

Engine No 416 came on at Salisbury for the less arduous but still by no means easy final stage to Waterloo, the time allowance being 91 minutes for the 83½ miles, representing an average start-to-stop speed of 55.1 miles an hour.[90] In this case again booked time was kept to the minute in spite of some rather serious delays, once for relaying, near Andover Junction as before, and twice for signals near Wimbledon and Vauxhall respectively, the latter involving a prolonged slack to walking-pace. These three delays, carefully computed, caused a total loss of slightly over 6 minutes, thus leaving the actual net travelling time from Salisbury to London 85 minutes, not far short of the mile-a-minute average. The uphill start from Salisbury was somewhat leisurely, the first 11 miles occupying exactly 16 minutes. Then came the hindrance near Andover, a bad prelude to the ascent of the succeeding rise at 1 in 178 to Whitchurch[91], which latter was performed at a minimum pace of 50 miles an hour. The remainder of the journey, however, was very easy work, and the next 52 miles, viz, to Wimbledon, occupied only 49 min 19 sec, in spite of the signal slack encountered at the latter station, from which we had not fully recovered when a much worse signal check near Queens Road brought us down to a crawl, which lasted past Vauxhall and cost us more than 3 minutes delay in getting into Waterloo. The engine, however, had not only performed the duty prescribed, but had gained fully 6 minutes in the unfavourable circumstances set forth. Mr Drummond may be complimented on the efficiency of his new engines.

---

[89] But what *was* the booked time? We are not told, nor are we given any actual times on the stage west of Salisbury—only speeds at a number of places.

[90] The distance is 83.8 miles, so the booked average speed was 55.25, not 55.1 mph.

[91] Rous-Marten should have written 'to Hurstbourne', not 'to Whitchurch'. Hurstbourne lies 1½ miles beyond the top of the 1 in 178—actually in a slight dip beyond it—and Whitchurch is 2 miles further on still, on a level stretch after a further rise at 1 in 194. If the 'minimum pace of 50' really was at Whitchurch, the engine has presumably gathered speed to reach it, so we are left unsure what the minimum at the top of the 1 in 178 really was.

LONDON, BRIGHTON AND SOUTH COAST RAILWAY

DECEMBER 1902

Performances of Billinton 'B4' 4–4–0s between London and Brighton

So soon as Mr Billinton had to build new express engines he at once adopted the leading-bogie type. He used coupled wheels 3 in larger than those of Mr Stroudley's engines, viz, 6 ft 9 in. Curiously enough, while increasing the diameter of the wheels he diminished that of his cylinders by ¼ in, making them 18 in by 26 in, and also the heating surface of the boilers, viz, from 1,485 square feet to 1,342 square feet. I do not doubt that there may have been some good reason for this apparent reversal of the usual course of action, but I am not aware of it and my readers will not need to be told that my own preference lies in another direction. However the new engines did some very good work and 'the proof of the pudding is in the eating'. The first came out in June 1895, and twenty-four in all were built, the last in January 1898. Perhaps the best-known of this class is No 206 *Smeaton*, which often ran the 60-minute 'Pullman Limited' between London and Brighton when that train was first put on. Testing this service, I timed *Smeaton* with 190 tons from Victoria to Brighton in 59 minutes 9 seconds and from Brighton to Victoria in 58 minutes 32 seconds, both creditable performances. A minimum rate of 45 miles an hour was maintained up the long bank at 1 in 264 approaching Merstham, and 49 miles an hour up that to Balcombe tunnel.

Early in 1898 Mr Billinton brought out a variant of this type, which differed, however, only in the very desirable respect of having a much larger boiler and firegrate. Thus, engine No 213 *Bessemer* was given 1,460 square feet of heating surface instead of 1,342 square feet, and 20.6 square feet of grate area instead of 18.7 square feet. With a load of approximately 200 tons behind her tender *Bessemer* ran from London to Brighton in 63 minutes 44 seconds, and taking the up Sunday Pullman she made the run from Brighton to Victoria in 57 minutes 44 seconds, the best I have ever recorded up to that date and, I believe, the best which had been done.

But Mr Billinton had realised that an engine of altogether larger dimensions and power had become indispensable to grapple with the increasingly heavy traffic of the London, Brighton and South Coast Railway. Accordingly in the early part of the year 1900 he introduced the very fine type which is now the standard on that line. There were three built in the first batch, Nos 52 *Siemens*, 53 *Sirdar*, and 54 *Empress*. To these some thirty have since been added, differing only from the first three in their boilers being pitched 1½ in higher above the rails, and in having a slightly varied design of casing for the safety valves, which in all these engines are placed over the firebox instead of being in the dome as previously. With boilers 4 ft 10 in in diameter, having a steam pressure of 170 lbs per square inch, 23 square feet of grate area, cylinders 19 in

LB & SCR 4–4–0 No 213 Bessemer, *the first of R. J. Billinton's 'B3s', built in 1898 for express passenger work. Rous-Marten mentions a run behind this engine on the 'Brighton Sunday Pullman' in the accompanying extract.* (NRM)

by 26 in and four-coupled driving wheels 6 ft 9 in in diameter, these new engines possess large tractive force, equal to 115.6 lbs for every lb of effective steam pressure in the cylinders. Their external appearance is extremely handsome and imposing, causing all other Brighton engines to look insignificant in size when compared with the newcomers. The question of interest, however, was whether these splendid-looking locomotives could do work proportional to their appearance, and that could only be determined by a direct test.

So, being courteously invited by the able General Manager to try for myself what the new engines could do, I made several journeys between London and Brighton with that object and had some very interesting experiences. It is desirable for my readers to understand that the principal expresses now run over the new

avoiding line between Croydon and Horley, which entirely avoids Redhill station and Junction and also that length of South Eastern line which used to provide so many vexatious blockings. Instead of ascending unbrokenly at 1 in 264 from East Croydon to the Merstham tunnel, the new line has for its final length to the summit $3\frac{1}{2}$ miles of 1 in 165, 1 in 125 and 1 in 100.[92] Also, in the opposite direction the line from Earlswood to the Merstham tunnel, instead of being on a steadily ascending grade of 1 in 264, rises at 1 in 162, 1 in 200, 1 in 230 and 1 in 205 for $3\frac{3}{4}$ miles continuously. Thus the new road is

[92] Rous-Marten has put these gradients in the wrong order. The 1 in 100 comes first and is only $\frac{1}{4}$ mile long; the 1 in 125 is even shorter; then comes a level half-mile before the final stretch at 1 in 165 to Quarry tunnel entrance.

manifestly a much steeper one and, comparing it with the official distance-scale which I have had for many years, the distance likewise seems to be increased. I make it 7 chains longer by the new way. If that be correct, the distance from Victoria to Brighton becomes extended to 50 miles 75 chains, or virtually 51 miles, while that from London Bridge is 50 miles 54 chains, or practically 50¾ miles. Consequently the engine has to do distinctly harder work than before. Still, this is a small matter as compared with the vexatious hindrances formerly experienced through blockings on the old line.

On the occasion of my first trip the engine, No 68 *Marlborough*, was not at her best owing to a leaky tube. Nevertheless she took a train weighing fully 250 tons behind the tender from

London to Brighton in 63 minutes 53 seconds . . . In the opposite direction, with a lighter load, approximately 160 tons, No 49 *Queensland* made a remarkably smart run from Brighton as far as Wandsworth Common, but took exactly 30 minutes to cover the remaining 4 miles to Victoria, owing to signal delays! The distance of 47 miles from Brighton to Wandsworth Common was run in the fast time of 50 minutes 41 seconds, start to stop, notwithstanding two bad checks near Merstham and Norbury respectively, the former being to a slow walking pace—almost a dead stand. These two slacks caused quite 4 minutes delay, so the run was virtually done at fully the mile-a-minute rate throughout. Haywards Heath, practically 13 miles from Brighton, was passed in 14

LB & SCR 4-4-2 No 41 at Victoria Station after bringing the 'Southern Belle' up from Brighton. It was designed by Earle Marsh, Billinton's successor, and closely resembled the large-boilered Great Northern 'Atlantics' in size and shape, which was not surprising as Marsh had been assistant to H.A. Ivatt at Doncaster before transferring to Brighton. The engine is liveried in the dark umber which succeeded Stroudley's more colourful ochre. Five of them were built in 1905 and another six in 1911. (NRM)

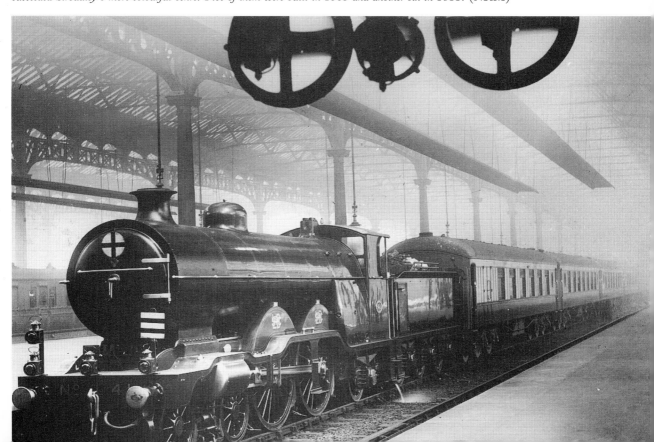

minutes 23 seconds from the start, in spite of the engine having to begin with the 5-mile climb to the Clayton tunnel, which was ascended at a steady rate of 60 miles an hour after full speed had been attained. Earlswood, 29 miles 2 chains, was passed in 29 minutes 58 seconds, but then came the bad check above referred to, in spite of which, with the later one at Norbury added, we averaged 55.6 miles an hour from the Brighton start to the Wandsworth Common stop.

More recently I made a trial trip with the 'crack' express of the London, Brighton and South Coast Railway, the 'Sunday Pullman Limited'. The train weighed 237 tons empty . . . every seat in the train was occupied, and, including the passengers, staff and baggage, the total load was slightly over 255 tons behind the tender. The engine was No 55 *Emperor*. The run was made from the Victoria start to the middle of the Brighton station in 56 minutes 51 seconds, but as the train continued to move forward at a walking pace nearly up to the buffer stops the inclusive time to the dead stop was 57 minutes 17 seconds, a very creditable run, accomplished by steady good work throughout, uphill and

downhill, without any extreme pace down falling gradients. The minimum rate up the grade of 1 in 100 was 36 miles an hour[93] and, up the 1 in 264, 55.5 miles an hour. The return journey was made with the same engine and train in 58 minutes 1 second exactly. A speed of 54 miles an hour was attained up the 1 in 264 to Clayton tunnel and was still rising when the summit was reached. Haywards Heath was passed in 15 minutes 49 seconds from Brighton, and Earlswood in 33 minutes 31 seconds; East Croydon, 40½ miles, in 45 minutes 7 seconds, and Wandsworth Common, 47 miles, where we began to ease down, in 51 minutes 53 seconds. This too may fairly be regarded as an excellent performance, and it should be noticed that the running of the train was throughout of the smoothest possible character, while the comfort of the magnificent Pullman cars is quite the climax yet attained in British travel.

[93] There are only two extremely short stretches at this gradient on the line, one just before Selhurst and one just past Coulsdon. Since Rous-Marten evidently had the order of the gradients confused on the approach to Quarry tunnel, possibly the minimum of 36 occurred on the 1 in 165 at the latter place.

LOGS OF THE LAST THREE RUNS DESCRIBED ABOVE:

Victoria–Brighton

Miles	Stations	Min	Sec
00.00	Victoria	00	00
02.72	Clapham Junction	05	12
04.09	Wandsworth Common	06	57
10.54	East Croydon	15	20
21.91	Earlswood	29	04
25.87	Horley	32	27
29.59	Three Bridges	35	59
34.15	Balcombe	40	57
38.05	Haywards Heath	44	23
40.92	Wivelsfield	46	43
41.75	Burgess Hill	47	28
43.86	Hassocks	49	23
50.94	Brighton	57	17

Brighton–Victoria

Miles	Stations	Min	Sec	Min	Sec
00.00	Brighton	00	00	00	00
07.08	Hassocks	09	10	10	15
09.19	Burgess Hill	11	06	12	15
10.02	Wivelsfield		–	12	57
12.89	Haywards Heath	14	23	15	49
16.79	Balcombe	18	38	20	41
21.35	Three Bridges	23	24	26	10
25.07	Horley	26	27	29	25
29.03	Earlswood	29	58	33	31
		Sigs			
40.40	East Croydon	43	53	45	07
		Sigs			
46.85	Wandsworth Common	50	41	51	53
48.22	Clapham Junction			53	39
50.94	Victoria			58	01

SEPTEMBER 1903

A record run from Victoria to Brighton and back

On Sunday, July 26th, at the courteous invitation of Mr William Forbes, General Manager of the London, Brighton and South Coast Railway, I was a passenger by the special train from Victoria which broke all records of that line. The expedition was not undertaken by the authorities of the London, Brighton and South Coast Railway for the purposes of amusement. For several years past threats have been heard of coming competition for the London and Brighton trade, and during the past two years these threats have taken more or less concrete form in the promotion of a Bill for an electric railway which, when completed, would convey passengers between London and Brighton in 50 minutes, or even less. Outside critics freely asserted that the present railway could not equal this, and even the authorities of the London, Brighton and South Coast Railway frankly admitted that they could not undertake to do it as a regular thing until the extensive alterations and widening of their line, which have long been in progress, should be finally completed. Nevertheless they were determined to make it plain that their only obstacle consisted in the difficulty of getting a clear line, owing to the great pressure of existing traffic, and that so soon as the newer line could be relied upon they would find no difficulty in rivalling the best speed that had been somewhat dubiously promised by the promoters of the electric scheme, and so the order was given that Brighton was to be reached in 50 minutes from Victoria, or as much earlier as might prove feasible.

Unfortunately the conditions at starting were highly unpropitious. Very heavy rain had fallen, the line was completely saturated and, although the weather cleared up soon after the start was made, the immediate effect was to give us a gradually-drying and, therefore, a greasy rail. All difficulties however were surmounted with triumphant ease and success. The engine, No 70 *Holyrood*, was one of the newest possessed by the Company, having only been running for a few months. She is one of Mr R. J. Billinton's latest design, having 6 ft 9 in driving wheels, four-coupled, inside cylinders 19 in by 26 in, a large boiler with about 1,700 square feet of heating surface and a steam pressure of 180 lbs. The driver, Thomsett, managed her remarkably well . . .

Very smart work was done from the start and throughout the entire trip. The load, as it happened, was almost exactly the same as that of the Great Western Royal record train, approximately 130 tons behind the tender. It consisted of three Pullman cars and two Pullman vans. The steep bank of 1 in 64 to Grosvenor Road was climbed with the utmost ease, and by the time Clapham Junction was passed we were going at 60 miles an hour. Up the long bank at 1 in 264 past Croydon we maintained a speed of 62.5 to 64.2 miles an hour . . . The gradients on the new avoiding line between Stoat's Nest and Earlswood . . . are far steeper than the uniform 1 in 264 which extends to the Merstham tunnel on the old line. For a considerable distance the rising grade is 1 in 165, 1 in 125 and even 1 in 100.[94] The descent from Merstham tunnel to Earlswood, although not so steep as this, is yet at 1 in 205, 1 in 230, 1 in 200 and even 1 in 162, as against the uniform 1 in 264 of the old line. Moreover it increases the distance by about $\frac{1}{4}$ mile[95] so that Brighton is practically 51 miles from Victoria, the shortage being only 5 chains. Up the gradients mentioned our speed never fell much below 60 miles an hour. Descending towards Horley we got up to 80.3 miles an hour, and then ascended the Balcombe bank, of 1 in 264, at a minimum of 66.6, and down the subsequent descent past Haywards Heath, which is at the same rate, our speed steadily rose until at the foot of the bank we just touched 90 miles an hour, this record being corroborated by another independent observer and also by the automatic register of Mr Billinton's speed recorder. The following short rise to the Clayton tunnel did not depress our rate much below 70, but the concluding descent into Brighton terminus was run down with special care, the rails being slippery, and the train was allowed to proceed slowly through the whole length of the station up to the buffer stops. This seemed rather a pity, as it might well have stopped just inside, . . . the final crawl need not have added to the transit time. As it was, however, the complete run from Victoria to Brighton was accomplished in 48 minutes 41 seconds from start to stop . . . and the length of 50 miles from Grosvenor Road was done in 46 minutes 11 seconds. Thus our average speed from start to stop was 63.4 miles an hour.[96]

Returning the same evening, the engine and train being identical with those of the morning, the journey up to town was done at a slightly slower average, but nevertheless broke all former records between the two termini, the en-

---

[94] See note 92 above.

[95] Rous-Marten indicated above that the new route was 7 chains longer. This is only just over a third of a quarter of a mile (see the fourth paragraph of the previous extract).

[96] A miscalculation. 50 miles 75 chains in 48 minutes 41 seconds works out as an average speed of 62.78 mph.

tire journey from dead start to dead stop occupying 50 minutes 21 seconds . . . The difference in the time was due partly to a very strong side wind having arisen during the afternoon and partly to some permanent way slacks. The actual travelling speed was generally about the same on both down and up journeys, but the maximum in the latter case did not exceed 85 miles an hour. In all respects both performances were not only a success but a triumph for the Brighton line, constituting a serious demonstration of the competitive force the old railway will be able to exercise so soon as its works at present in progress shall be completed, and in case its supremacy in respect to the London and Brighton traffic should ever be seriously threatened by electricity or otherwise. Mr Forbes may be cordially congratulated on the success of his judicious strategy.

SOUTH EASTERN AND CHATHAM RAILWAY

JUNE 1905

Journeys on the South Eastern line behind Stirling 'B' class and Wainwright 'D' class 4–4–0s

I made two up journeys from Folkestone Central to Cannon Street within the space of a few days, and each proved alike creditable and interesting. On one of those two occasions the engine was of Mr James Stirling's latest type, No 453, with 7 ft coupled wheels, leading bogie and cylinders 19 by 26, having a somewhat larger boiler than the earlier engines of the same type . . . The load consisted of six eight-wheeled Pullman cars, weighing with passengers and luggage close on 200 tons behind the tender. No fewer than four rather bad relaying slacks and one signal check were encountered. Nevertheless we made the run of 69 miles in 87 min 24 sec start to stop. We duly observed the service slack, to 30 miles an hour, past Tonbridge Junction, and slowed down to walking pace between London Bridge and Cannon Street. The minimum rate up the bank at 1 in 120, between Hildenborough and Sevenoaks, was 31 miles an hour. Our lowest approaching Knockholt was 40. The descent after Polehill tunnel was made at a uniformly steady pace; altogether the performance was a distinctly good one.

It was bettered, however, a few days later by one of Mr Wainwright's latest express engines with cylinders 19¼ by 26, 6 ft 8 in coupled wheels, 1,500 square feet of heating surface, No 745, hauling precisely the same load. There was a still worse relaying slack near Smeeth, our speed being reduced to 10 miles an hour for more than a minute. Some fast running was done between Ashford and Tonbridge, the distance of 26½ miles being covered in 25 min 16 sec—exactly one minute quicker than on the previous occasion—while a speed of 73.8 miles an hour was attained as against 70, the previous maximum. The lowest rate up the 1 in 120 after Hildenborough was 32 miles an hour, which increased later to 33 up the same bank but then dropped again to 32, and finally to 31 after slipping in the long Sevenoaks tunnel. Up the shorter rise at 1 in 143 to the Polehill tunnel our rate never went below 45 miles an hour, and when we were badly slowed for relaying at Orpington—after running the 56 miles from Folkestone in 1 hour 8 min inclusive—we still had 22 minutes left to run the remaining 12½ miles to Cannon Street; consequently the subsequent downhill running was necessarily a mere amble, at 52 to 55 miles an hour, and even then we reached a point just outside Cannon Street station, where we were stopped by signal, only 84 min 11 sec from Folkestone, or nearly 6 minutes under booked time. It is not easy to work out the net results because of the long downhill dawdle after Knockholt, but roughly it may be estimated that, eliminating the delay near Smeeth, and maintaining after Knockholt the rate that would ordinarily have been run, Cannon Street would have been easily reached in less than 80 minutes from Folkestone.

SE & CR 4-4-0 No 156, one of James Stirling's 'F' class, of which the first appeared in 1883; 88 were built in all. Like his brother on the Great Northern, Stirling preferred domeless boilers and cut-away cabs. The prominent brake-rodding below and outside the driving-wheel bosses hardly improved their appearance, and at least once led someone to report to the railway that the coupling rods had come adrift. (NRM, Chisholm Collection)

SE & CR 4-4-0 No 740, of H.S. Wainwright's 'D' class of express passenger engines — in the writer's opinion the most handsome steam locomotives ever built. The actual designer was R.R. Surtees, Wainwright's Chief Draughtsman; Wainwright himself, however, inaugurated the superb livery which (to use his own words) was 'Brunswick green relieved with broad bands of light green lined out with yellow and red; frames are dark red, picked out with yellow and red lines'. Though he consented to modify this with his freight engines he maintained the full livery, with domes and splasher beadings of polished brass, as long as a disapproving Board of Directors would let him. While they were intent on economy, he maintained that a splendid livery inspired the shed and footplate staff to keep their charges clean and had definite publicity value. Rous-Marten had many runs behind engines of this class and one is described here. (NRM)

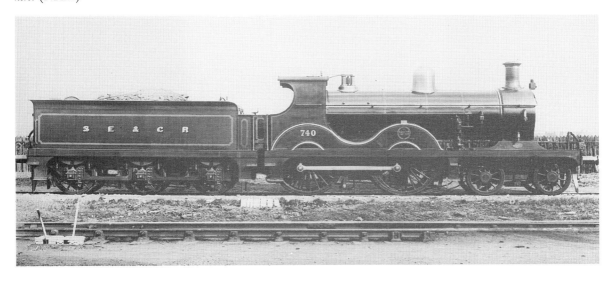

Two later journeys by the same trains during the Easter holiday season are not worth describing in detail. The down train, hauled by a Stirling engine, No 456, consisted of thirteen vehicles, seven being eight-wheelers. It was consequently reckoned as '20 coaches' but except on the South of England lines would have been called '16½'.[97] It was much impeded by signals and unavoidably arrived late. The return journey, with six Pullman cars and one ordinary eight-wheeler was performed by No 75 (Stirling)[98] in 89 minutes, ie one minute under booked time. One other journey by the down train is perhaps worth mentioning. The engine was No 727 (Wainwright) and the load six Pullmans, two ordinary eight-wheelers and one six-wheeler, the last three vehicles being slipped at Ashford. The total load to that point was therefore well over 250 tons. The work done as far as Tonbridge was excellent; the time to that station, almost the

whole distance being on a steep up-grade[99], was exactly 40 minutes. The lowest speed up the bank at 1 in 118 near Elmstead was 33 miles an hour. At Chislehurst it had risen to 36, at Orpington to 41, and the minimum in the Polehill tunnel was 34.[100] On the short downhill stretch near Dunton Green it increased to 56, after which it did not go below 50 on the short uphill stretch approaching the Sevenoaks tunnel, which was threaded in 2 min 26 sec, the distance being 1 mile 1691 yards.[101] After Tonbridge, however, there seemed to come a curious temporary collapse, the speed dropping from 60 miles an hour at Paddock Wood, and 69 at

---

[97] At a guess, this would amount to about 240 tons.

[98] A mistake. No 75 was a 'D' class Wainwright engine, the first of a batch of two built by Dübs & Co in 1903. But it could have been No 175, which *was* a Stirling 4-4-0, and Rous-Marten may have mistaken the number.

[99] Rous-Marten does not often deviate into complete nonsense, but that is what this statement is! From Knockholt to Tonbridge, 13 miles, the line is, apart from a short length before Sevenoaks, steeply downhill all the way.

[100] The minimum was surely *before the tunnel was entered*, at the summit, Knockholt. All the way through the tunnel the line is on a down gradient of 1 in 143.

[101] If the speed did not go below 50 mph on the up-grade before Sevenoaks tunnel was entered, it seems very strange indeed that the average speed through the tunnel, on a down gradient of 1 in 144, should be as low as 48.4 mph.

SE & CR 4-4-0 No 36, built in 1908, one of a batch of 26 locomotives made slightly more powerful than the 'D' class in order to cope with increasing loads; it had a slightly larger boiler and Belpaire firebox, and some, like the one illustrated, also had extended smokeboxes. (NRM)

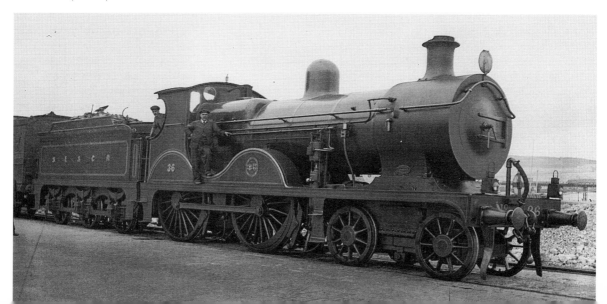

Marden, to 56 and finally 49 before Ashford. Thus the distance of 26½ miles of very easy road between those stations occupied 30 minutes[102], certainly very poor work indeed. The fault seemed to me to lie not with the engine but with

the sluggish driving. I suspect that the driver failed to notice how seriously his speed was dropping, and although he pushed along briskly after Ashford and made a very quick stop at the Folkestone Central station our arrival was 2 minutes late. We could easily have been in as much before time.

The following are the 'logs' of the two up journeys by the Folkestone Pullman Car express:

[102] The stretch can scarcely be called 'very easy road'. After Headcorn, 6 miles beyond Marden, it rises for 9 miles to Chart Siding, with gradients of 1 in 280 or steeper for nearly half that distance. The minimum of 49 was presumably at Chart.

Locomotive		Stirling Class 'B' 4–4–0 No 453		Wainwright Class 'D' 4–4–0 No 745	
Approximate load		200 tons		200 tons	
Miles	**Stations**	**Min**	**Sec**	**Min**	**Sec**
00.0	Folkestone Central	00	00	00	00
05.8	Westenhanger	09	17	09	20
09.6	Smeeth	13	14	13	02
		PW slack		PW slack	
13.9	Ashford	18	24	18	44
19.5	Pluckley	24	12	24	26
24.7	Headcorn	29	09	29	08
28.1	Staplehurst	32	09	31	58
30.6	Marden	34	35	34	22
35.1	Paddock Wood	38	58	38	30
40.4	Tonbridge	44	40	44	00
43.0	Hildenborough	48	40	48	03
47.9	Sevenoaks	57	39	57	03
49.4	Dunton Green	59	32	58	53
53.4	Knockholt	64	58	64	24
56.2	Orpington	68	03	67	31
		PW slack		PW slack	
58.7	Chislehurst	71	30	70	58
		PW slack		PW slack	
60.9	Grove Park	74	44	73	49
62.8	Hither Green	76	41	75	45
65.1	New Cross	79	57	79	20
		Sigs		Sigs	
68.8	Cannon Street	87	24	84	11[103]

[103] Time to a stop just outside Cannon Street station.

CALEDONIAN RAILWAY

AUGUST 1903

Performances of McIntosh 4–6–0s on the main line between Carlisle and Glasgow

I went to Scotland expressly to test the actual working of Mr J. F. M'Intosh's twin giants on the Caledonian Railway, Nos 49 and 50. I travelled to Glasgow by the 2 pm London and North Western corridor-diner from Euston . . .

At Carlisle Mr M'Intosh's Caledonian colossus, No 50, came on under the admiring gaze of a large crowd of eyes, there being quite a big assemblage of spectators kept within bounds by a policeman. The vast size and magnificent ap-

pearance of the new engine were very striking, especially in comparison with the relatively small engines of the six other railway companies that run into Carlisle, some even of the newest of which looked mere pigmies when passing near her.

The load continued to be 330 tons behind the tender. A speed of 60 miles an hour was attained by the time we passed the first station out of Carlisle (Rockliffe) and that had increased to 65

CR 4–6–0 No 50 Sir James Thompson, *one of two locomotives built by McIntosh in 1903 to cope with the heaviest Anglo-Scottish expresses, particularly the famous 'Corridor', which left Euston at 2 pm each weekday and returned the next day at the same time from Glasgow Central. This train could load up to 400 tons, which was more than a 'Dunalastair' could manage and still keep time. Four more were subsequently built, including the famous* Cardean, *which monopolized the 'Corridor' in both directions for many years.* (NRM)

when we started the Gretna bank, 8 miles on end at 1 in 200 up.[104] This was ascended without the speed dropping below 50, and that experience was repeated up the subsequent 4 miles of 1 in 200 past Ecclefechan. Down the 7 miles of easily falling grades past Lockerbie the big engine ran very freely, the maximum rate keeping a little below 70 miles an hour. Beattock, 39¾ miles from Carlisle, was passed in the quick time of 43 minutes 10 seconds, and 'then came the tug of war'—otherwise the Beattock incline, beginning with 2 miles at 1 in 88, 2 miles of 1 in 80 following, and 6 miles continuously of 1 in 75, completing the rise to the summit. This length of 10 miles occupied 23 minutes in the ascent, the minimum speed point touched being 22 miles an hour. I may observe here that this performance was not so good as a subsequent one by the same engine, when that distance was covered with the same load in 4 minutes less time. The explanation of the longer run on the occasion in question was that through a slight disarrangement of the dampers, which had not been noticed till after the train was started, the engine was working under adverse conditions, which necessarily hampered her in attacking so heavy a climb at high speed. But, even as it was, the summit, 49¾ miles, was passed in 66 minutes 9 seconds from the Carlisle start— 1080 feet vertical climb—and the stop at Strawfrank Junction (73¼ miles) was made in 89 minutes 21 seconds from Carlisle. The descent from the summit was rapid but not exceptional, the train being in good time. At Strawfrank the Edinburgh coaches were cut off, leaving the Glasgow portion, about 240 tons, with which No 50 arrived at Eglinton Street 2 minutes before booked time.[105]

My next experience was with the 2 pm corridor diner from Glasgow. This was a very much heavier train, its weight being officially reckoned as 395 tons. After leaving Glasgow the up train has to face a series of heavy adverse gradients extending for 23 miles in virtually unbroken succession; the ruling grade over this length is 1 in 100. Nevertheless No 49, the earlier-built of the two giants, tackled it without faltering. The first 5 miles were done in 8 minutes 1 second, and Carstairs (29½ miles)[106], almost all on heavy up grades, was reached in 48 minutes 38 seconds. Here we encountered a special stop for signals, due to an extra train having got in the way of the Edinburgh express which preceded the Glasgow to Carlisle. We were detained for 5 minutes at Carstairs and after getting away again, while we were going at 50 miles an hour up 1 in 200, we were badly checked at Symington[107], and only 'got the road' once more to meet with another signal check between that station and Lamington. Thus we had to start the final climb to the Beattock summit going quite slowly. Nevertheless we got up to 56 miles an hour on the easier part—about 1 in 300—maintained 47 miles an hour up the 1 in 150 near Elvanfoot, and sustained a persistent 33 miles an hour up the final 2½ miles to the summit. In fact our speed showed a tendency to increase instead of diminish as the top was approached. Our time from the Carstairs start to the summit pass, 23½ miles, with two bad checks, was 34 minutes 8 seconds. No exceptional speed was run down the Beattock bank; in fact the brakes were applied at five different points; and the 10 miles to passing Beattock occupied 9 minutes 23 seconds. It was down the more moderate 8 miles of 1 in 200 near Gretna that we did our fastest running, three successive quarter-miles being covered in 11.8, 11.6 and 11.4 seconds respectively, or at speeds of 76.3, 77.6 and 79 miles an hour. If any doubt had remained as to the capacity of a six-coupled engine for attaining high velocities, that doubt was definitely set at

---

[104] Actually only 7½ miles, but the first two are inclined at 1 in 193.

[105] Eglinton Street, now demolished, was immediately before the terminus, Glasgow Central; the train halted there to put down passengers.

[106] A mistake; Carstairs is 28½ miles from Glasgow.

[107] There is no such gradient between Carstairs and Symington, but there *is* a 1¼-mile stretch at 1 in 100 just before the latter; no doubt this is what Rous-Marten refers to. The 50 mph was probably reached at the *foot* of this incline.

rest. Ultimately we stopped at Carlisle at our exact booked timing, in spite of having made a dead stop of 5 minutes at Carstairs and having experienced two other signal checks, the total delays amounting to fully 11 minutes. The entire journey of 103 miles from Glasgow to Carstairs[108] therefore occupied 2 hours 4 minutes net, and this with a load of 395 tons behind the tender.

My third experience was once more with the corridor diner from Carlisle back to Glasgow. Its make-up was virtually identical with that of the corresponding train in the opposite direction, and its weight almost exactly the same . . . The start from Carlisle was 3 minutes late owing to the train from the south being somewhat behind time, and it now became a serious question whether the Beattock bank could be faced unassisted without risk of time loss, it being the rule with that train, in case of late arrival at Carlisle, to make up as much as possible before reaching Glasgow and Edinburgh respectively. No doubt whatever existed as to the ability of the engine to take even that enormous train up that terrific ascent; the only doubt was whether this could be done in such time as to be consistent with the punctual arrival at the train's destination after 3 minutes late start.

Once more a very smart start was made out of Carlisle, and Rockcliffe, 4 miles 2 chains, was passed at the rate of 60 miles an hour in 5 minutes 57 seconds. Up the 8 miles at 1 in 200 past Kirkpatrick and Gretna[109] the speed never went below 47 miles an hour; indeed, only for a single

quarter-mile dropped to that point, subsequently rising to 48 before the top of the bank was reached. Down the easy descent past Lockerbie the speed rose to 69 miles an hour, but it soon became evident that none of the late start could be made up by the time Beattock was reached, and so, approaching that station, the engine whistled its signal for a 'banker' and we stopped at Beattock, having covered the 39¾ miles from Carlisle in 44 minutes 28 seconds start to stop, with just under 400 tons behind the tender, 16 miles of the distance being on rising grades of 1 in 200. A tank engine, No 443, stationed at Beattock for this particular service, then came on in our rear, and the ascent of 10 miles to the summit was done in 18 minutes 32 seconds, the minimum speed being 28 miles an hour. Then the bank engine left us and a swift descent of 21 minutes 50 seconds followed to the stop at Strawfrank, which was reached in 87 minutes 28 seconds inclusive from the Carlisle start, or in 84 minutes 51 seconds actual running time, deducting the stop at Beattock, or in 81¾ minutes net for the 73¼ miles. The highest speed touched on the downhill length was just 75 miles an hour. At Strawfrank the Edinburgh coaches were detached and the rest of the train, weighing 280 tons, ran swiftly forward to the Eglinton Street station in Glasgow, arriving 2 minutes before time in spite of the 3 minutes late start, 2½ minutes stay at Beattock and two signal stops just outside the arrival point—another clearly admirable performance, notwithstanding resort being had to a 'pusher' up Beattock.

[108] Probably a typesetter's error; it should of course be *Carlisle*. Also, the distance from Glasgow is not 103 but 102¼ miles.

[109] See above, note 104. Also, going north Gretna comes before Kirkpatrick.

GLASGOW AND SOUTH WESTERN RAILWAY

JANUARY 1906

Performances of newly-built 4–6–0 express engines on the Glasgow–Kilmarnock–Dumfries–Carlisle route

It is some years since I described any locomotive work of the Glasgow and South Western Railway. The reason is that until quite lately no fresh locomotive type has been introduced, nor has there been any actual acceleration of the services . . .

Two years ago, however, Mr Manson, recognising the need of increased locomotive power in dealing with the severe gradients of the Glasgow and South Western main line—which on the Barrhead section are as steep for nearly 4 miles on end as 1 in 67, 1 in 69 and 1 in 70, with a considerable length at 1 in 75[110]—decided upon following the example already set by the North Eastern, Great Western and Caledonian lines, of introducing six-coupled bogie engines for express service. Accordingly he brought out a very handsome design of this type and 10 engines were constructed to that design. They have 6 ft 6 in coupled wheels, cylinders 20 by 26, 1,850 square feet of heating surface and 180 lbs steam pressure. Mr Manson did not follow his Caledonian *confrère* in using inside cylinders driving the front coupled wheels. Like the North Eastern and Great Western chiefs he preferred the outside position for his cylinders and the middle pair of coupled wheels for the drivers. With 124 lbs of tractive force for every pound of effective steam pressure on the pistons, and the adhesion of six-coupled wheels, these engines possess very large theoretical power, and my own experience with them goes far to show that they exercise it in practice also. My chief difficulty proved to be to get trains of just the weight which they could haul unassisted up those gradients of 1 in 67, etc, *and no more*, for the principal expresses between Glasgow and Carlisle were far in excess of the nominal '15 coaches', which load was understood to be the limit to be taken unpiloted. That represented a weight behind the tender of more than 280 tons, no trifle of a 'pull' on such grades. But in most of my journeys the trains were reckoned as 19 to 21, and once even $22\frac{1}{2}$ coaches, or 370 to 430 tons, which no self-respecting locomotive could be expected to take up grades of 1 in 67, 1 in 69 or 1 in 75 at express speed without the aid of a pilot or 'banker'. Upon this section of the main line, viz between Glasgow and Kilmarnock, I only once succeeded in getting one of the ten-wheelers on a fair load unpiloted. The train was estimated at '13 coaches' and weighed approximately 250 tons behind the tender, including passengers, luggage, etc. It was booked to run from St Enoch to Kilmarnock, $24\frac{1}{2}$ miles,

---

[110] The gradient profile does not agree with Rous-Marten's figures; it shows two-figure gradients beginning just south of Barrhead, at 1 in 67, 1 in 78, 1 in 69 and 1 in 70 over a distance of $3\frac{1}{4}$ miles, with no slope of 1 in 75 at all, though there is a mile and a half at this inclination downwards some miles further on, beyond Dunlop.

in 33 minutes, over the terrific grades already mentioned, averaging 44.5 miles an hour start to stop. The run was made by No 383 in 32 minutes 9 seconds, the lowest speed up 1 in 67 being 24.3 miles an hour, while down the falling grade at 1 in 75 toward Kilmarnock the rate was never allowed to exceed 66.1 miles an hour. No 390 of the same class, piloted by a four-coupled engine and hauling 350 tons, gave me almost exactly similar figures over that trying stage. No 389, six-coupled, piloted, and pulling 360 tons behind the second tender, took 32 minutes 54 seconds for the same run. In this case the minimum up 1 in 67 dropped to 23.6 miles an hour owing to a drizzling rain with strong side wind, but the speed down the falling grade rose to 77.5 miles an hour.

But although the severe 'pinches' on the Barrhead line are the worst the locomotives have to face, the long stretches of 1 in 100 to 1 in 99 from Kilmarnock to New Cumnock going south, and up Nithsdale to the same point going north[112], are almost equally arduous owing to their lengthened continuance. Thus the $20\frac{3}{4}$ miles from Kilmarnock to New Cumnock occupied 27 minutes 38 seconds, the engines being No 389 and a pilot with 360 tons behind. The minimum speed was 33 up the 1 in 99 and 50 to 53 up 1 in 150. The pilot went off at New Cumnock summit and thenceforward to Carlisle No 389 ran alone. Now the descent of the Nithsdale slope from New Cumnock to Dumfries is, one may admit, an easy run, but nevertheless it was to the credit of Mr Manson's engine that a stage of 37 miles was done from start to stop in 36 minutes 27 seconds with 360 tons behind the tender. Once more a maximum of 77.5 miles an hour was attained on easily-falling grades.

It is customary to talk about the 33 miles be-

[112] Going north, the steepest gradient is 1 in 150, for $5\frac{1}{2}$ miles south of Drumlanrig tunnel.

LMSR 4–6–0 No 14672, formerly one of the '381' class of G & SWR outside-cylinder express engines built by James Manson for the heavy expresses between Glasgow and Carlisle by way of Kilmarnock and Dumfries, a route with severe gradients north of Kilmarnock. The picture has a melancholy interest, since the engine is lined up with others destined for scrapping (what looks like coal on the tender is actually part of the background). (NRM, M.D. England Collection)

tween Dumfries and Carlisle as 'a very level length'. But although relatively easy as compared with the Dumfries–Glasgow length in either direction it is assuredly by no means a level road. It certainly has an easy start each way, but it has considerable distances of such gradients as 1 in 300, 1 in 200 and even 1 in 170[113], each extending quite far enough to 'stall' an engine that had not the capacity of grappling with them when hauling a heavy train. There was therefore an abundance of interest in observing the behaviour of Mr Manson's ten-wheelers with such a load as 360 tons behind the tender, and in distinctly unfavourable weather.

This is what happened. The booked time for the 33 miles was 40 minutes start to stop. This was exactly the time we took. But out of it we were at a dead stand for nearly a minute—51 seconds to be quite exact—at Gretna Green owing to signals being adverse. Thus the actual travelling time for the 33 miles of undulatory road was 39 minutes 9 seconds and the net time $36\frac{1}{4}$ minutes. The distance of $23\frac{1}{2}$ miles from Dumfries to Gretna Green was covered in 26 minutes 49 seconds start to stop and the $9\frac{1}{2}$ miles, nearly all uphill thence to the Carlisle stop[114], in 12 minutes 20 seconds. I should mention here that the train was the Midland-Scottish afternoon dining train, the fastest on the Glasgow and South Western system, due to leave St Enoch, Glasgow, at 1.30 and reach St Pancras at 10.20 pm. We had to make a special stop at New Cumnock to drop the pilot, and another at Gretna Green for signals, and also the optional stop at Dumfries, yet our actual travelling time from Glasgow to Carlisle was only 2 hours 15 minutes 7 seconds for the $115\frac{1}{2}$ miles, with four intermediate stops, 70 miles of the total being run without a pilot.

This was very creditable work under such conditions, but it did not stand alone. Returning from Carlisle to Glasgow by the 3.52 pm train,

the Glasgow and South Western continuation of the 9.45 am from St Pancras, the train was a tremendous one, the longest I ever saw on that railway. According to information supplied to me from official sources it was reckoned as '21 coaches', or approximately 400 tons, from Carlisle, and '$22\frac{1}{2}$ coaches', or 425 tons, from Dumfries. The engine was another of the ten-wheeled six-coupled type, No 384. No pilot was taken. Getting away very smartly from Carlisle we passed Rockcliffe, 4 miles, in 6 minutes 11 seconds; Floriston, 6 miles, in 8 minutes 25 seconds; and Gretna, $8\frac{1}{2}$ miles, in 11 minutes 5 seconds. Most of this distance is on a slightly falling gradient; nevertheless the rapid acceleration with so huge a load was worthy of very favourable notice. Then came the 6 miles to Dornock, of which half is on a rising grade of 1 in 200 to 1 in 170, the rest being level.[115] This was done in 6 minutes 59 seconds, the speed never going below 45 miles an hour on the up grades and rising to 60 on the level. Up the $5\frac{1}{2}$ miles at about 1 in 200 to Ruthwell[116] the speed did not drop below 50 miles an hour; on the final level approaching Dumfries it rose to 67.2 and kept steadily at that point[117], a remarkable achievement for one engine hauling 400 tons on the level. Dumfries was reached in 38 minutes 4 seconds, start to stop, from Carlisle, the average speed being thus 52.1 miles an hour.

At Dumfries the load was augmented to 425 tons, and a pilot—one of the late Mr Smellie's 6 ft 6 in four coupled class—came on for the remainder of the journey. Then came the long and trying climb of 37 miles up the Nithsdale bank to New Cumnock. This occupied 47 minutes 48 seconds, the lowest speed

[113] There is no 1 in 170, but there is a 2-mile pitch at 1 in 150 between Racks and Ruthwell going south.

[114] Only very slightly uphill, and with $1\frac{1}{2}$ miles at 1 in 193 down from Gretna, to help to get the train on the move.

[115] This, and all gradient indications onward to Glasgow, are Rous-Marten at his misinformative worst. Between Gretna and Dornock (a village close to the line just beyond Eastriggs station) the line, after a mile at 1 in 193 up, falls steadily.

[116] Only 2 miles, past Ruthwell, are so inclined.

[117] Rous-Marten omits to mention that one-third of the distance after Ruthwell summit is downhill—in one place at 1 in 150 for 2 miles.

up 1 in 100[118] being 33 miles an hour, while up the 1 in 200 and 1 in 150 it was 50 and 44 respectively. No stop was made at New Cumnock. The subsequent downhill speed was kept at a very moderate point, the 22¼ miles occupying 21 minutes 25 seconds to the Kilmarnock stop, while the total run of 58½ miles from Dumfries[119] was done in 69 minutes 18 seconds, thus averaging just 51 miles an hour.[120] After leaving Kilmarnock the long rise at 1 in 75 past Stewarton had to be faced.[121] It was ascended at a steady rate of 25 miles an hour except for a single quarter-mile, in which the speed dropped to 24.3, from which, however, it promptly recovered—still on the 1 in 75 grade—to 25, and then 26 miles an hour before the summit was attained. We then ran at 65 to 70 miles an hour to near Pollokshaws where we eased down careful-

ly. At Strathbungo we were stopped dead for 2 minutes by signal, having come from Kilmarnock, 22½ miles, in 30 minutes 21 seconds. This delay made us slightly late into St Enoch station, but our actual travelling time from Carlisle had been 2 hours 22 minutes 43 seconds with that enormous load, or 2¼ minutes under booked time. Even taking into account the pilot assistance after Dumfries I regard this as an excellent performance.

It will be observed that all these were 'surprise' trips, made without any previous intimation being given that those engines or their drivers would be under special observation on the occasions referred to. Thus the results must be regarded as showing the normal work done. Quite possibly Mr Manson's ten-wheelers may yet give me even finer achievements when specially 'put to it', but the instances which I have adduced go far to prove that Mr Manson's judgement was quite sound when he arrived at the conclusion that the time had come when such heavy and fairly fast-timed trains as the Midland Scottish expresses . . . must be worked by six-coupled engines . . . He may justly be complimented on his locomotives and congratulated on their achievements. That the Glasgow and South Western ten-wheelers will be multiplied, I entertain no doubt whatever.[122]

---

[118] There is *no* gradient at 1 in 100 on this stretch of line anywhere. So where did the speed fall to 30 mph? Probably before Drumlanrig tunnel. But the approach to that is at 1 in 150. Where the 50 and 44 speeds were reached is anybody's guess.

[119] Actually the distance is 58.1 miles.

[120] Actually 50.3 mph. Rous-Marten had calculated it on the basis of 58½, not 58.1, miles having been covered.

[121] There is no gradient pitched as steeply as this until Stewarton station is reached, after which there are 1½ miles at 1 in 75, ending at the summit.

[122] In fact, only seven more were built.

INDEX

General

Adhesion, remarks on 41, 42
Allen, Cecil J., railway writer 12, 13
Aspinall, J.A.F., loco engr 27, 35, 39, 40, 45, 55, 63, 129, 132

Billinton, R.J., loco engr 27, 38, 55, 139, 144
Bouch, W., loco engr 27
Brighton Sunday Pullman 16, 142, 143

Charlewood, R.E., railway writer 9
Churchward, G.J., loco engr 32, 35, 38, 45, 46, 48, 66, 71–75, 85, 89
Conyers, W., NZ railway engr 11
Crampton, T.R., loco engr 31

Dalby, Professor 9
Dean, W., loco engr 23, 25–27, 38
Deeley, R.M., loco engr 67, 68
Diamond, E.L. 9
Drummond, D., loco engr 27, 29, 32, 35, 38, 55, 60, 134, 136, 138
Drummond, P., loco engr 27, 39
Dübs & Co, locomotive builders 32

Fletcher, E., loco engr 27
French compounds, CR-M's advocacy of 13
Funeral of CR-M 13

Gooch, D., loco engr 31, 38
Gooch, J.V., loco engr 73

Hickson, Emily J., married to CR-M 11
Holden, J., loco engr 27, 38, 45, 49
Holmes, M., loco engr 27, 39
Hoy, H.A., loco engr 131

Ivatt, H.A., loco engr 27, 35, 38, 39, 73, 109, 111

Johnson, S.W., loco engr 27–30, 32, 35, 39, 40, 45, 55, 70

Kirtley, M., loco engr 27

Latin quotations, CR-M's fondness for 18
Locomotive types: See separate index below

Macdonald, N.D. 9
McIntosh, J.F., loco engr 27, 35, 39, 43, 46, 74, 150
Manson, J., loco engr 27, 29, 39, 46, 153, 154, 156
Marsh, D., loco engr 141
Marten, W., father of CR-M 11
Monkswell, Lord 9

Neilson, Reid & Co, locomotive builders 32

Priming in locomotive boilers, remarks on 74, 75

Queen Victoria's funeral train 16

Railway Museum Association 76
Railway Race to Edinburgh, 1888 16
Railway Race to Aberdeen, 1895 13, 16, 33, 98
Record runs: by NZ locomotive 1892 12
   GWR *City of Bath*, 1903 83
   London-Brighton, 1903 143
   Plymouth-Waterloo, 1904 133
   GWR, *City of Truro*, 1904 12, 55, 56
Report by CR-M on UK railway system 12
Robinson, J.G., loco engr 27, 39, 46, 55, 64, 68, 116

Scott, Rev. W.J., railway writer 13, 19
Single wheelers, general remarks on 41
Sleeping cars on L&SWR 17
Slipping, locomotive 42
Smellie, H., loco engr 73
Smith, W.M., loco engr 66, 126
Stirling, J., loco engr 27, 35, 40, 73, 74, 146
Stirling, P., loco engr 15, 26, 27, 32–35, 38, 39, 41, 42, 73, 74
Stroudley, W., loco engr 63
Sturrock, A., loco engr 34, 35, 73, 76
Surtees, R., loco engr 141

Tractive force, general remarks on 43

Locomotive types

LOCOMOTIVE PRACTICE AND PERFORMANCE

Highlights from the celebrated *Railway Magazine* articles

by O.S. Nock

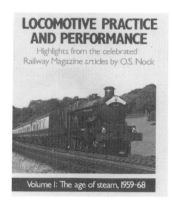

Volume 1: The age of steam, 1959–68 'We were doing 100 mph as early in the descent as Little Bytham, and the rate of acceleration was steady and swift. The engine was riding with the utmost steadiness, and the only minor and incidental discomfort was an absolute whirlwind of coal dust on the footplate...'

'...I can now tell also that we arrived in Victoria with all the metal out of one of the side-rod bushes, and a red-hot smokebox door!'

'Good though the work was up the Grayrigg bank, it was put completely in the shade by a terrific attack upon Shap...'

Exhilarating, incisive, expert, authoritative — O.S. Nock brought all these qualities to his articles during his 22 years as author of *The Railway Magazine*'s 'Locomotive Practice and Performance' column. And now, 30 years after his first article appeared, he has made a personal choice of 27 covering the years 1959–68, chronicling the last decade of British steam, and comparing its performance with that of the new diesels and electrics that were gradually replacing it on Britain's main lines.

THE NORTH WESTERN AT WORK

A portrait of the LNWR

by Dr R. Preston Hendry and R. Powell Hendry

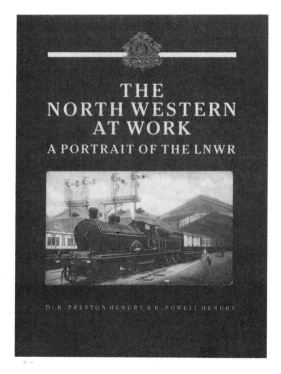

Until the railway Groupings of 1923, the London & North Western Railway was Britain's largest railway company, and with its regal air, magnificent trains and 'dustless tracks' was justifiably dubbed 'The Premier Line'. But what was it like to actually work for the LNWR in its heyday during the early years of this century, whether as axlebox greaser or top link locomotive driver or Chairman?

Drawing on a vast personal collection of contemporary photographs, books, official reports and ephemera, as well as first-hand reminiscences, the authors paint a remarkably vivid picture of the everyday working lives, attitudes and aspirations of the men and management of an Edwardian railway at its prime.